JOHN WAYNE BOBBITT
CHARGE: SEXUAL ASSAULT
VERDICT: NOT GUILTY

LORENA LEONOR BOBBITT
CHARGE: MALICIOUS WOUNDING
VERDICT: NOT GUILTY BY REASON OF
TEMPORARY INSANITY

WAS JUSTICE DONE?
COME TO YOUR OWN CONCLUSIONS WITH:
THE BOBBITT CASE—YOU DECIDE!

THE BOBBITT CASE
YOU DECIDE!

Peter Kane

PINNACLE BOOKS
WINDSOR PUBLISHING CORP.

Author's Note

What follows is what the jury heard, taken from court transcripts of the eight-day trial of Lorena Bobbitt. They have been edited only for redundancy and length. In the interest of readibility, some of the less significant testimonies and arguments between the attorneys over certain legal technicalities have not been included.

Detailed testimony regarding the psychological evaluations done on Lorena Bobbitt using clinical tests, personal interview with Ms. Bobbitt and others, police reports and witness depositions was heard from Dr. Susan Feister (for the defense), and "state doctors" Dr. Henry O. Gwaltney, Dr. Miller Ryans and Dr. Evan Nelson. The testimonies of Dr. Feister and Dr. Nelson has been condensed and included in this volume as representative of the psychological theories and findings introduced during the trial. Dr. Feister found Ms. Bobbitt to have suffered from acute psychosis and "irresistible impulse."

The Cast of Participants includes every person who testified during Lorena Bobbitt's trial as well as some who are mentioned throughout the trial. Those testimonies that have not been included in this volume are designated by an asterisk.

Cast of Participants—
In Order of Appearance

HERMAN A. WHISENANT, JR., on the circuit bench since 1980, he was Prince William County's chief judge at the time of the trial.

PAUL EBERT, Prince William County's Commonwealth Attorney, the equivalent of a District Attorney or county prosecutor in other states. Elected to the county post in 1968, he supervises a staff of 13 prosecutors and also tried the Bobbitt case.

MARY GRACE O'BRIEN, an Assistant Commonwealth attorney since 1985 who specializes in adult sex offenses. She also argued the commonwealth's case.

BLAIR HOWARD, Lorena Bobbitt's lead defense attorney from Alexandria, Virginia. In 30 years of practice he's forged an impressive record of criminal case acquittals.

LISA KEMLER, a ten-year veteran Alexandria criminal defense attorney who served as second counsel to Lorena Bobbitt's defense.

JAMES LOWE, a 24-year veteran criminal and personal injury attorney from Alexandria, Virginia who served as Lorena Bobbitt's original lawyer and also helped argue her defense.

LORENA LEONOR BOBBITT, the defendant accused of "malicious wounding" when she cut off her husband John's penis as he slept off a night of drinking and bar hopping on June 23, 1993. Born in Ecuador, she came to the U.S. in 1989. The couple married June 18, 1989, three weeks after he'd proposed to her in a Manassas ice cream parlor. She is 24.

JOHN WAYNE BOBBITT—The victim, a 26-year-old former Marine. He'd been raised by his aunt and uncle in Niagara Falls, New York after his father left home. John suffered from a learning disability as a child and worked hard to move from special education to regular classes.

ROBERT JOHNSTON, a 22-year-old engineering student from the University of Buffalo. A boyhood friend of John Bobbitt, he'd come to Virginia for a visit and was sleeping on the Bobbitt's couch the night of the attack.

*CECIL DEAN, a Prince William County police officer dispatched to the hospital where John Bobbitt was taken for his injury.

HOWARD PERRY, a Manassas volunteer fireman who searched the Bobbitt apartment after the incident.

WILLARD HURLEY, a Prince William County police sergeant who supervised the search of the intersection where John Bobbitt's penis was found.

JAMES SEHN, a Manassas urological surgeon who reattached Bobbitt's penis in a nine hour operation at Prince William Hospital.

PETER WEINTZ, a Prince William County detective who took Lorena Bobbitt's statement four hours after the assault.

*JANNA BISUTTI, Lorena's friend, boss and confidant. She did not testify but is frequently mentioned in the trial as the owner of the Nail Sculptor, the shop where the defendant worked as a manicurist.

KATHLEEN WILLIAMS, a Navy social worker who responded to a spouse abuse complaint involving the Bobbitts in 1990.

JOHN WHITAKER, a 19-year-old Stafford, Virginia man who played basketball and lifted weights with John Bobbitt at the Quantico air base.

ELLA JONES, a Jehovah's Witness who lived below the Bobbitt's Manassas apartment. She gave Lorena religious brochures on marriage and spouse abuse.

BOBBIE JO LORE, a Centreville, Virginia woman who worked at the Nail Sculptor and sometimes socialized with the Bobbitts.

*GARY BODMER, a Prince William County police officer who investigated a report of domestic violence at the Bobbitt residence.

TERRI MCCUMBER, a nail technician who worked with Lorena and went on a weekend outing to Ocean City with the Bobbitts and John's cousin Todd.

*RICHARD BORZA, a Virginia man who bought the Bobbitt's former home on Pine Street in 1992.

SUSAN INMAN, a family physician who treated Lorena Bobbitt.

*MICHAEL DIBBLE, a flight attendant who lived in an apartment adjacent to the Bobbitts. He was home the night of the knife attack.

LYNN ACQUAVIVA, a long-time customer of Lorena Bobbitt at the Manassas nail salon where she worked.

ROMA ANASTASI, another regular customer of Lorena Bobbitt at the Nail Sculptor.

MARY JO WILLOUGHBY, a neighbor of the Bobbitts when they lived in their home on Pine Street.

*BONNIE ALEXANDER, manager of the Maplewood Park Apartments where the assault took place.

BETH ANN WILSON, the assistant apartment manager of Maplewood Park.

MERCEDES CASTRO, the 24-year-old daughter of woman who took Lorena into her home after she moved to Virginia from Venezuela.

CAROL PALMER, a forensic scientist who analyzed the body and clothing evidence from Lorena Bobbitt for evidence of sexual assault.

MARGARET MCGARY, a woman who worked with Lorena Bobbitt for four years at the Nail Sculptor.

SANDRA BELTRAN, a Spanish-speaking friend of Lorena Bobbitt who let the Bobbitts live in her Stafford home for six months beginning in the fall of 1992. An interpreter was needed for her testimony.

IRMA CASTRO, the daughter of a Stafford woman who took Lorena Bobbitt into her home soon after she emigrated from Venezuela.

*REGINA KEEGAN, a Centreville housewife who got a manicure and eyebrow waxing at the Nail Sculptor from Lorena Bobbitt days before the attack.

BARRY WHITE, a Baptist minister who Lorena sought out to talk about domestic violence.

SUSAN FEISTER, medical director of Psychiatric Institute of Washington, D.C. The psychiatrist evaluated Lorena Bobbitt on behalf of the defense.

SHERRY BIRO, the wife of Bud Biro, John Wayne Bobbitt's brother.

BRETT BIRO, a 25-year-old cousin of John Bobbitt who served as a surrogate brother to Bobbitt as he grew up in his mother and father's Niagara Falls home.

TODD BIRO, another cousin Bobbitt called his brother. He lived with the Bobbitts briefly in 1989.

MARYLYN BIRO, John Bobbitt's aunt and surrogate mother. She and her husband William raised John since the age of 5.

DAVID CORCORAN, a Prince William Hospital emergency physician who examined Lorena Bobbitt for evidence of rape hours after the knife attack.

DIANE HALL, an apartment complex neighbor who socialized with the Bobbitts and offered Lorena a place to stay.

CONNIE JAMES, the wife of another Marine who discussed with Lorena what the consequences would be if she found her husband had been unfaithful.

*HENRY O. GWALTNEY, a forensic psychologist on the staff of Central State Hospital in Petersburg, Virginia. He conducted a psychological evaluation of Lorena Bobbitt.

*MILLER RYANS, a psychiatrist at Central State Hospital who also evaluated Lorena Bobbitt for mental illness.

EVAN NELSON, a clinical psychologist and the third Central State Hospital mental health professional who examined Lorena Bobbitt.

Introduction

On January 10, 1994, Lorena Bobbitt went on trial in a Manassas, Virginia courtroom for cutting off her husband John's penis with an eight-inch kitchen knife. She did it, she said, after he came home drunk on the night June 23, 1993 and raped her.

Five lawyers assembled to argue the case in front of small courtroom audience and hundreds of journalists housed with TV monitors in a vacant office building across from a Manassas court house.

But the battle lines were drawn months before the trial began.

By trial time, feminists had elevated Lorena Bobbitt to an icon, her attack representing a defining moment in the women's movement, some said. She had realized "every woman's fantasy," committed the ultimate escalation in the battle between the sexes. With one cut, she had said "enough" for every woman who had endured physical and mental abuse, it was said.

Many men, on the other hand, condemned the attack as "jungle justice." Reaction exceeded shock. The mutilation of John Wayne Bobbitt's body forced men everywhere to ponder a condition many considered worse than death. And as feminists embraced Lorena, the incident struck a deeper fear. Men already feeling psychologically emasculated by the women's movement now were forced to consider a very tangible loss.

The two participants in the drama seemed to be cast specifically for the debate. John Wayne Bobbitt was a strikingly handsome former Marine who could have graced recruiting posters in post offices across the U.S. He carried the name of the actor that epitomized manhood—before all the roles got changed. Lorena Bobbitt was a petite, seemingly shy woman of only 95-pounds, a manicurist, raised in a traditional Catholic family in Venezuela.

In homes and businesses across America debate continues to rage at a pitch not heard since the Anita Hill-Clarence Thomas affair. Did any man deserve John Wayne Bobbitt's fate? Was Lorena Bobbitt justified in extracting retribution for what she claimed were years of abuse.

Simply, the Bobbitt case was changed from a criminal case to a phenomenon. Lorena Bobbitt's trial on charges of "malicious wounding" loomed as landmark moment in the ongoing struggle by the sexes to define their roles in contemporary America.

On January 10, 1994, these forces seemed to be sweeping down on the town of Manassas, Virginia, like the armies of the North and the South did more than a century ago in two of the Civil War's greatest battles.

But beneath all the sociological and political hoopla, another story would be told, one of crime and punishment and tragedy. It would be a story of ordinary people caught up in extraordinary events.

The Bobbitts achieved equality in their marriage in at least one respect. Both were charged with crimes.

After the attack, the Commonwealth of Virginia charged John Wayne Bobbitt with raping his wife. He was tried on those charges in November of 1993. However, evidence and public access to the proceeding was limited by state law covering rape cases. The evidence focussed only the five days preceding the mutilation. Rulings barred testimony about their stormy four-year marriage. When it was over, John Wayne Bobbitt was acquitted by a jury of fellow Virginians.

In 1993, the Commonwealth also charged Lorena Bobbitt with malicious wounding, an offense that carried a penalty of up to twenty years in prison. In January, a trial entirely different from her husband's would unfold. Lorena Bobbitt's defense of temporary insanity would allow attorneys to call dozens of witnesses who were familiar with the couple's relationship. Secret materials and intimate details about the couple would be made public for the first time. As with most trials, it all would boil down to credibility: Whom the jury would believe.

Was John Wayne Bobbitt the abusive, insensitive hunk who battered his wife for years and raped her at will? Did Lorena Bobbitt cut off her husband's penis because she was overcome with an "irresistible impulse," caused by the trauma such repeated abuse? Was it vengeance or crippling mental illness? Did she even remember the act itself, or had she conveniently lost her memory to bolster her insanity defense?

Other motive had to be considered. The prosecution seemed to argue that Lorena wielded her knife because she was obsessively possessive of her husband. John Bobbitt testified that he experienced physical violence at the hands of his sexually demanding wife. Did she attack her husband because she suspected him of being unfaithful and planning to divorce her? Was she the sexually aggressive wife who once complained to police that he failed to give her orgasms? And, if she was a battered wife, why didn't she leave Bobbitt? Why didn't she take advantage of offers by friends for shelter and support?

As with any criminal case, the battle was not fought not on the editorial pages of newspapers or on sensational magazine news shows or in the press releases of special interest groups. The battle was waged in the courtroom with physical evidence and sworn testimony.

Then, on January 21, after only seven and a half hours of deliberation, a Prince William County jury of seven women and five men found Lorena Bobbitt not guilty by reason of temporary insanity. She was immediately taken to Center State Hospital in St. Petersburg to undergo a 45-day psychiatric evaluation.

Despite the verdict, the controversy continues to rage. To help men and women across America settle the dispute, here are the actual transcripts from Lorena's trial, with all the facts and most of testimony that the jury used to arrive at their final verdict.

Now, America, you decide.

Monday,
January 10

OPENING STATEMENTS

PAUL EBERT: Ladies and gentlemen, let me begin by thanking you for coming here and giving up your valuable time to perform what I'm sure all of you will agree is one of our most important functions as citizens.

This case is not a civil case. It's not a divorce case. It's not a media event. It's a criminal case. And my job is to prosecute criminal offenses. In this matter it's your job to judge this case on the evidence that you will hear, and apply that to the law that you will get at the end of this proceeding.

Now, the evidence in this case really, as to what happened, is not in much conflict. The evidence will reveal to you that John Bobbitt, the victim in this case, and Lorena Bobbitt were married. That they lived together in Manassas at 1874 Peekwood Court at the time of this alleged offense. And the evidence will reveal to you that they planned to separate and probably divorce.

The evidence will further reveal to you that just prior to the day in question—and the Commonwealth's evi-

dence in this case will be very narrow at the onset, that
a Mr. Robbie Johnston, a friend of John Bobbitt's, had
come to visit. He will tell you that he didn't know
whether he would be here for a long period of time or
a short period of time. But, nevertheless, he knew that
he would probably be here for at least, at the very minimum, a few days.

But on the 22nd of June of last year, he'll tell you that
for whatever reason John came home early [He worked
at Atlantic Foods, unloading trucks.] and they decided
they would go out on the town, so to speak, and visit a
number of bars.

And they'll tell you that in the course of the evening
both of them consumed five beers. John had, in addition
to that, two B52s, which is sort of a mixed drink, and
Robbie had one B52. John will tell you—the both of
them will tell you that they started to come home, they
stopped over on the way home and went to Denny's and
had something to eat.

Now, within the apartment and you'll see a diagram
of that apartment. It was a one bedroom apartment and
there was a couch which could be made into a bed, and
that's where Robbie was to sleep.

When they got home Lorena was already in bed. John
will tell you that he was tired, having worked, really, from
the early morning hours and then going out on the town.
And when he came home he got in bed. Now, he will
tell you that after he got in bed that he was—approached
Lorena in an amorous way.

And it may be hard for you to understand from all of
the evidence as to why these people who were going to
separate, perhaps never live together as man and wife
would have anything to do together with each other. But

nevertheless, he will tell you that that's what happened on this occasion.

He will tell you that he started to respond after they started to have sex. And, quite frankly, he will tell you that he doesn't recall ever having any sex. He thinks that he fell asleep. And it will be uncontradicted that whether he had sex or not, no doubt the defense will tell you that it was forcible sex, and against her will, it was a rape.

Whether that's true or not he will tell you that he fell asleep and that he had the sheet over him.

He will tell you that out of a dead sleep he was awakened by what he believes someone grabbing and ripping his penis and that he felt a sharp pain. He awakened, looked down to see what had happened, and he saw Lorena leaving rapidly. He got up, examined himself, went in and woke up Robbie.

Now, Robbie will tell you that he was in a dead sleep. And he thought it was time to go to work again. This is in the early morning hours of the 23rd, after three o'clock. He saw blood on John's hands. John was completely nude, as he stood over him. John examined himself and knew he no longer had a penis. They will both tell you that John asked Robbie to take him to the emergency room when that happened.

You will hear that when they arrived at the emergency room, Dr. Sehn examined his patient. He was familiar with cases where people had, for whatever reason, lost their penis, and that he had a discussion with John. And he will tell you that John was surprisingly somewhat upbeat.

He'll tell you that he told John that this could be life-threatening. He'll tell you that John Bobbitt had lost a third of his blood capacity at that point in time. And that he told John that he would no longer be able to stand up and urinate as most men do. He'd no longer be able to enjoy sex. And at that point in time they went into the operating room.

In the meantime, and you'll hear other evidence, that Mrs. Bobbitt had left. That when she left she took John's penis, a kitchen knife that she had used to sever his penis and a Gameboy, which apparently was put into her purse in some manner. And prior to that leaving she had taken a $100 bill out of Robbie's wallet.

But, in any event, Mrs. Bobbitt on the way, leaving the apartment, at one point in time discarded his penis off to the right on the grassy area, I think some 24 feet as I recall, from the center line of the road on which she was traveling. She took the knife that she used to amputate her husband and left that in a trash can outside the place where she worked. She went to her boss's home. Eventually, of course, the police were involved. They had gone to the apartment to search, for the remains. She [later] provided the exact information as to where the appendage was located.

Very briefly that will be the evidence that you will hear. You will hear that a sleeping man had his penis amputated, and that will, as I say, be the Commonwealth's evidence.

Now, the defense in this case. We know from question that they asked you, and notice that they have given us prior to this date, they will tell you about a marriage that, at best, was up and down. They will tell you that there was verbal, physical, sexual abuse of the Defendant by John Bobbitt.

And I suggest to you that the evidence is in hopeless conflict. And you folks are going to have a task to determine who you believe and what you believe, and even if you believe her evidence at its very best as to whether or not what she did was justifiable or excusable.

The defense will tell you that she acted, has already told you that in effect, by asking you certain questions, in self defense. And if you don't like that defense, then they will tell you she suffered an irresistible impulse. And they will have a doctor who will say that.

There will be other doctors who examined the Defendant, people employed by Central State Hospital, which is an agency of the Commonwealth, who will tell you that she certainly suffered depression, [and] that in their opinion, she did not suffer a known disease, a disorder and certainly did not suffer an irresistible impulse at the time this act occurred.

So, you folks will have to judge and be the judge as to whether or not what this woman did to her husband was justifiable or excusable. And you'll have to base that on what you hear in this courtroom.

And I feel confident that after you've heard all the evidence you will believe that there is no justification, was no justification or excuse for taking the law into her own hands, for maiming her husband.

And that she acted in anger or out of revenge and as a result she has violated the laws of this Commonwealth. Thank you.

LISA KEMLER: Good afternoon. This is a case about a young, petite, delicate and naive woman, Lorena Bobbitt, who for four years, the evidence will show, suffered extreme brutality and violence perpetrated against her by the very person who, when she and he took their wedding vows, promised to protect and honor her.

The evidence will show that everyone agrees that jus
in only the six months immediately preceding June 23rd
1993 that she endured this violence at the hands of he
husband as frequently as two times a week.

This violence, ladies and gentlemen, the evidence wil
show was characterized by brutality, which included
things such as rape, beatings, kickings, punching, shov
ing, slapping, dragging, choking, and threats of more vio
lence.

And this 92 pound woman reacted to defend hersel
against the brutal violent and primitive assault, that i
the rape that was committed against her by her husband
on June 23rd, 1993. She reacted to defend her life, t
defend her physical integrity, and to defend her dignity

But as I told you at the start of my comments to you
that this story, this tragedy didn't begin with only wha
occurred during the last six months of their marriage
prior to June 23rd. You will hear testimony about Lorena
Bobbitt's upbringing, in which the evidence will show i
both material and relevant to your assessment of wha
happened here and why it happened.

Lorena Bobbitt was born in Ecuador. Her family sub
sequently moved to Venezuela where she was raised. She
comes from a very close-knit, traditional, strict Catholi
household. You will hear testimony about the cultura
mores that Lorena grew up with, which place an empha
sis on the woman's role in the family. You'll hear tha
the woman is considered the backbone of the family. An
it is the woman, who is blamed if the marriage fails.

The evidence will further show that Lorena Bobbit
grew up fairly sheltered, in an overly-protective environ
ment, never experienced or saw any violence in the family

Now, you will hear that when Lorena was 18 she came to live in this country.

You will hear testimony from the members of the Castro family with whom Lorena lived after her parents and her sister and brother returned to Venezuela.

For Lorena the Castro family was very much like her own in Venezuela, in that Mr. and Mrs. Castro are Latin-American, they share the same cultural experiences. And, like Lorena's parents, the Castros and their two daughters were very protective of Lorena.

It was during this time that Lorena met John Wayne Bobbitt, her future husband. The evidence will show that when she first met John she fell head over heels in love with him. He was, you might say, her knight in shining armor. During the ten months that Lorena and John dated she experienced no violence on his part, nor had she seen any indication that he might be violent or abusive in any way.

You will hear that when he asked her to marry him, she immediately accepted, and June 18th, 1989 at the age of 19, Lorena married John Wayne Bobbitt. You will hear, ladies and gentlemen, that within the first month of their marriage, Lorena suffered the first violent episode in what was to become a reign of terror in the marital home. Beginning in July 1989, her husband began to physically beat, and kick, and punch, and slap, and shove her.

You will hear that at first these brutal and vicious assaults occurred only occasionally. But that as time went on they began to increase in frequency and in severity to once a month, and ultimately to twice a week. Countless witnesses personally saw occasions when he committed violence against her and observed the injuries that

she sustained as a result of the violence perpetrate
against her by her husband.

These included such things as knots to her head.

In addition to the physical abuse that Lorena Bobbi
endured, the evidence will show that John subjecte
Lorena to constant and relentless verbal abuse, verba
badgering. He would hurl insults at her, make degrading
and derogatory, and demeaning, and demoralizing com
ments to her.

This verbal badgering in combination with the physica
violence caused Lorena, the evidence will show to de
velop feelings of hopelessness, and helplessness to th
point where she believed that the situation she was i
was such that she had nowhere to go; nowhere that sh
could be safe.

You will hear about the embarrassment, the humili
ation and the shame she felt and how her self-esteer
was reduced to blaming herself for the beatings that sh
was enduring. Lorena became psychologically depender
upon her husband, this man who was abusing her an
committing violence on her.

And you will hear evidence that during the course o
the marriage, in about the spring of 1990, Lorena becam
pregnant. She was thrilled, excited. She hoped that Joh
would be just as excited as her and thrilled. And tha
perhaps it would bring them closer together, maybe
would stop some of the violence. Much to her shock an
dismay and surprise, that John reacted very badly an
ultimately, after much verbal badgering, Lorena felt tha
she had to choose between whether to carry the baby t
term or her husband. She ultimately gave in, the evidenc
will show, to his demands that she abort the baby, an
she submitted to unwanted abortion. This event, the ev

dence will show, was a crushing and lasting blow for Lorena Bobbitt.

In addition to the physical injuries that she sustained, beginning in the last six months she began to suffer physical manifestations of this abuse. She began to have gastrointestinal problems, experience hyperventilation, cramping in her fingers. She began to express to some people what was happening to her.

You will hear from the state's doctors that not only was Lorena Bobbitt a battered woman, but as a result she was suffering from a major mental illness on June 23rd, 1993, and that illness is major depression; a major depressive illness.

You will hear about how major depression can affect a person's behavior from a Dr. Susan Feister, a psychiatrist who has had experience working with and treating battered women. She will also tell you that Lorena Bobbitt, at the time that she cut off her husband's penis, suffered from major depressive illness. She will also tell you that she suffered from two other significant psychiatric disorders.

She will talk to you about Post Traumatic Stress Disorder and she will talk to you about Panic Disorder. Both of which she believes, it's her opinion, that Lorena was suffering from in addition to major depression at the time that she cut off her husband's penis.

There will also be evidence that in the state doctors' report they conclude that Lorena Bobbitt suffered from the symptoms of PTSD. Although they don't think that she suffered from it at the time of the incident, they don't think it was significant, but they conclude that she suffered some symptoms of Post Traumatic Stress Disorder.

What the evidence will show, ladies and gentlemen, is

that the psychiatric disorders were the product of the years of violence and abuse that she had suffered at the hands of her husband, and that they combined to cause her to experience what Dr. Feister will tell you was an acute psychotic break.

And it was as a result of that that she was unable to overcome any ability to control her impulse to defend herself, against what Lorena Bobbitt perceived was a serious threat against her body and to her personal security and safety.

Now, by the time Lorena Bobbitt got to June 23rd, 1993, the evidence will show that Lorena Bobbitt believed that she had no real means of escape. John Bobbitt had told her, the evidence will show, and he threatened her that if she tried to leave, if she tried to divorce him, it wouldn't matter, he'd follow her, he'd find her, he'd surprise her, and he would force her to have sex any way he wanted it.

What you need to know about the violence that Lorena Bobbitt suffered at the hands of John Bobbitt, her husband, is rape. Beginning in 1990 John decided it was okay to force Lorena to have sex with him whenever he wanted it, and whenever he desired it. You will hear, there will be testimony, that the rapes became more violent and more vicious, and the force was escalated.

She believed, ladies and gentlemen, she had no avenue of escape. Her family was more than 3,000 miles away. The times she had sought help from law enforcement had not stopped him from hurting her.

The evidence will show that just prior to June 23rd, Lorena had taken some steps to try to extricate herself from this awful, horrible, hideous situation. She had begun to pack some bags. She even moved some things out from the apartment, some clothes.

She was beginning to come to the realization that maybe this wasn't going to work, that she was going to have to give up on her marriage. She had even talked to John about it, to some degree.

She had even taken some steps to obtain a restraining order. She had gotten some pamphlets and some advice from a neighbor about shelters for battered women and rape.

The evidence will show that she went home the night of the incident, decided she could stay there because she felt safe, in that there was a third person staying at the apartment that night. That third person was John's friend, Robbie.

For the most part, the violence that she had sustained had been perpetrated between her and John in the absence of any witness.

So, she went home thinking that she was probably going to be okay. Lorena was home, she had worked, and she went to sleep.

The evidence will show that when John and his buddy Robbie came home, they had been out having a night of partying and drinking. That when John came home and into the bedroom he brutally raped Lorena again.

The evidence will show that this 92 pound woman perceived, it was her state of mind, she believed that she could not escape. She was not going to be permitted the dignity of an escape. And on this night, not only did he once again rape her, but the evidence will show that he did it knowing that his friend was right outside the bedroom door. For Lorena, ladies and gentlemen, this last offense of sexual violence was more than she could endure.

And ladies and gentlemen, what we have is Lorena Bobbitt's life juxtaposed against John Wayne Bobbitt's penis. The evidence will show that in her mind it was his penis from which she could not escape, that caused her the most pain, the most fear and the most humiliation.

And I submit to you, that at the end of this case you will come to one conclusion, and that is that a life is more valuable than a penis. Thank you.

JOHN WAYNE BOBBITT
DIRECT EXAMINATION

BY MR. EBERT:

Q: State your full name, please and give your address.

A: My name is John W. Bobbitt, John Wayne Bobbitt.

Q: And to whom are you married?

A: Lorena Bobbitt.

Q: And when were you married?

A: In June of '89; June 18th of '89.

Q: Now, directing your attention to the 22nd day of June of last year, where did you and she live together?

A: Pine Street, Maplewood Apartments in Manassas.

Q: Now, I'm going to show you a diagram I think you've seen prior to this time and ask you if you can identify that.

A: That was our apartment.

MR. EBERT: Could this be marked, Your Honor, for identification? I don't know if it will be objected to or not.

MR. HOWARD: No objection, sir.

THE COURT: It will be admitted, Commonwealth's Number 1.

Q: And how many bedrooms does that apartment have, Mr. Bobbitt?

A: Just one.

Q: And was there any other area which could be used for sleeping?

A: Well, yes, we had a sofa couch or a sofa bed in our living room.

Q: And on the 22nd day of June was there anyone else staying there with you, other than you and your wife?

A: Yes, at the time my best friend, Robert Johnston.

Q: Now, did you and your wife have any plans to separate and divorce on that date?

A: Yes.

Q: And how long had Robert Johnston been there at your home?

A: Since Sunday, two days prior.

Q: And what day, do you recall, was the 22nd of June?

A: It was a Tuesday.

Q: At that time where did you work?

A: Well, in the morning I worked at a warehouse in, you know, early in the morning . . . Atlantic Food Warehouse Distribution.

Q: And what type of work did you do there at Atlantic Food?

A: I first started working, you know, driving forklifts. And then I switched and then I started unloading trucks, unloading tractor trailer trucks.

Q: And how would you be paid for unloading these trucks?

A: Cash.

Q: Did you work anywhere else on that day other than at Atlantic Foods on the piecemeal basis?

A: I was supposed to work that evening at a new job I had as a host at Legends a nightclub.

Q: And where's that located, sir?

A: Directly, right across from our apartment.

Q: All right, sir. Now, after Robbie came to visit you on this occasion did he likewise work with you?

A: Yes, in the morning.

Q: Did you in fact work that night?

A: No, I didn't.

Q: And why not?

A: My boss said that they were going to be slow that night and they wouldn't need me. So I said okay, you know, thought to myself, well, good, because Robbie my best friend just got here, and I thought to myself, well, I'd show him around Manassas.

Q: Did you return home?

A: Yes, I returned home after my boss said I didn't have to work.

Q: And was Robbie there when you returned home?

A: Yes.

Q: And was Lorena there when you returned home?

A: No, she wasn't, sir.

Q: And after you returned home what did you do?

A: I told Robbie, I told him that I don't have to work, so why don't we go out. He said, "Great."

So, he got dressed, I changed, and we went back to Legends.

Q: Was Lorena home when you left?

A: No, she wasn't.

Q: Was there any reason why you left as early as you did?

A: Not really. Well, one of the main reasons was that I didn't want to have any conflict with Lorena before she got home. So, I wanted to leave, you know, before she got home. I didn't want her to be upset that, you know, that we were going to go out together.

Q: Do you know how she felt about, at that point in time about your working at the Legends as a host?

A: Yes. She opposed of it because she said she didn't want me working there because she thought women would be hitting on me or vice versa.

Q: And how long did you stay at Legends, approximately?

A: Stayed there about half an hour.

Q: Have anything to drink while you were there?

A: Yes, we both had a beer and I had a B52.

Q: And you had what?

A: A B52, it was a shot. It's like Kalua and cream and Grand Marnier.

Q: And so, after you left there where did you go?

A: We went to a place in Fairfax called Champions. It was empty. We didn't stay. Then we went to a place next door called PJ Skidoos. We stayed there for a while and talked, and you know, had a few drinks.

Q: What did you have to drink there, sir?

A: We had three beers each and we both had a B52.

Q: Then what happened?

A: We left there about 1:30—no, well—we left— yeah, we left there around 1:30 and we went to a place called O'Toole's. But, you know, same thing, there was no one there, so we left and we went to Denny's. We had breakfast and coffee and we stayed there for a little while.

Q: And then where did you go?

A: Then we went directly home after that, back to the apartment.

Q: And do you know approximately what time it was when you arrived home?

A: We arrived home around 3:15, around there.

Q: And then what happened?

A: When we arrived home Robbie, you know, I made sure he was set up. I pulled out the sofa bed and, you know, made sure he was comfortable. And he went to bed, and I went in my room.

A: Yes.

Q: And where was Lorena when you went to your room?

A: She was sleeping on the right side of the bed, laying on her side.

Q: Now, looking at that diagram, could you point approximately to the area that you're mentioning now? First show us where Robbie was sleeping.

(The witness left the witness stand.)

A: Robbie was sleeping right here—(indicating). There was the sofa couch pulled out—(indicating).

Q: And where was the bed located in your bedroom?

A: It was right here—(indicating). Lorena was sleeping on this side of the bed—(indicating) on her side. I walked in, you know took off my clothes, folded them up, put them on the ironing board, walked around the bed and got in bed.

Q: You folded your clothes up and put them on the ironing board; is that correct?

A: Right.

Q: Did you put on any nightwear of any kind?

A: No.

Q: You sleep naked?

A: Well, occasionally I do. Well, in the summertime especially.

Q: Is that your normal practice to sleep naked?

A: Not really, I usually sleep in my underwear.

Q: But on this occasion you slept naked; is that correct?

A: Correct.

Q: Then what happened?

A: Then got in the bed and then I just fell right to sleep.

Q: You fell asleep?

A: Fell asleep, because I was tired.

Q: And at some point in time after you had gone to sleep did something occur?

A: Yes, I woke up about, I don't know, I'd say an hour later, being restless I just rolled over. I rolled over in bed. And as I was rolling over I was adjusting the covers, I was rolling over. I saw Lorena laying on her back.

Q: How was she dressed?

A: She was dressed in silk lingerie; like a top and underwear.

Q: Did she customarily dress that way when she slept?

A: Yes.

Q: Then what happened?

A: Then next thing I remember, I remember caressing her. Well, I was laying on my side. But, you know, but part of me was asleep and part of me wasn't. I mean, I wanted to perform but I was too exhausted. I was too tired. And I remember, touching her and then I remember rolling over on top of her.

Q: Now, you say you wanted to perform, you mean sexually?

A: Correct.

Q: Then what happened?

A: Anyways, I was too exhausted to like, get up to perform. But I wanted to. I rolled over and I was on top of her. And then I just remember that she put her knees up, and she put her arms around me, and then I just fell back off to sleep. And I don't remember anything else happening after that, until I was just laying on my back. I mean—then at that point I opened my eyes because I seen her sitting on my side, like checking me and seeing if I was able to perform for her.

Q: Again, when you say perform, sir, you mean perform sexually?

A: Yeah, because I remember I wanted to but I was just too exhausted, and I said there's no way I can do this, because I was so exhausted that evening that I just couldn't, you know, I was just laying, you know—

Q: How much had you had to drink that night?

A: I had about, between four and five beers and like two shots of B52s.

Q: Now, did you or did you not have sex with her that night?

A: Well, I just, I don't really know, sir, if I did or not.

Q: You don't have any recollection of it, that's what you're saying?

A: No recollection of it at all, sir.

Q: Now, you say you were then over on your back, and what happened?

A: Well, I remember her, she was sitting on my left side and I just remember I opened my eyes barely, just to see what she was doing.

Q: What was she doing?

A: Just like—I don't know, just checking my midsection to see if I was able to perform, but I felt too exhausted to.

Q: Let me ask you, did you have an erection at that point in time, sir, or do you know?

A: I believe I didn't.

Q: All right. And then after you say you recall that what happened?

A: After that I just closed my eyes and went to sleep because I couldn't even—I couldn't stay awake, I was too exhausted. The next thing I remember is she was sitting on my left side again. I woke up a little, I opened my eyes just barely. I just noticed what she was doing, just sitting there, and she just pulled up on my groin area.

Q: She did what?

A: She pulled on my groin area twice, I think. I felt a couple jerks. And then after that she just like cut it off.

Q: Now, what did you feel at that time, sir?

A: I was laying on my back in a deep sleep. I just sprang up like I wanted to, you know, scream but there was nothing there. I was bleeding and she just—

Q: What did you feel, sir?

A: Pain. A lot of pain, like it really hurt, it hurt real bad but—to try to explain—

Q: Tell us what you thought, sir, if you don't mind.

A: Okay. I thought she just, you know, grabbed it and just pulled it right off my body. I didn't see a knife. I didn't see nothing.

I just sat up real quick, like I was in real pain, a lot of pain. And I held myself. I was bleeding. I was confused. I was like hysterical. And I was like, I don't know—I didn't—I was confused, I didn't know what was going on.

Q: Did you see her after that when you felt that pain?

A: Vaguely. I just caught her out of the corner of my eye just dashing out of the bedroom. And after she did it she gave like a—she gave it a grunt like when she did it and just ran.

Q: Where was it approximately that you have this recollection of seeing her? Point that out to the ladies and gentlemen of the jury.

A: Well, when I sat up real quick she just, you know, dashed right out the bedroom door, real quick, she grunt[ed], and ran out the door. (indicating).

Q: What did you do then?

A: I felt dizzy. I felt like, you know, weird. But then I collected myself. I knew I was bleeding. I knew I had to get some help. So I went out into the living room and I woke my friend Robbie who was sleeping. I used my foot to wake him up, while I held myself and applied pressure. So, at that point—

Q: You say you were holding yourself?

A: Correct.

Q: How were you holding yourself, sir?

A: Just with my hands.

Q: With your hands?

A: Over my groin—yeah. Holding both hands and pressing.

Q: Pressing on your groin area?

A: Right, pressing, you know—

Q: Let me stop you. At that point in time you knew that your penis was missing, is that correct?

A: Well, correct.

Q: All right. Go ahead.

A: Well, anyways, he woke up and he was kind of like in a daze. He thought I was getting him up to go to work.

But I told him, you know, my wife had cut me. And I didn't know how to explain it to him and I was kind of embarrassed at the time. And he said, well, you know—well, anyways, I went in my bedroom. I was naked still. And got a pair of sweat pants off my dresser and put them on.

And then my friend went into the bathroom and he brushed his teeth. And I guess, I went out here and I was talking to him, "Robbie, you have to take me to the hospital." And in the rear view of the mirror he seen the blood that was, you know, was dripping and stuff.

And he got hysterical, he said, "Oh, my God." So, I slipped on a pair of shoes and we ran out the door and down the stairs into his car. And then I directed him to the hospital, you know, the best way I could.

Q: You went from there to the hospital; is that correct?

A: Correct.

Q: And what happened after you arrived at the hospital?

A: We arrived at the hospital. He ran in front of me, he told the people in the emergency room that, you know, I guess he was hysterical. He said his wife tried to kill him or something like that, and I walked in behind him—

MR. HOWARD: Your Honor, excuse me, I'm going to interrupt.

THE COURT: Sustain the objection as to what he said.

BY MR. EBERT:

Q: Go ahead, don't tell us what he said, sir, just tell us what you did.

A: Okay. I walked in the hospital. And as I passed a room there was a person I knew, I just looked at him. And he was, you know, I asked him what he was doing here. It was real brief. He said, "They're going to let me out of here."

Then at that point the doctor said—"Get in this room. Let me see where you're cut."

So I pulled down my pants and I showed him. And he like kind of stepped back, you know, like "Wow." Then he got an orderly to put me on a table to apply pressure. And then I guess I must've passed out.

But the doctor came back later, I guess he put a tourniquet on, and then he explained procedures. At that time, you know, there was nothing they could do, just close it up, you know, I wouldn't be normal anymore. I'd have to sit down to urinate, and, you know—

Q: Do you remember what doctor that was?

A: It was Dr. Sehn, the urologist.

Q: And did there come a time when you were operated on that night?

A: Yes. I was taken to the operating room yes, for surgery.

Q: And you underwent an operation; is that correct?

A: Correct.

Q: And as a result of that operation your penis was re-attached; is that correct?

A: Correct.

Q: Now, what is your condition now, sir, relative to your injuries?

A: Pretty stable now. I mean, I'm getting back—well, the doctors are pretty sure that I'll be fully functional.

Q: Now, in your apartment, did you have certain kitchen knives there?

A: Yes.

Q: And where were they customarily kept?

A: Right in here in the corner—(indicating). This is the kitchen sink over here in the corner—(indicating).

Q: And what kind of container, if any, were they kept in?

A: It was a regular cutlery container, a knife set.

Q: Do you know how many knives were in that set?

A: I think six, or five. I don't know how many exactly but there were five or six knives, different knives.

Q: And the person that you identified as the person that did this to you, is she in the courtroom today?

A: Yes.

Q: Would you identify her for the record?

A: It's my wife, Lorena Bobbitt.

Q: Is she the lady at counsel table to your far left?

A: Yes, sir.

MR. EBERT: Would the record indicate he has identified the Defendant.

That's all I have of this witness at this time.

THE COURT: Mr. Howard

CROSS EXAMINATION

BY BLAIR HOWARD:

Q: Mr. Bobbitt, my name is Blair Howard and I'm representing your wife in this matter. I'm going to ask you some questions. If I ask you any questions, sir, that confuse you, please stop me and let me know that. And I'm going to take my time and give you plenty of time to answer my questions; is that okay?

A: Yes, sir.

Q: Mr. Bobbitt, I'm happy to hear that you made a good recovery in this case. You say at this time you feel like your condition is stable?

A: Yes.

Q: As a matter of fact, isn't it true that you've made a rather remarkable recovery up to now?

A: Yes.

Q: And I believe you spent some time out west on a ranch, haven't you?

A: Yes.

Q: Done a lot of horseback riding out there in recent time?

A: Yes.

Q: You've done some calf roping out there?

A: Right.

Q: Made a number of television appearances?

A: Correct, sir.

Q: And you've spoken very positively about this operation, and insofar as the results of that operation.

A: Right.

Q: And you've thanked, on national television, your surgeons for doing such an excellent job; is that basically correct?

A: Yes, sir.

Q: On the evening of June 22nd, Mr. Bobbitt as I understand it you went to Legends. You worked at Legends at that time.

A: Correct.

Q: How long had you had that job at Legends?

A: I started June 14th. I mean, we trained—we were in training.

Q: Okay. So you went there that night with your friend, Robbie and you expected to work and you were advised that you weren't needed that night, so that you and Robbie could go out; is that right?

A: Correct.

Q: And it's my understanding from your testimony that you had at least five beers during the course of the evening?

A: Correct.

Q: And you had approximately two B52s?

A: It wasn't approximately. It was exactly two.

Q: You have a very vivid recollection, do you not, of exactly what you drank and what bars you drank in?

A: Yes.

Q: Is it fair to say then that your recollection about the events of the evening is very clear?

A: Yes.

Q: After you finished bar hopping, you then had some breakfast at Denny's, and then you went back to the apartment with Robbie?

A: Correct.

Q: Now, would you tell the members of the jury what your frame of mind was at that point? Did you feel any effects from the alcohol at all?

A: No.

Q: None whatsoever?

A: No.

Q: No effects from the alcohol, clear recollection of everything that occurred that evening?

A: Yes.

Q: When you went into the bedroom and you undressed, you looked down on the bed and what state of dress did you say your wife was in?

A: She wore her silk lingerie.

Q: Now, would you tell the members of the jury, do you have a recollection of what kind of lingerie she was wearing?

A: Yeah, Victoria's Secrets.

Q: And you didn't have any problems identifying that?

A: Yeah, I remember the top, and, you know, and the bottom, clearly. She was like wearing purple, like a purple-like blouse and like a beige like cream-colored silk underwear.

Q: And that's just as vivid and clear to you now as it was as if it happened yesterday; isn't that correct?

A: Correct.

Q: All right. You caressed your wife at one point.

A: Yes.

Q: And in terms of some advance on your part to try to have sex with her, or to let her know that you were trying to stimulate her to have sex. Is that fair to say?

A: Yes, sir.

Q: And that was because you wanted to perform sex.

A: Well, like I said, one part of me wanted to have sex but I was asleep, basically. I vaguely remember knowing what I was doing, you know, I was like in a deep sleep.

Q: Wait a minute now. You have a clear recollection of what she was wearing. You have a clear recollection of caressing her. You have a clear recollection that you wanted to have sex. And then suddenly we're into sleep? Now, are you still aware of what you were doing?

A: I don't think you understand. When I rolled over I was, like, yeah, I remember, because in our room it's lighted. You know, like we have a light that reflects, that illuminates the room, and our whole room is white. And when I rolled over my eyes were open and I seen what she were wearing. And I gradually closed my eyes and began to caress her.

Q: And you know what you saw. You've told us that.

A: I know what I saw and—

Q: And you know what you felt in your mind.

A: Yes.

MR. EBERT: Let him answer the question.

THE WITNESS: He's trying to twist it.

BY MR. HOWARD:

Q: Is that true, sir, you know what you saw next to you on that bed, that's correct?

A: That's correct, sir.

Q: And you know what thoughts were going through your mind. And those thoughts were you wanted to have sex with your wife; isn't that correct?

A: Yes, I mean, because of the silk underwear, I mean, it just turned me on.

Q: Sure. And you were turned on by the underwear, and you touched her, and caressed her to let her know that you wanted to have sex with her.

A: Yes, sir.

Q: And then you got on top of her; isn't that correct?

A: Correct.

Q: And then you got on top of her, you have a specific recollection she put her knees up on either side of you.

A: Yes.

Q: That's correct, isn't it, sir?

A: Yes.

Q: She put her hands around your back.

A: These are vague recollections, not a solid recollection. I vaguely remember, you know, when I rolled over on top of her, her knees were up, her arms were around me, and then I just fell asleep, you know, at the same time.

Q: Now, while you were doing these things was she fondling you also, sir?

A: Fondling?

Q: Yes, sir.

A: Not at that point, no.

Q: Did she fondle you sometime during the activity?

A: After. I remember waking up and that she was fondling me. I mean, I was like really, really tired, and I was trying to but I couldn't.

Q: You have a recollection of her fondling you, sir?

A: Yes.

Q: Okay.

A: But when I was laying on my back.

Q: Let me ask you this, Mr. Bobbitt. We've gone through this story on direct examination, we've gone through it on cross examination. Have you ever given the police or the Commonwealth Attorney a different version than you've just given to this jury of the events in that bedroom that night?

A: Yeah, I probably left out one thing that I forgot to tell you. But as I was laying on my side and before—after I caressed her, I slid her pants down, her underwear, down to my foot and slid them off the rest of the way. And then I rolled over on top of her.

Q: Let me take you back, Mr. Bobbitt, let me take you back in time. Do you remember on June 24th, 1993 talking to Investigator Morgan, Sergeant Morgan and Detective Weintz, Prince William County Police Department, June 24th?

A: June 24th? Oh, yeah. They came to me, you know, in the hospital when I was laying there.

Q: Let me ask you a few questions about that interview. There was Sergeant Morgan and there was Detective Weintz; isn't that correct, sir?

A: Yes.

Q: On that occasion isn't it true that you told those two gentlemen that you didn't have any sex with your wife that night?

A: Nope.

Q: Now, excuse me. Did you tell those gentlemen the same story you just told this jury on June 24th?

A: Well, yeah, but, you know—I don't remember what

they said. I didn't think I had sex with her, you know, I didn't really remember. I didn't give them an accurate statement.

Q: You weren't asleep then when Detective Weintz and Sergeant Morgan were talking to you, were you?

A: But I was drugged. I just got out of a major operation.

Q: Did you tell Detective Weintz and Sergeant Morgan on June 24th, 1993 that you had a clear recollection of all the events that evening?

A: I don't remember.

Q: Did you tell Detective Weintz and Detective Morgan that you had no effects from the alcohol when you went in there to your wife's bedroom?

A: See, I don't remember that interview with those detectives at all. I don't remember what I stated or what I said.

Q: Let me just ask you this, sir. The truth of the matter is that on that occasion when you talked to those two detectives, you told them that you had no recollection of sex at all. And in addition to that, you told them that the reason why you didn't remember having any sex with your wife that night was because you had had too much to drink. Isn't that what you told them on June 24th, 1993?

A: I might have.

Q: You might have said. You're not backing away from that now, are you, Mr. Bobbitt?

A: No, I'm not. I'm just telling you I don't remember that interview.

Q: You're certainly not going to deny those things that I've just asked you about are you?

A: No, no, I won't deny it.

Q: Now, that's story number one.

Story number two. Do you remember talking to them again on July 13th?

A: July 13th?

Q: Do you remember having an interview with Detective Weintz and Sergeant Zen?

A: Yes, I remember, they came back—

Q: That was on July 13th, 1993?

A: Yes, sir.

Q: Do you remember that occasion? Were you awake on July 13th, 1993 when you talked to Detective Weintz? And with Sergeant Zen?

A: Right.

Q: On that occasion did they ask you anything about what your wife was wearing when you went into the bedroom?

A: Yes, and I told them.

Q: What did you tell them on July 13th, 1993?

A: I told them that she was wearing silk underwear.

Q: Now, let me refresh your recollection about that, sir. Didn't you tell Sergeant Zen and Detective Weintz on July 13th, 1993 that you didn't see what your wife was wearing because she was covered up with the sheets?

A: Nope.

Q: You didn't tell them that, is that what you're saying?

A: No, I told them that—exactly what I told you.

Q: And you never said that you couldn't give them any information about what she was wearing because she was under the covers, on that interview of July 13th; is that your testimony here today?

A: Right.

Q: Is that a maybe, or a might, or is that an unequivocal "No, I didn't tell them that?"

A: Yeah.

Q: You're the only person there other than those two detectives, it doesn't help you to look at Mr. Ebert.

A: I remember, you know, clearly what she was wearing. So, if I, you know, I said something different—

Q: So, if you told them that—

MR. EBERT: Well, wait a minute now, Your Honor, he's getting ready to explain that he didn't know until he pulled the sheet back what she was wearing. She had the sheet on and he couldn't see.

THE WITNESS: Oh, yeah, that's right.

THE COURT: All right, sir.

THE WITNESS: He's trying to twist it. He's trying to twist this whole thing around.

THE COURT: Answer the question.

THE WITNESS: All right.

BY MR. HOWARD:

Q: My question to you, sir, is did you make that statement to them that she was under the covers and you couldn't tell what she was wearing?

A: Right.

Q: Oh, you did make that statement? Okay.

A: When I entered the room.

Q: All right, sir.

Now, did they ask you on July 13th whether you had had sex with her?

A: Whether I had—

Q: Yeah, sex with your wife.

A: Yes.

Q: The same night she cut your penis off.

A: Yes.

Q: And what did you tell them?

A: That I don't remember having sex with her at all.

Q: Okay. So, on July 13th in the beginning of that interview you reiterated what you had told them on June 24th that you didn't have any recollection?

MR. EBERT: And what he told this jury, he doesn't know whether he had sex or not.

THE COURT: All right, sir. Go ahead. Go ahead Mr. Howard.

BY MR. HOWARD:

Q: Well, let me ask you about that. After you made this statement that you didn't have any recollection about sex, didn't Sergeant Zen confront you with the test results that they had taken of your wife showing that she had recently had sex; isn't that right?

A: Correct.

Q: Okay. And after they confronted you, you told them you didn't want to lie to them.

A: Right.

Q: You then admitted to them that you had gotten on top of your wife and that you had had an orgasm; isn't that true?

A: Nope.

Q: Okay. Now, I want to be certain about this. Do you remember being confronted with the fact that they had run tests on your wife and determined that she had in fact had recent sex? You remember them confronting you about that?

A: Can I run this conversation through that I had with them?

Q: Yes, sir.

A: Okay.

Q: Did they tell you that they had evidence that she had had recent sex?

A: Yes.

Q: Okay.

A: Then I said I didn't remember. Well, if I did, you know, I don't know. And I told you, you know, I didn't have sex with her.

Q: All right. It was only after they confronted you with hard evidence that you admitted, for the first time, that you had gotten on top of your wife; isn't that true?

A: No.

Q: You never told them after they confronted you with that evidence that you got on your wife?

A: I don't remember.

Q: Did you ever tell them after they confronted you with hard evidence that you had had an orgasm that evening?

A: No, I told them I might have. I just didn't remember. I didn't remember any sex.

Q: But you don't recall telling them specifically that you had an orgasm?

A: No. I didn't tell them, no, "Yeah, I had an orgasm," because I don't remember.

Q: Do you remember them asking you about foreplay, after they confronted you with hard evidence?

A: Foreplay? I don't remember.

Q: Do you remember telling them that there was no foreplay that night, that that just wasn't part of the scenario between you and your wife? Do you remember telling them that?

A: Right. Actually—

Q: That's what you told them back on July 13th.

A: Me and my wife didn't really get into much foreplay.

Q: Well, excuse me, you told us here today, before I confronted you with these earlier statements, that you had caressed your wife, that she had fondled you, and that there was some fondling—

A: That's not a lot of foreplay.

THE COURT: The jury heard his previous answer, let's proceed.

BY MR. HOWARD:

Q: Did you ever tell the police that you might have had sex with your wife while you were sleeping, on any of those occasions?

A: See, I don't know. I don't remember these interviews with the detectives that well.

Q: As a matter of fact, you told them when confronted with hard evidence, that you often are asleep when you have sex with your wife. Isn't that what you told them? That maybe that was the reason why you didn't remember?

A: This is really the only solid time that I really had sex with my wife while I was sleeping. It was the most exhausting day of my life, really. It was a long day. I had been up for 24 hours, and I was just plain old tired.

Q: Let me ask you this, Mr. Bobbitt. You mentioned that your wife was upset at the fact that you had gotten a job at Legends. And, I believe, according to your testimony it was because she thought some girls might hit on you.

A: Correct.

Q: Well, she had every reason to believe, based on your conduct toward her, that you were seeing a lot of girls, didn't she?

A: No.

Q: You made up a list of ladies, did you not?

A: Right.

Q: And let me show you a copy of that list.

MR. EBERT: Well, I'm going to object. This is outside the scope of direct examination. There's no indication that that list had any bearing whatsoever on the night in question. He can bring that out later on if he wishes to.

THE WITNESS: He can bring the list out.

MR. EBERT: This has nothing to do with his wife's attitude about him working in a bar.

THE COURT: I'll sustain the objection, Mr. Howard. I'll let you bring it out in your case in chief.

BY MR. HOWARD:

Q: Is it your testimony, sir, that you and your wife never engaged in foreplay?

A: Not much at all.

Q: Not much at all.

Do you remember getting a book entitled *How to Satisfy a Woman Every Time and Have Her Beg for More?*

A: Yes.

Q: Is this the book—(indicating)?

A: Yes.

Q: This is like an encyclopedia on foreplay, isn't it?

A: It's techniques, I guess.

Q: All the techniques of foreplay and arousal.

A: This is just teasing, it's not foreplay.

Q: And you and your wife went over this together, didn't you?

A: Yeah. We both read it together.

Q: And, basically, is what you're telling this jury is that you bought the book, you and your wife read it together, giving all the techniques of foreplay and teasing but you never engaged in any of that. You never put the teachings of the book to practical use?

A: Just a couple times.

Q: Just a couple times.

A: Well, you know, we didn't get along well. We just didn't communicate.

Q: Let me just ask you this, sir. Is it your position in this case that you did not have any sex with your wife that night, in the early morning hours of June 23rd?

A: Correct.

Q: Is it your position that you did not try to forcibly have sex with her in the early morning hours of June 23rd?

A: Correct.

Q: Is it your position that you never tried to have forcible sex with your wife?

A: I never did.

REDIRECT EXAMINATION

BY MR. EBERT:

Q: The book that Mr. Howard asked you about— Where did you get this book, sir—(indicating)?

A: It was at Sandra Beltran's house, one of Lorena's friends where we stayed at for a few months—well, several months.

Q: What was the name of the party that provided this book to you?

A: Sandra Beltran and Raymond Beltran. They—

Q: Beltran?

A: Beltrans, yeah.

MR. EBERT: I'd like to have that marked for identification purposes.

THE COURT: It will be marked for identification as Commonwealth's Number 2.

BY MR. EBERT:

Q: Sir, just a couple of questions. Mr. Howard asked you about fondling on the night in question, the early morning hours of the 23rd. When did that occur? Did your wife fondle you at any time, in your recollection, on that night?

A: Yes. After I fell asleep, you know, after I initially tried to have sex and just, you know, fell asleep. Just right after that, laying on my back. I woke up noticing that she was, you know, just fondling with my midsection. Just, you know, I thought she was—wanted to continue, wanted to have sex or whatever. I, you know, just couldn't perform. I was way too exhausted to do anything.

Q: In any event, when you got between her legs, what have you, did she have—her pants were off, is that what you testified to?

A: Yes, I mean, I was laying on my side.

Q: Did she have her top on?

A: She had the top on, yes.

Q: Did you take that off?

A: Oh, no.

RECROSS EXAMINATION

BY MR. HOWARD:

Q: In light of Mr. Ebert's questions are you telling this jury that you didn't have sex with your wife but you took her pants off?

A: Correct.

Q: Okay. Is there any other reason in the world you can think of that you can tell this jury why you would take her pants off if you didn't want to have sex, and didn't have sex with your wife?

MR. EBERT: Well, Your Honor, he's arguing with the witness. He said he wanted to have sex—

THE COURT: Sustain the objection. I think you're arguing with the witness.

THE WITNESS: I wanted to, yeah, but I couldn't, I was too exhausted.

MR. HOWARD: That's all I have.

Tuesday, January 11

ROBERT JOHNSTON
DIRECT EXAMINATION

BY MR. EBERT:

Q: Directing your attention to the 20th day of June of last year, did you come to the Prince William County area?

A: Yes; I did. I came to visit John. John was planning on getting a divorce and I wanted to look at some schools in the area and if I could find a school, I was going to stay there and finish my last year of school in Virginia.

Q: What day of the week was it you arrived, sir?

A: It was on a Sunday.

Q: And did you come to the apartment?

A: Yes; I did.

Q: Who was there when you arrived?

A: Lorena answered the door and John was in the bedroom.

Q: And did you have a conversation at that time?

A: Yeah, Lorena said John will be happy to see you and she went and got John.

Q: Then what happened?

A: Well, Lorena asked me to leave. She said she needed some privacy.

Q: She asked you to leave?

A: Yes.

Q: And did you bring any belongings with you when you came?

A: Yes; I did.

Q: What was your intention; how long were you to stay?

A: Well, I figured, well, I would stay for two weeks, two months or—or a year, at least, until I finished my schooling.

Q: What, to your way of thinking, would depend on the length of your stay?

A: Well, if John and Lorena didn't get divorced, I'd probably stay for two weeks. If I couldn't find a school, I'd stay for two months, go back to Buffalo and finish school there.

Q: When she asked you to leave, did you, in fact, leave?

A: Yes; I did.

Q: What did you do when you left?

A: I went—I called my parents, so I went down to the 7-Eleven. To tell them I arrived safely.

Q: Then what did you do?

A: Then I came back.

Q: What happened then?

A: Well, John and me went down to the pool.

Q: And when you got to the pool, what did you do?

A: I laid down on a chair and John went into the pool.

Q: How were you dressed?

A: I was wearing shorts, T-shirt.

Q: How was John dressed?

A: The same.

Q: Then what happened?

A: Well, John disappeared and I went looking for him.

Q: How long would you say you were at the pool?

A: I'd say like between ten minutes and an hour.

Q: Were you sleeping or dozing?

A: I probably dozed off for a few minutes, yes.

Q: Where did you go when you went looking for him?

A: I went to the—there's a little room, there's like a little sauna area, I went looking through there and I went back to the apartment.

Q: What happened when you got to the apartment?

A: Lorena answered the door. John and Lorena were in there.

Q: Did you notice anything unusual about them?

A: They were kind of like smirking.

Q: Both of them?

A: Yes.

Q: What happened then?

A: Lorena asked me to leave again. She said she needed some privacy.

Q: What did you do as a result of that request?

A: I left again.

Q: And were did you go?

A: I went to get some lunch at the McDonald's and I went to call my parents again, because the first time it was busy.

Q: Did you get through on this occasion?

A: No; I didn't.

Q: What happened then?

A: I came back to the apartment.

Q: And what happened at that point in time?

A: At that point, Lorena was moving boxes out of the apartment.

Q: Moving boxes out of the apartment?

A: Yes.

Q: And do you know where she was going with those boxes?

A: That was to the apartment below, Diane's apartment.

Q: Taking them to the apartment below their apartment; is that right?

A: Yes.

Q: Do you know what was in those boxes?

A: I didn't really look.

Q: What happened then?

A: Then Lorena left and I guess me and John went— we were just hanging out together.

Q: And did you spend the night there that night?

A: Yes; I did.

Q: Who slept there that night?

A: Well, Lorena came back later that night and went into the bedroom and I slept on the sofa couch in the living room and then John then went to the bedroom too and slept with Lorena.

Q: When Lorena came back, were you and John in the front room or the living area?

A: Yes.

Q: Approximately what time did you go to bed on that night?

A: I'd say between 11:00 and 12:00.

Q: And Monday, what happened?

A: Me and John woke up about 6:00 o'clock and we went to work.

Q: And was that pre-arranged?

A: Yes.

Q: Where did you go to work?

A: A place called Atlantic Food Services.

Q: And what was your type of work that you performed there?

A: We were called lumpers. We unloaded trucks.

Q: And how long did you work on that day?

A: Until the afternoon.

Q: When you got back to the apartment, what did you do?

A: I cooked—I cooked some dinner.

Q: What did you cook; do you remember?

A: Yeah, it was chicken, some chicken.

Q: And was Lorena there when you arrived back at the apartment?

A: No; she wasn't.

Q: Did she come in while you were there?

A: Yes.

Q: And what happened then?

A: I think John offered her some chicken.

Q: Did she accept it?

A: No; she didn't.

Q: Did you notice anything unusual about the relationship between the parties at this time?

A: They didn't seem to be talking, kind of ignoring each other.

Q: And did you stay in the apartment?

A: Yes; I did.

Q: Did Lorena stay in the apartment?

A: Yes.

Q: Did Lorena spend the night there that night?

A: Yes; she did.

Q: Who went to bed first that night?

A: Lorena did. She left the apartment and came back later that night and went right to the bedroom.

Q: And you slept—

A: On the sofa couch.

Q: Then what happened; did you wake up the next morning?

A: Yeah, we woke up again around 6:00 o'clock, went to Atlantic Food Services.

Q: What time did you return on that day?

A: Afternoon.

Q: Was Lorena home at that point in time?

A: No; she wasn't.

Q: And when you got home, what did you do?

A: I cooked some dinner.

Q: What happened then?

A: Well, later that night, John had to go to work.

Q: How long was John gone?

A: Probably not more than fifteen minutes; he came back.

Q: When he came back, did you and he make some plans?

A: Yeah, he said, you know, get ready, let's go out. They didn't need me at work.

Q: Did you, in fact, do that?

A: Yes; I did.

Q: And was Lorena home when you left?

A: No; she wasn't.

Q: Did you have any discussion about leaving before she got home?

A: Yeah, John said let's get ready before Lorena gets back, get out of here.

Q: Where did you go?

A: We went to Legends . . . then we went to a couple of bars called, I think it was P.J.'s and Champions . . . and about—probably about maybe 1:00 or 1:30, we left to go home.

Q: How were you traveling, sir?

A: I was driving my car.

Q: And in total, how much would you say you had to drink on this occasion?

A: I had five beers and that one B-52.

Q: How much did John have to drink?

A: John had the same amount as me, except he had one more B-52.

Q: Now, sir, were you feeling the influence of what you had to drink?

A: Sure.

Q: Where did you go from there?

A: Well, we went to Denny's.

Q: Was John awake during the entire time that you were driving back or do you know?

A: I think he had probably fallen asleep.

Q: And leaving there, how did you feel?

A: You know, better. I wasn't as intoxicated as I was before.

Q: And from there where did you go?

A: We went back to the apartment.

Q: And what happened then?

A: Well, then I went into the bathroom and then John made the sofa couch which was in the living room.

Q: And did you go to sleep?

A: Yes; I did.

Q: What did John do?

A: John went into the bedroom.

Q: Did you hear anything after you went to sleep until you awakened?

A: No; I didn't.

Q: And did there come a time when you were awake.

A: Yes.

Q: And describe for the ladies and gentlemen of the jury what happened.

A: Well, John woke me up. He kicked me and said, "Get up, Rob; get up." And I woke up.

Q: And when you woke up, what did you think?

A: Well, I was tired, I had only been asleep a couple of hours and I saw John there. He was naked and his hand was covering his groin area and you could see blood around his hands which really didn't make sense to me.

I didn't really understand and I actually went into the bathroom and started brushing my teeth because I had thought that he was waking me up to go to work.

Q: And when you started brushing your teeth, what happened?

A: Well, then John followed me in and I saw his reflection in the mirror and I saw the blood and it just kind of shook me, shocked me a little bit. I kind of woke up.

He said, "You'd better take me to the hospital. I've been cut."

Q: What happened then?

A: I spit out the toothpaste. John went and got some jogging pants on. Then I took him to the hospital. Prince William Hospital.

Q: And after this occurred, how long did you stay in the area?

A: I believe a couple of months. I left on August 23rd.

Q: You stayed in the apartment; is that correct?

A: Yes.

Q: Was there any furniture in the apartment?

A: Well, all of the furniture was taken out of the apartment. Somebody took it. There wasn't even a bed. The dresser, the bed, even the food out of the refrigerator was taken.

Q: Did you stay there despite that?

A: Yes.

Q: Where did you sleep?

A: I had to sleep on the floor.

Q: Now, before going out on that night, the Tuesday night, did you have any property that you left there?

A: Yes; I did.

Q: Did you have your wallet with you when you left to go on the town that night?

A: No; I didn't.

Q: Where did you have your wallet?

A: I put it in my bag that I brought with me, a big duffle bag.

Q: And did you have any money in it?

A: Yes; I did.

Q: How much money did you have in it?

A: Approximately $300.

Q: Where did you keep that within your wallet?

A: Well, I had probably $200 in assorted bills in the billfold itself and I had a $100 bill which I pulled it out and tucked it away in the wallet.

Q: Do you mean in a little compartment other than in the folding opening?

A: Yes.

Q: Why did you do that, sir?

A: For safekeeping.

Q: Why is it that you did not take the wallet with you when you went out that night?

A: Because I didn't want to spend all of my money. I took $20 out and put it in my pocket and my license out for ID.

Q: And when you came back, or did at some point in time did you discover that that $100 bill was missing?

A: Yes; I did.

Q: When was that?

A: That was Wednesday in the morning sometime.

Q: And did you discover whether anything else was missing?

A: Yes. I had a Game Boy I brought with me that was missing also.

Q: Do you know where that was located when you last saw it?

A: It was probably somewhere in the living room area, I don't know exactly where.

Q: And have you recovered the $100 bill and the Game Boy since then?

A: Well, I got the $100 back and the Game Boy, yes.

Q: How did you come to get that back, sir?

A: From Detective Weintz.

Q: Did you contact him?

A: Yes; I did.

Q: When was it that you contacted him and told him those items were missing?

A: It was about 11:00 o'clock on Wednesday.

Q: And when was it that Detective Weintz returned the $100 and Game Boy to you?

A: I believe it was a few days later.

Q: Did you discover whether or not anything else was missing thereafter?

A: A couple of weeks later, I noticed a battery charger was missing also.

Q: A battery charger?

A: Yes.

Q: And where was that kept?

A: That was also kept in my gym bag.

Q: What was that used for?

A: That was used for charging the batteries for the Game Boy.

Q: You have not recovered that; have you?

A: No; I haven't.

Q: When John woke you up, was Lorena in the apartment?

A: I didn't see her, no.

Q: When was it that you first discovered, sir, that John's penis had been amputated?

A: On the way to the hospital, John had said to me, "They better be able to make me a new penis," and that's when I kind of found out what had happened—really happened.

CROSS EXAMINATION

BY MR. LOWE:

Q: Robby, when did you first decide to come down to Virginia?

A: Probably in May of that year.

Q: And you communicated in early May with John about coming down here?

A: Yes, we talked about it.

Q: On the day you went to Legends and bar hopping with John—

A: On Tuesday?

Q: Tuesday, yes, sir.

John had indicated to you that day or had indicated to you by that day that they were separating?

A: That they planned on getting divorced, yes.

Q: And there was some disagreement over who would keep the apartment?

A: Yes.

Q: Now, you have indicated that that evening, you had some six or seven drinks?

A: No, six drinks.

Q: Now, did you keep a score card as you were going along?

A: I can remember the night.

Q: Now, when you came home at 3:00 o'clock in the morning, you went immediately to bed and to sleep?

A: No; I didn't.

Q: Did you stay up for a while?

A: Well, I had to go to the bathroom.

Q: After you got rid of some of the beer and the coffee, did you go immediately to bed?

A: Well, yeah, after John finished making the couch.

Q: How long did that take?

A: A few minutes.

Q: How long did it take you to go to sleep after that?

A: A few minutes.

Q: Are you a heavy sleeper normally?

A: Real regular sleeper.

Q: And you are a heavier sleeper when you are under the influence; aren't you?

A: Well, I was tired, yes.

Q: Tired and under the influence?

A: Probably, yes.

Q: You didn't hear a single thing then until John woke you up?

A: No, sir.

Q: When you woke up, you thought you were being awakened to go to work?

A: Yes; I did.

Q: You didn't understand John when he was saying—

when he was standing there next to you, obviously badly injured; did you?

A: No, it's kind of like a bad dream almost.

Q: So, you went into the bathroom and go ahead and start getting ready for work?

A: Yes.

Q: Didn't recognize that he was—the significant—

A: It didn't click right away, no.

Q: And only after you had been in the bathroom for a while—

A: No, for a minute or two.

Q: —that you notice it?

A: For a minute or so, yes.

Q: Now, when we come back to this Game Boy, did Lorena ever play with the Game Boy?

A: No; she didn't.

Q: And you left the Game Boy in the dining room area; did you not?

A: Well, in the living room area.

Q: Right next to where she left her purse and keys?

A: It could have been, yes.

Q: And as far as the $100 that was in your wallet, when did you last check the wallet to see that it was there?

A: Oh, it was there that day.

HOWARD PERRY
DIRECT EXAMINATION

BY MS. O'BRIEN:

Q: Would you please tell the jury how you are employed?

A: I'm a police officer with the City of Manassas Park

(and) I am a volunteer at the Yorkshire Volunteer Fire Department.

Q: Let me direct your attention to the early morning hours of June the 23rd and ask you if in that capacity if you received a call on that day?

A: Yes; we did.

Q: And based on the information you received from the call, where did you go, sir?

A: I believe it was 8174 Peekwood Court, Apartment Number 5.

Q: Did you learn whose residence that was?

A: Yes; I did.

Q: Who was that?

A: John Wayne Bobbitt.

Q: And for what purpose did you respond to that residence?

A: We were looking for an extremity.

Q: And what was that extremity?

A: A penis.

Q: And did you, in fact, conduct a search of the apartment?

A: Yes; we did.

Q: Were you successful?

A: No, ma'am.

Q: How long were you at the apartment?

A: About a half an hour.

Q: And did you make any observations of the condition of that apartment while you were there?

A: Yes, ma'am.

Q: What were they?

A: There was a large amount of blood on the bed leading to the bathroom, down the stairs to the parking lot.

There was a butcher's block in the kitchen with some knives missing.

Q: Did there come a time then when you left the apartment?

A: Yes, ma'am.

Q: Where did you go when you left the apartment?

A: To the intersection of Old Centreville Road and Maplewood Drive.

Q: For what purpose did you go there?

A: We had received information that the penis was at that intersection.

Q: And did you assist in conducting a search of that intersection?

A: Yes, ma'am; we did.

Q: Describe if you would for the jury the terrain in that area.

A: Mostly residential. There is a Patty Cake Day Care Center, a 7-Eleven, some field and it's a grass area, little bit of woods.

Q: Were you present when the penis was recovered there?

A: Yes, ma'am.

Q: In fact, did you recover the penis?

A: Yes; I did.

Q: At whose direction was that?

A: Sergeant Hurley.

Q: What did you do, sir?

A: I picked up the penis and placed it in a clear, plastic bag and packed it in ice.

Q: Wrapped it in ice?

A: It was an ice pack.

Q: And then what did you do?

A: We got in the ambulance and proceeded to Prince William Hospital.

Q: And approximately how long after you arrived at the location you described was the penis located?

A: Within five minutes.

CROSS EXAMINATION

BY MR. LOWE:

Q: The location that you found the penis in is about a city block and a half or so away?

A: Yes, sir; approximately that.

Q: And it is at an intersection; is it not?

A: That's correct.

Q: On the left-hand side of the street is a 7-Eleven?

A: Yes, sir.

Q: And the right-hand side of the street is a stop sign?

A: Yes, sir.

Q: You found it on the right-hand side of the street just off of the pavement?

A: Yes, sir.

Q: And that is a two-lane road; is it not?

A: It is.

Q: It is about twenty or twenty-four feet wide on the road?

A: Approximately, yes, sir.

Q: A little bit of a shoulder on the side?

A: Yes, sir.

Q: And the shoulder—the road is ten or twelve feet and the shoulder is probably five or six feet?

A: About four or five feet, yes, sir.

Q: And somebody measured the distance from the center line to the point where the penis was found; didn't they?

A: I don't know. I was gone when they did the actual crime scene.

Q: It was within a few feet of the side of the road, wasn't it, that you spotted it?

A: To where the penis was found, sir?

Q: Yes.

A: It was about twelve feet from the road, yes, sir.

Q: And much of that—half of that is the shoulder?

A: A little less than half, yes, sir.

Q: You never would have found it there if you hadn't had specific information on where to go look for it; would you?

A: That's correct, sir.

A witness, was called for examination by counsel on behalf of the Commonwealth, and, after having been duly sworn, was examined and testified, as follows:

WILLARD HURLEY
DIRECT EXAMINATION

BY MS. O'BRIEN:

Q: Sergeant Hurley, were you on duty in the early morning hours of June the 23rd, 1993?

A: Yes, ma'am.

Q: In the course of your employment, did you respond to a call that you received at approximately 5:20 in the morning?

A: Yes, ma'am.

Q: Where did you go when you received the call?

A: I went to 8174 Peekwood Court, Apartment Number 5.

Q: Were you supervising a search which was conducted at that residence?

A: Yes, ma'am.

Q: Did there come a time, sir, when you responded to Maplewood and Old Centreville Road?

A: Yes, ma'am.

Q: Sergeant, let me show you a street map of that location and ask you if you can identify that?

MS. O'BRIEN: I would ask, Your Honor, that the map be admitted into evidence and posted for Sergeant Hurley to testify.

THE COURT: It will be so admitted into evidence as Commonwealth Exhibit Number 4.

BY MS. O'BRIEN:

Q: What did you do at the location of Maplewood and Old Centreville Road?

A: Myself and some rescue personnel searched for Mr. Bobbitt's penis.

Q: Were you in contact with anyone by radio transmission?

A: Yes, ma'am. I had an officer at the hospital who was regularly in contact with me by radio.

Q: And did he advise you of the location?

A: No, ma'am, actually that was Lieutenant Prillerman who was at headquarters who spoke to Mrs. Bobbitt at headquarters.

She had given him the location for us to search and that's where we left the apartment and went to that intersection.

Q: Did you actually find the penis, sir?

A: Yes, ma'am.

Q: And did you call Officer Perry over and direct his attention to it?

A: Yes, ma'am.

Q: Subsequent to that time, did you have occasion to be aware of some measurements of exactly where the penis was located with relation to distance from the road?

A: Yes, ma'am, myself and Sergeant Zinn did that.

Q: Would you tell the jury where it was located with relation to the road.

A: It was located approximately thirteen feet off of Maplewood Drive. Mrs. Bobbitt would have been probably traveling towards Old Centreville Road.

Q: How far back from the stop sign is that?

A: Approximately forty-five feet.

Q: Did you say thirteen feet off of the road?

A: Right, from the side of the pavement.

Q: Do you know how far it was then from the center of the road?

A: It would be in the mid twenties, something like that, twenty some feet.

CROSS EXAMINATION

BY MR. LOWE:

Q: Officer, it was in low brush that it was found; wasn't it?

A: Yes, sir, about eight to ten inches of grass.

Q: It wouldn't have been very visible there without knowing where to specifically go look; would it?

A: No, sir, you wouldn't have—we didn't have any specifics as to where to look, we just knew in that vicinity.

JAMES SEHN
DIRECT EXAMINATION

BY MR. EBERT:

Q: What is your occupation, sir?

A: I'm a urological surgeon.

Q: Now, sir, did there come a point in time in the course of your occupation that you had occasion to be called to Prince William Hospital to see one John Wayne Bobbitt?

A: Right.

Q: And when was that, sir?

A: This past June, the day of this event. I was called shortly after 5:00 o'clock in the morning by the ER physician to see Mr. Bobbitt.

I was on call that morning as the urologist for the hospital.

Q: What did you observe when you arrived?

A: When I arrived, I observed Mr. Bobbitt lying on a stretcher on his back and upon examining him, it appeared that he had a complete amputation of his penis.

There was nothing more than a red clot of blood left where the penis should have been. He was, however, despite a degree of blood loss, coherent and quite cooperative at that point.

Q: And you were able to communicate with him and he was coherent; is that correct?

A: Yes, sir, quite so.

Q: And you say his penis was missing, could you determine at what portion or where it had been severed from his body?

A: Yes, it appeared to be—had been severed right at the body wall.

Q: And do you know whether or not he had lost any blood?

A: At that point, there was considerable blood about the wound and as I took the history, it was clear that the wound had been inflicted at least an hour prior to his arrival in the emergency room.

And, so, yes, he had lost a fair amount of blood. In fact, the first hematocrit which we obtained was approximately thirty percent which would indicate that he had lost about a third of his blood volume.

Q: And had that wound not been treated or had he not received immediate attention for the wound that he had suffered, do you know whether or not that was potentially life threatening?

A: It is certainly a potentially life threatening injury. If a wound of this sort is neglected over a period of time, a patient would be expected to elapse into a hemorrhagic shock and could suffer morbid complications in that event.

Q: When you say hemorrhagic shock, what you do you mean by that?

A: Simply continued blood loss would cause a compromise of the vascular system and lead to other complications, cardiac arrest, et cetera.

Q: And what did you do upon seeing the patient?

A: Well, I first was able to stabilize John. He had an IV started by the emergency room staff and I was able then to counsel him as to what I could and couldn't do for him surgically.

Q: What was your counsel, sir?

A: I counseled John as to our options at that point given the fact that we did not have the amputated penis.

And it was clear at that point that perhaps the best we

could do for him would be to simply close over the stump of the penis and this is an operation not uncommon in urology which we do with patients with penal cancer.

We are able to close over the remaining stump. And I explained this to John and that he would have to spend the rest of his life voiding like half the world does sitting down and would never know sex again quite as he had known it.

And obviously he was quite upset and basically I said I would do my best that I could for him. And John understood that. He understood what we could and couldn't do.

And with that, he signed a permit and we were off to the operating room. And it was only on our way to the operating room that, in fact, the organ was retrieved.

Q: Now, you determined—was a blood alcohol done on Mr. Bobbitt at that time, sir?

A: I don't believe so, Mr. Ebert.

Q: From your observation, did anything indicate to you that he was unable to communicate or were there any impairments by virtue of ingesting alcohol at the time you saw him?

A: Not to my observation, no.

Q: What was his attitude and his communication to you, sir, when you advised him of these things?

A: He was an exceptionally stoic patient and quite cooperative and I believe he understood the possibilities at that point.

And I think in every way he was before and after the surgery a very cooperative gentleman.

Q: Now, sir, would you tell the ladies and gentlemen of the jury after you got into the operating room, you say the appendage or the end of his penis had been recovered; is that correct?

A: That is correct.

Q: And what did you do, sir?

A: I first—fortunately it had been brought to the hospital on ice by the police department in very good condition and the first thing, of course, I had to inspect it and it appeared very clean and very undamaged in every respect apart from obviously this cut.

And it appeared like we had a good chance to re-implant it.

Q: I will show you three photographs which the Court has allowed to come into evidence.

You have seen those photographs before, have you not?

A: Yes, sir.

Q: They were taken in the course of your procedure?

A: That's correct.

Q: Would you tell the ladies and gentlemen of the jury what they depict?

A: The first photograph depicts the severed penis.

Q: Would you show that to the ladies and gentlemen of the jury, please, sir?

A: This (indicating) is the severed part as I received it that morning, quite intact, a very clean cut at the proximal end of the penis, in every way a very acceptable organ for replantation.

Q: Now, the fact that it was a very clean cut, does that have any bearing or any meaning to you as a physician?

A: Well, yes, it certainly increases the possibility technically to replant it.

Q: Sir, in your professional opinion, in order to inflict such a cut, would someone have to hold the organ on the end in order to cut it from the body assuming that the penis was flaccid or soft?

A: In my opinion, I don't believe this particular injury could be inflicted unless the organ were held in some tension with one hand and with the other hand, with a knife, a clean cut were made with some force, in my opinion.

Q: All right, sir.

MR. EBERT: I would like to offer that into evidence, Your Honor.

THE COURT: This is marked as Commonwealth's 6A.

BY MR. EBERT:

Q: Tell the ladies and gentlemen of the jury what the other photographs are.

A: This particular photograph was a photograph of the patient after I stabilized him, I place a tourniquet here above the stump.

The stump had actually inverted into the body wall slightly.

Q: Why was that, sir?

A: Partly because of retraction of tissues, arteries, vasal restrict, tissues retract as a physiological way for the body to hang onto blood.

And once this was averted out of the body wall, the penial stump, this a Penrose drain to be placed around it and a Kelly clamp used to secure that tourniquet to stench the bleeding, to stop the bleeding.

MR. EBERT: I'd offer that into evidence, Your Honor.

THE COURT: You've marked it Commonwealth's 6B. It will be admitted at this time.

THE WITNESS: And this last photograph details the first part of the operation when the urethra tube, which can be seen here (indicating), was first approximated end to end and it's surrounding corporal tissues are beginning to be approximated as the organ is replanted.

And again, here (indicating) is the tourniquet that you saw before and the amputated part here (indicating), distally.

MR. EBERT: I would like to offer that photograph into evidence.

THE COURT: It is marked as 6C and be admitted as same.

BY MR. EBERT:

Q: Describe for the ladies and gentlemen of the jury in layman's terms as best you can, what you did and how you were able to reattach the penis.

A: Well, the penis is attached in several steps. The first step has—involves attaching the urethra which transports urine and semen and that's the largest tube.

And that's attached over a catheter which acts as a splint at the lower end of the penis. Nature, fortunately, has reserved the top of the penis for all the very difficult smaller structures, the small arteries and nerves and veins.

And so, once the lower, the ventral half of the penis has been reattached successfully, we turned our attention to the very small structures at the top and began with the deep dorsal vein which is a very important structure to re-approximate so that we have good outflow of blood.

The arteries though also were attached dorsally. One deep corporal artery was reattached as well as the dorsal nerves.

And the entire surgery took approximately nine hours to do following which the tourniquet was removed and it was apparent that there was good flow.

Q: Did you ask for assistance in the course of your operation?

A: I certainly did. Dr. David Berman assisted me and we worked again through the micro-vascular nastro-mosis. Dave has training in micro-vascular nastromosis.

As I mentioned, I'm a urologist and it was a team effort. We both worked steadily through the day under the microscope to complete the repair.

Q: What would you say the prognosis is as a result of your operation?

A: I would say the prognosis is quite good for return of functions.

Q: And you say it will take some period of time before you know the extent of the success of the operation?

A: I believe that is still an open-ended question at the moment.

Q: Is this an unusual operation, sir, that you performed, you and Dr. Berman?

A: It's a very unusual operation. There have probably been less than fifty in this century.

Q: And prior to this, had you ever done one of these, sir?

A: No, sir.

Q: And what was John's attitude during the course of your treatment of him?

A: John's attitude was very cooperative. He had to lie on his back for virtually for a week following the surgery while he recovered . . . a very cooperative and willing patient.

Q: Was he on medication while he was there?

A: He may have been on a mild sleeping pill at night, but beyond that, really very little.

Q: And do you know what his attitude toward his wife was during this period of time?

A: I did have an opportunity as I got to know John

during that period to ask him about his feelings. And it was clear—he showed me a picture of Lorena, and I sensed that there was even some lingering affection at that point that he had for her.

He did not seem—while he was upset, he did not seem overly hostile or inappropriate to me. We had a psychiatric evaluation which he declined.

And I think in every way, John seemed fairly appropriate given the nature of the injury.

CROSS EXAMINATION

BY MR. LOWE:

Q: You talked to him after the surgery; didn't you?

A: I did.

Q: Did you explain to him that the surgery was at least technically a success and you would have to wait a while to know whether it was going to be—

A: Yes. The first he knew that the penis had been found was when he woke up. He went to anesthesia without the knowledge that he might have regained his organ.

Q: And his response was appropriate when told that; wasn't it?

A: Yes.

Q: Pleased?

A: Yes.

Q: Appeared to understand?

A: Yes.

Q: And when did you finish surgery?

A: Approximately 4:00 o'clock that afternoon.

Q: When did you next see John?

A: I saw him in the Intensive Care Unit shortly there-after following the recovery from anesthesia.

Q: Did you see him the next day?

A: Oh, yes.

Q: What time did you see the victim?

A: I would imagine around 9:00, 8:00 to 9:00 that morning.

Q: Describe his condition then, sir.

A: Again, he was lying as we asked him to on his back. He had a styrofoam collar about the replantation site.

There was an umbrella cage to protect this from sheets and John was cooperative that morning. I believe he had something to eat.

And we did through that period doppler testing of the replanted organ. The doppler is a little sound probe we use to check for blood flow velocity and that seemed quite secure all through the night and continued to be so the next day.

Q: Did you discuss with him what you were doing?

A: Yes, sir.

Q: Were his answers—did he appear to understand what you said?

A: I believe so.

Q: Were his answers appropriate to what you said?

A: Yes, sir.

Q: How much medication was he on at that point?

A: As I say as I recall, and I have to go back to medi-cal record, I don't believe he was on anything to speak of at that point.

He really required very little by way of analgesia.

Q: So, a couple of hours later, was he still in the con-dition of not having much in the way of medication?

A: Yes.

Q: And he was still at the point where he was making sense, understanding what was said to him and so forth?

A: Oh, yes.

Q: Were you present when Detective Weintz interviewed him?

A: I was not.

Q: Do you know when that was?

A: I understand there was an interview, but, I don't remember.

Q: Did you see him again later in the day?

A: Yes.

Q: Was he still cooperative and making sense?

A: Yes.

Q: When did you next see him?

A: Probably saw him late afternoon.

Q: Did you have any reason to believe that he became incoherent during that time frame?

A: No, no; I have no such reports.

REDIRECT EXAMINATION

BY MR. EBERT:

Q: When he came to the hospital, was there any indication to you that he was drunk?

A: He didn't appear to me to be drunk.

Q: Would you have done surgery on him in the manner that you did had he been drunk?

A: He certainly needed surgical intervention and the anesthesiologist would have helped me out with that aspect of his care.

Q: But, from your observation, you didn't feel that was a concern; did you?

A: It wasn't a concern for me that morning, no.

PETER WEINTZ
DIRECT EXAMINATION

BY MR. EBERT:

Q: State your full name, sir, and give your place of employment.

A: Peter Weintz, I'm with the Prince William County Police Department.

Q: How long have you been so employed?

A: Twenty-three years.

Q: And were you on duty on the 23rd day of June of last year?

A: Yes, sir; I was.

Q: And in that capacity, were you called to headquarters?

A: Yes, sir; I was.

Q: And upon arriving there, did you have occasion to see the Defendant?

A: Yes, sir; I did.

Q: And at that point in time, did you have any opportunity to talk with her?

A: No, sir; I did not.

Q: Soon thereafter, did you and she and another officer leave for the Prince William County Hospital?

A: Yes, sir.

Q: And what was your purpose in going there?

A: Mr. Bobbitt—I had originally been called there. While at headquarters, I had been advised that Mrs. Bobbitt had appeared at the front desk area on the other side of the building and she at that time was being sent to the hospital for a PERK exam.

Q: What is a PERK exam?

A: That's a rape exam done by the doctors to establish fluids, hairs, fibers.

Q: And to your knowledge, that was done on her; is that correct?

A: That's correct.

Q: And then there came a point in time, sir, that you returned back to headquarters; is that correct?

A: Yes, sir; I did.

Q: And did you have occasion to talk with her at that time?

A: Yes, sir; I did.

Q: And was she under arrest in anyway at that time?

A: No, sir; she was not.

Q: And where was the interview held?

A: In the interview room at the Detective Bureau at Manassas Headquarters.

Q: Who was present at that time?

A: Myself, Mrs. Bobbitt and Mrs. Bobbitt's employer, Mrs. Janna Bisutti.

Q: Did she appear to comprehend and understand everything that you told her?

A: Yes, sir; she did.

Q: And would you tell the ladies and gentlemen of the jury, you can refer to the tape if you would, what you asked her and what her responses were.

A: Let's see, "A taped interview with Lorena Bobbitt in reference to a felonious assault. It is now 9:50 a.m. hours.'

'We are at Prince William Police Headquarters. Present at this time of the interview are myself, Detective

Peter Weintz, Mrs. Bobbitt and a personal friend of hers, her employer, Mrs. Janna Bisutti, from Fairfax."

I started, "Okay, Lorena, what I'm going to ask you to do is I want you to start again from the time that you went to bed last night, Tuesday night, and then or early this morning, and tell me what you know happened."

Lorena stated, "Okay. He came, he slammed the door and that's when I wake up. I look at the clock and, you know, it was like around 3:00, I don't remember exactly. So, I went and tried to—well, go back to the sleep again when he took his clothes off but he kept his underwear on."

And I asked, "He kept his underwear on?"

Mrs. Bobbitt stated, "Yeah, yes, he kept his underwear on and I asked him if he worked. If he finished work late and he said, 'No, I didn't have to work today, I went out.' "

"And I asked him when did he go out and he said he went to the Holiday Inn and I just went back to sleep. And maybe like an hour later, he jumped on top of me.

"And he also was naked and he started to take my clothes off very fast and I said, I don't want to have sex and then just tried to pull my pants on.

"And he kept take it off real quick. And he tried to take my underwear off and I try to put it and he forced me to take the underwear off, but he used his legs and his feet also to take it off.'

"And I was just struggling and trying to keep my underwear on. I don't know. He opened my legs and that's how he forced—he already was on top of me. I couldn't move.

"My arms couldn't touch him because there was—I was like this and that's when he had intercourse.

"And I was—I tried to scream or do something or push him, but I couldn't because he's so heavy for me.

"And his shoulder is right—shoulder was pushing my mouth so I couldn't. I couldn't talk or breathe through my mouth.

"And I remember he kissed me or tried to kiss me putting his tongue inside my mouth and that's how I tasted that, that he had, you know, was drinking and it was alcohol.

"And he put it so—so low that I wanted to throw up.

"And he kept it like that."

I then asked, "Okay, you've been tested then at the hospital. Results we'll have later."

Mrs. Bobbitt responded, "Yeah."

I then inquired, "Robert didn't hear anything outside?"

And Mrs. Bobbitt said, "No."

I asked, "You couldn't scream?"

Mrs. Bobbitt's response was, "It was closed, no."

Q: What was she referring to then, if you know, the door?

A: The door, I believe.

Q: Okay, go ahead.

A: I asked if something similar to this had happened on Saturday or Friday night, Saturday morning and Mrs. Bobbitt responded, Friday.

I asked, "Is it before Robert?"

Mrs. Bobbitt responded, "Before, yeah."

I stated, "The same thing, he came home from work?"

And at that point, Mrs. Bobbitt responded, "Yeah, but he wanted to have sex and I said no, I don't want to have sex. He just only wanted to have sex because he—he wanted his own satisfaction and that's not fair. Sex should be mutual and then—then we had sex, but I didn't really want to.

"And I tried to push him out and I asked him and he said that that kind of sex, forced sex that he called it, he—excites him and I said, it's not fair, I don't get excited like that.

I then stated, "Okay, you were ready to leave the house. He has thrown you or is that—"

Mrs. Bobbitt responded, "Yeah."

I stated, "What happened to the house on Pine Street?"

Mrs. Bobbitt responded, "They foreclosed on that house because I couldn't make the payments and he was out of work."

I stated, "Okay."

I stated, "Are you still paying all the bills?"

Mrs. Bobbitt responded, "Yes."

I then asked, "What does John do with his money when he does work?"

Mrs. Bobbitt responded, "I don't know. He said that he told me one time that he—I shouldn't ask him anything because it's none of my business.

"And I said, 'I'm your wife, I should know why you don't share with me anything.' And he said, 'That's the way it is. I want you to support me.' I don't think he's right. And he said I have—"

I interrupted, "Okay. Was there something that happened to a car here just a little while ago?"

Mrs. Bobbitt responded, "Yeah, his car was repossessed."

I asked what kind of car was that and Mrs. Bobbitt responded an Escort.

I stated, "Escort."

And Mrs. Bobbitt responded, "1989, he was very late on his payments. My car was repossessed also."

I stated, "Yours was too?"

Mrs. Bobbitt stated, "Yeah. But I never told him that it was repossessed because I was afraid that he was going to hit me or something because of the anger or whatever."

I stated, "Okay."

And Mrs. Bobbitt went on, "So, I told him that my car was in the mechanic, but I got my car back thanks to my boss, Janna. She gave me an advance money, you know."

I stated, "Okay."

"After, and then you know—"

"Please take a couple of minutes if you need it."

After a response, I then stated, "After you and John, after he forced you to have sex this morning—

Can you tell me what happened then?"

Mrs. Bobbitt responded, "Yes, he pushed me away like when he finished like he did it before. Sometimes he just push me away, make me feel really bad because that's not fair, that's not nice.

"I don't feel good when he does it. I came back to pick up my clothes looking for my—my underwear and I didn't even have my shirt off. And I put my underwear back, my other shirt, spandex shirt on and I was hurt.

"I went to the kitchen to drink water. I opened the refrigerator and I got a cup of water and then I was angry already.

"And I turned my back and I—the first thing I saw was the knife. Then I took it and I was just angry. And I took it and I went to the bedroom and I told him I—he shouldn't do this to me.

"Why he did it. Then I said I asked him if he was satisfied with what he did. Then he said he doesn't care about my feelings. He did say that and I ask him if he has orgasm inside me because it hurt me when he made me do that before.

"He always have orgasm and he doesn't wait for me to have orgasm. He's selfish. I don't think it's fair, so I pull back the sheets and then I did it."

I stated, "All right, you cut him?"

And Mrs. Bobbitt said, "I, yes."

I said, "All right, how? You didn't know what you were doing?"

Mrs. Bobbitt's response was, "No, I guess not."

I stated, "So, you were talking to him and he was talking back to you when it happened?"

Mrs. Bobbitt's response was, "No, he was sleeping. He just say, 'I don't care, leave me alone.' "

I then asked, "And he went back to bed or back to sleep?"

Mrs. Bobbitt responded, "Yes."

I asked, "Did he have any clothes on when this happened?"

Mrs. Bobbitt responded, "No."

I asked, "Did he have his underwear off? Did you say you pulled back the sheet?"

Mrs. Bobbitt responded, "He had his underwear off when he was ready to—when he jump on top of me. He—he took his underwear off and then took my clothes, the bottom part."

And I responded, "Okay."

Mrs. Bobbitt then went on, "If he wanted to make love, he should have asked me or took, you know, everything off."

I stated, "All right, it is now 10:05," and at that time, I concluded the interview.

Q: Did you allow her to leave the police headquarters after she gave the statement?

A: Yes, sir; I did.

Q: And there came a point in time later when you obtained a warrant for her arrest?

A: That's correct.

Q: Did there come a point in time later that you had occasion to call her and ask her about certain items that she had allegedly taken from one Robert Johnston?

A: Yes, sir; I did.

Q: When was that?

A: I believe it was the following day, it would be the 24th.

Q: And how did you come to make that call?

A: Mr. Johnston, when speaking to him, the second time we spoke, and advised that he was missing some money from his wallet and also a Game Boy machine was missing from the apartment, his personal things.

Q: And did you call Mrs. Bobbitt as a result of what he had said?

A: Yes; I did.

Q: Did she agree to return those items?

A: Yes, sir.

Q: And did she—when did she do that and how did she do it?

A: She brought them to the station and met me at the back of the building and turned them in.

Q: Did she tell you how she had come into the possession of those items?

A: Yes, sir. When I asked her what she had taken them for, she advised that Mr. Bobbitt had given Mr. Johnston money to hold for him.

She felt like it was John's money and he was having

Robert keep it for him so that she couldn't have access to it.

Q: Did she tell you where she took the money from?

A: Mr. Johnston's wallet.

Q: And with regards to the Game Boy, did she have an explanation for how she came to take possession of that?

A: No, sir; she did not. She just stated that it was picked up on her way leaving the apartment.

CROSS EXAMINATION

BY MR. LOWE:

Q: Officer, you spoke to her at more than one place, both at the hospital and at the station?

A: That's correct.

Q: And you took some time to attempt to calm her down when you spoke to her at the station and at the hospital; didn't you?

A: That's correct.

Q: What was her condition at the time that you spoke to her first?

A: Very emotional state. She was crying. She appeared to know where we were and what we were doing and I went on to explain [the] procedures and what we were to do next.

Q: You were aware that she had given the location of the knife and of the penis?

A: I was not at that time, no, sir.

Q: You became aware of it later?

A: Yes, sir.

Q: That she actually volunteered that information?

A: That is my understanding.

Q: During the course of talking to her, it became clear that English was her second language; did it not?

A: That's correct.

Q: And even though she speaks English with some fluency, she did not understand everything that you said to her; did she not?

A: Yes, sir.

Q: You were able to obtain a good bit of detail during the course of this statement that you took from her; weren't you?

A: That's correct.

Q: And all that checked out; didn't it?

A: It has, yes sir.

Q: Did she tell you either in the earlier statements or in this statement that forced sex excited him?

A: That had come up on several occasions, both—to my knowledge, I can't specifically recall whether it was before this. It certainly did during this and—

Q: Did she indicate whether it excited her?

A: She stated it did not.

Q: Did she indicate during the course of your conversations with her that she feared her husband?

A: I don't recall; no, sir.

THE COURT: Your next witness, Mr. Ebert.

MR. EBERT: No more questions.

JOHN WAYNE BOBBITT
DIRECT EXAMINATION

BY MR. HOWARD:

Q: Mr. Bobbitt, when I called you yesterday to the

stand, I think one of the last questions I asked you was concerning physical activities between you and your wife.

I want to ask you this, during the course of your marriage, sir, did you ever strike your wife?

A: No.

Q: That's certainly been your position all along not only in court proceedings but in the interviews you've given on numerous television shows?

A: Correct.

Q: Did you ever do anything that in your opinion angered her?

A: Well, I believe I did.

Q: Were there ever occasions when you would be in the same room with her and you would be angry and stomp out of the room?

A: Yeah, I believe I did.

Q: Did you ever insult or swear at your wife?

A: I may have a few times.

Q: Let me ask you this, when you were living at the Beltran residence, did you ever say things about her physical appearance or her heritage?

A: I remember commenting about her—

Q: Breasts being too small?

A: No. Her butt being too big, but it was joking.

Q: And that was something that you said to your wife often?

A: Well, not often. I said it a few times, but—

Q: What was her reaction to that comment when you would tell her that her butt was too big?

A: Well, she would get upset. I guess the reason why I told her that was, she sits all day long and she does nails.

Q: You say she sits all day long. The fact of the matter is during the marriage, she was working six days a week as a nail sculpturer; wasn't she?

A: Well, yes.

Q: And she'd work up there ten hours a day as a nail sculpturist; didn't she?

A: Yeah, sometimes. It depends on how busy she was.

Q: And the fact of the matter is, you told people in the past that it was upsetting to you and embarrassing to you that your wife was earning more money than you; isn't that correct?

A: Yes, I think I said that.

Q: Did you ever tell your wife when she wanted to leave or go visit friends and go out to do things without you that you did not want her to leave and did you ever restrict her from seeing certain people?

A: Did I restrict her from seeing certain people, no, never.

Q: And you never told her during the marriage that she couldn't leave?

A: No, I didn't say anything like that. I didn't restrict her from anything at all.

Q: And you never said either in writing or to anyone anything to the contrary, have you, Mr. Bobbitt?

A: No.

Q: Have you ever smashed any objects or kicked or hit any objects in her presence?

A: I'm not sure if I did or not. But, I remember one day, you know, she locked me out of the house, so I broke open the back door. You know, I kicked the door and broke it off the hinges.

Q: There was an occasion on Pine Street when you

lived next to the Willoughby's when you kicked the door in; isn't that true?

A: Yeah, her mother was there at that time. I kicked it, it swung open and it almost hit her. I told her mother, "I'm sorry" and I fixed the door. She locked me out of the house because we were fighting over the TV. I went outside and she locked me out and I kicked the door in to get in the house.

Q: Did you ever threaten to hit your wife or throw anything at her?

A: No.

Q: And you've never said that to anybody; have you, Mr. Bobbitt?

A: No.

Q: You've never put that in writing over your signature that you did something like that; have you?

A: When she pressed charges against me, I had to go to court for a domestic situation. I might have signed something, I don't know, but I never pled guilty to about hitting my wife at all and nothing.

Q: Have you ever pushed, restrained, grabbed or shoved your wife?

A: Yes; I have.

Q: On how many occasions have you done that?

A: Many—many times. Most of it was just restraining, you know, holding her down.

Q: And to say that you grabbed her or shoved her would not be appropriate?

A: Well, I shoved her once, one time. One time I was sitting down on the couch because we had a fight and I didn't want to go to bed with her. We weren't getting along so I slept on the couch. She came out and I remember she pulled the covers off of me. She wanted me to go to bed. I didn't want to go to bed. I was upset and I wanted to sleep on the couch. She just kept on ripping the covers off. She was upset and just wouldn't leave me alone and I pushed her away.

Q: And that's the only incident of shoving that you can recall in the entire marriage?

A: Yes.

Q: Did you ever drive recklessly to scare your wife?

A: No. I mean, I drove fast a few times which makes her upset. [But] not to scare her, no.

Q: Did you ever throw her bodily down or against the wall or at any place at all during the marriage, throw her bodily?

A: No way.

Q: And you've already told us that you simply never hit your wife?

A: Right.

Q: Mr. Bobbitt, let me take you back, you remember talking to Kathleen Williams with the Family Advocacy Group Quantico Marines about an allegation of abuse involving your wife?

A: I remember I talked with a priest.

Q: Do you remember an incident the Thanksgiving of 1990 in which you drove an automobile with the door open and knocked your wife to the ground?

You accelerated the automobile, backed up, she was standing by an open door, you knocked her to the ground and then you drove off in your car?

A: I remember that, but not the way you are putting it.

Q: You remember basically the incident?

A: Yes; I do. Can I describe that incident?

Q: As a result of that, your wife filed a complaint with the Marine Corps; is that correct?

A: Yeah, I believe I remember something like that. When I went to work one day, I remember my staff officer said that your wife called and said you had marital problems. Then he suggested that if you want to, you can talk to the base priest. So, I said that would be a good idea and I told him I was going to have a talk with him.

Q: Are you telling this jury that you never talked to a female social worker with the Family Advocacy Council of Quantico as a result of the incident involving striking your wife with an automobile?

A: I don't remember talking to a woman. I remember talking to a gentleman.

Q: Do you remember this form (Indicating), sir, that you filled out and signed in front of Kathleen Williams?

A: I can't say. I don't remember the form at all.

Q: Are you denying that you filled that form out?

A: I don't know. I don't deny doing it, I just don't remember this form.

Q: And you don't remember the lady?

A: I—you know—I mean, I might have filled it out, I don't know. I just don't remember. I don't remember the form at all.

Q: Do you remember telling anybody on an interview as a result of the incident where you struck your wife with that automobile that you grew up in Niagara Falls, New York?

Do you remember an interview in which you gave that family history?

A: I—I remember something like that, but I remember talking to a male priest.

Q: Okay, do you remember that you went to live at an early age with your aunt and uncle who had three children; is that true?

A: I may have, but I don't remember the conversation. I remember going there, but I don't remember the details of all the—you know, what was said.

Q: Do you remember saying that the household that you lived in as a young man, there was a lot of fighting?

A: There was never a lot of fighting in our house.

Q: And you don't remember telling that to anybody concerning this incident?

A: There was a lot of love in our family. There was no fighting, ever.

Q: And was there any problem in that house with alcohol when you were a youngster?

A: Yes, well, my father, he had a problem with alcohol, but he stopped about seventeen years ago.

Q: Do you remember telling anyone on an interview about the alcohol problem in the family growing up?

A: No; I don't.

Q: All right. Do you remember discussing with anybody in the Marine Corps that you were to see a Dr. Giovanni, a psychologist?

A: No; I don't remember.

Q: Were you ever asked to give the telephone number of your wife in connection with a complaint involving the car door and the striking of her with the automobile?

A: I ain't struck her with an automobile.

Q: And you never told anybody that?

A: I don't remember.

Q: Did you get any counseling while you were in the Marine Corps?

A: No—well, no. Just that one time that I went to

the priest, the base priest for counsel. Throughout the course of our marriage, I did everything I could to make it better.

Q: Was it ever determined while you were in the Marine Corps that you had abused your wife?

A: No, no.

Q: When you left the Marine Corps in January for terminal leave, you never were involved in any other activity associated with the Marine Corps in terms of counseling; is that correct?

A: That's correct, after I left the Marine Corps.

Q: On February 21, 1991, a month after you got out of the Marine Corps, you were charged with assault and battery of your wife; isn't that correct?

A: She didn't press charges and the State did, I believe.

Q: First of all, let me show you a copy of the complaint and ask you if you recognize this, sir?

(Mr. Howard handed a document to the witness for his examination.)

A: Okay, I can remember this, yes.

Q: You remember that complaint?

A: Yes, well, I remember reading it, but, you know, I remember the incident and what happened that day.

Q: Do you remember entering a plea of guilty in the court for these charges?

A: Well, I didn't plead guilty to it. I just said, you know, I denied what she stated in this (indicating) here. I didn't do nothing. I didn't hit my wife or anything. This is what they got from her.

Q: If the court records indicated that on March 4th, 1991, that you entered a plea of guilty after a partial hearing on those charges that are in front of you, then the court records are wrong; is that your testimony?

A: Well, they said that. But I had to go to a release program. But I never signed, I never pleaded guilty to nothing. They just said that I was.

Q: My question to you, sir, is if the court's record show that you entered a plea of guilty to the charge that is on the piece of paper in front of you, are you saying that the court's records are in error?

A: Not really. But what was explained to me at the time was that, you know, this is not a criminal thing. It will be thrown out after six months.

Q: And you didn't understand this was a criminal proceeding?

A: No, it was just—it was a quick thing.

Q: Look at the piece of paper on your right right in front of you, sir, doesn't it say in bold face capital letters, Criminal Complaint?

A: Criminal Complaint, Bobbitt, John Wayne, yes.

Q: Are you John Wayne Bobbitt, 7712 Pine Street, Manassas, Virginia?

A: Yes, Mr. Howard.

Q: You are one and the same with the man on that criminal complaint; aren't you?

A: Correct.

Q: And as a matter of fact, you went down and when you got out of jail, you swore out a warrant against your wife; isn't that true?

A: Yes, because I was upset and I didn't start this whole thing, she did and I swore out a warrant for her.

Q: When you came to court to plead guilty, they dropped the charges against your wife; isn't that true?

A: They dropped the charges against both of us. I remember both of us standing in front of the judge and he said that if you can't reconcile your marriage, you can get a divorce.

Q: And the judge told you to stay away from your wife until further notice; isn't that true?

A: No.

Q: You violated the judge's order in that regard too; didn't you?

A: He didn't say stay away from my wife. He said both of the charges were dropped.

Q: That's your recollection?

A: That's my recollection.

Q: Now, Mr. Bobbitt, the first incident of assault involving you and your wife was about a month after the marriage. Do you remember an incident when you were driving down the road and you punched your wife, after the Chelsea Restaurant?

A: No, that's not what happened. Well, we were getting ready to go out, me and my wife and my brother, Todd. I was wearing sneakers and jeans and a nice shirt. But, my wife was dressed up and she had her heart set on going to this restaurant. It was a Spanish restaurant and she wanted to go there. None of us had been there before. When we got there, the door man wouldn't let me in because I was wearing sneakers. My wife got very upset. She started swearing and ranting and raving.

I said I was sorry. I didn't know what kind of place this was and I wasn't prepared for it. So, we got in the car and driving home, I just apologized to her and she just got so irate, she started swinging and punching me in the face. She punched me about three or four times and I told her to stop. I had to pull over and just hold her until I said, "What are you doing, I told you I was sorry."

And then I started driving again and she started hitting me again, and [I] just pushed her. After that she stopped. My brother is sitting in the back seat and I remember looking in the rearview mirror and he was just nodding his head.

Q: So, your recollection on that occasion was all this behavior came from your wife and it was inflicted upon you?

A: Yeah, and I couldn't drive. I mean, how can you drive when somebody is slugging you in the face.

Q: Now, you remember that same summer, the summer of 1989, taking a trip to Ocean City, you, your wife, your brother and a girl by the name of Terri McCumber?

A: Yes; I remember that.

Q: Do you remember a problem that developed up there at Ocean City that weekend?

A: A problem?

Q: Do you remember a situation in which some men whistled at Terri and your wife and that you got very upset about that?

A: This is in the early part of our marriage. I remember that, yeah.

Q: When this whistling took place, did that upset you, sir?

A: I think you've got it wrong. It wasn't on the beach. It was when we were driving and there was a couple of guys, you know, driving in the same lane and they were looking at, you know, Terri and Lorena in the back seat and were kind of flirting.

Q: And did that upset you, sir?

A: Yes.

Q: And you got angry on that occasion?

A: Angry, well, I just got upset.

Q: Did you strike your wife on that occasion?

A: No. I was driving.

Q: Do you remember taking your wife abruptly back to the room and getting your belongings and leaving Ocean City very abruptly on that occasion?

A: I don't remember; it was like three, four years ago.

Q: Do you remember returning back to the Northern Virginia area with your wife and Terri McCumber earlier than what had been planned?

A: No.

Q: Well, the fact of the matter is, Mr. Bobbitt, you were angry all the way back; isn't that true?

A: Nope.

Q: Did you threaten at any time to put Terri out of the vehicle?

A: No; I didn't.

Q: When you got back home, you let Terri off some place before you and your wife went home?

A: Yeah, we dropped her off at her house.

Q: Later that night, at some point, you assaulted your wife after you got home, isn't that true?

A: No; that's not true at all.

Q: Do you recall an occasion down where you lived on Ashton Park?

A: That was our first apartment.

Q: Do you remember an occasion down there in July of 1989 when you assaulted your wife and an Officer Francis, Manassas Park Police came to the door?

A: I remember somebody coming in the door, but we were having a big argument. He just knocked on the door and said is everything all right and he just left.

Q: Do you remember him showing a badge to you?

A: No.

Q: Had you been yelling and screaming at your wife just before he came to the door?

A: I know we were arguing. We were yelling at each other, but I don't know.

Q: You were drinking heavily on that occasion; weren't you, Mr. Bobbitt?

A: No.

Q: Do you deny having any alcohol when he came to the door on that occasion?

A: July, July—No. I mean, there is really like one time first after our marriage that we really went out and drank, me and Lorena with my brother, Todd.

Q: Do you know what might have caused that person to come to the door on that occasion and—

A: You know, he was walking by and we were yelling at each other really loud and he just stopped and said, "Hey, what's going on." He was just curious.

Q: And the incident involving your automobile, that occurred Thanksgiving 1990. Suppose you tell the jury what happened on that occasion with the automobile?

A: She was getting ready to go out with her mother, but she don't know how to drive [my] standard car and I didn't want her going out, you know, since she didn't know how to drive a standard. But she wanted to leave anyway since her car wasn't, was totalled. So I got in my car and she was getting upset because she wanted to use the car to go out with her mother.

So, as I was backing out, she opened the door and as I was backing up, she fell down and then I pulled forward to close the door and she stood in the back part of the driveway so that I couldn't get out. But, I diverted that by cutting through the neighbor's yard and going out of his driveway and just leaving.

Q: And that statement that you just gave to this jury—

A: That's what definitely happened.

Q: Have you ever told anyone about this particular event differently than what you've just told to this jury?

A: No.

Q: Let me ask you about Amaline Hoyt; do you know her?

A: Hoyt, no.

Q: Do you remember Christmas 1989? Do you remember giving a present to your wife, a pair of bikini panties in a small box at a Christmas party?

A: Yes, it was a teddy. It wasn't my idea, she picked it out.

Q: Okay. And on the occasion that you presented this little gift to her, were there some people standing around?

A: I have no idea; I can't remember.

Q: Do you remember your wife being embarrassed because of that gift?

A: She might have, but this is a teddy she wanted from Victoria's Secret.

Q: Mr. Bobbitt, do you remember when she opened that box, when she hid the box behind her?

A: No.

Q: Do you remember an association with those bikini panties and what I've just described your grabbing her by her dress around the throat and throwing her up against the wall?

A: No.

Q: Mr. Bobbitt, I asked you yesterday at the conclusion of the hearing whether or not you had ever forced sex upon your wife.

A: True.

Q: I'm going to ask you that question again.

Did you ever forcibly have sex with your wife?

A: No; I didn't. I never forced my wife to have sex ever.

Q: Did you ever tell anybody that you enjoyed forceful sex?

A: No.

Q: Do you remember an occasion when you were in the Beltran residence when you came into Renzo's room and it was John Whitaker, Renzo, and Mr. Kaopua and they were sitting around talking about girls and sex?

A: They always used to do that.

Q: And you remember on that occasion expressing yourself that the way that you get excited about girls is hitting them in the behind, make them scream, making them bleed and making them crawl?

A: No.

Q: That never happened?

A: No; never happened.

CROSS EXAMINATION

BY MR. EBERT:

Q: Mr. Bobbitt, I want to ask what happened on Thanksgiving, and correct me if I'm wrong about the dates.

I think you said you were fighting over the TV on that occasion?

A: Yes, there was like a football game that was almost over that I wanted to finish watching, but I went to the bathroom and Lorena changed the channel and she put on the Thanksgiving Day Parade. She really got upset because, you know, the game was almost over, and I wanted to finish watching the game. There was only five or ten minutes left.

Q: And then sometime thereafter, she fixed dinner for all of you; right?

A: Yes—well, her mother and her were fixing dinner.

Q: You didn't eat dinner with them because of this fight; is that right?

A: Yes. Lorena said that I couldn't have Thanksgiving Dinner with them because she cooked the food. She said make your own food. So, I just made a sandwich or something, but I didn't eat. But, later on, her mother was really upset about how Lorena was acting and she made me a plate of food.

Q: And then there came a point in time when Lorena and her mother wanted to leave the premises and go to a movie; isn't that right?

A: Yes.

Q: And you were not included in that?

A: Right.

Q: And how were they to go to this movie, what means of transportation were they to take?

A: The only means was my car and it was a standard car and Lorena she couldn't drive it. Her mother was, you know, kind of upset that I wasn't going [and] that Lorena was acting hostile towards me.

Q: For whatever reason, you went out and got in the car?

A: Well, yeah. I knew they were leaving. I just got ready to leave myself.

Q: And during the course of this, somehow or another, you backed into her or hit—the car struck her or the door struck her in some way; is that right?

A: Right, I was trying to back up. She knew I was

going to leave. She ran out of the house and tried to open the door and while she was doing that I was backing up and she fell.

So, you know, I stopped and I pulled the car forward, I closed the door. She got up around the car—the back of the car and if I backed up again, she tried to stop me from backing up out of the driveway. I pulled forward and then drove through my neighbor's yard and left.

Q: You are aware that after that, she filed a complaint concerning that and saying that you had whatever, assaulted her, struck her with the car; is that right?

A: I guess so, yes.

Q: And as a result of that, you went to see a priest?

A: Yes, sir.

Q: Now, there came a point in time when she obtained a warrant for you; I think Mr. Howard asked you about that and you went to court. You had an attorney; did you not?

A: A court appointed attorney. I'm not sure. It was a long time ago. When they brought me in, they explained that it was an assault charge, it was a domestic thing and that it's not a criminal record.

It's just that I had to go to a police program and after six months, it would be thrown out. And I didn't plead guilty to it. It's just a mandatory.

Q: Can you tell us, sir, what happened the night that gave rise to the arrest warrant.

A: I don't remember what it was about. You know, the police were called, we were separated and they talked to us and then they told me they had to bring me in because this [was] like the fourth of fifth call.

Q: Lorena had certain bruises on her lip or something

and then on her arm or foot, I think, when the police came on that occasion; did she not?

A: Yes.

Q: How did that happen?

A: I don't know what the argument or the fight was about, but I remember pushing her and then she jumped on my back and I was trying to get her off of me and push her away.

Sometimes I would hold her down and then she would get really, really angry because I was holding her down. Then after that I said, I can't be holding her or pushing her anymore because she just gets anger, more angry. So, I just said, well, from now on, I'll just walk away, go on outside, go for a run or a drive until everything cools down. I said I was using the wrong kind of method trying to handle the conflict.

Q: Did you ever restrain or do any type of physical, have any physical contact with your wife other than when she was attacking you?

A: Physical contact, yes, just push her away or fend her off. Sometimes I hold her down. That's all. I could never hit my wife. I'm afraid to hurt her if I hit her, you know. So, I never hit her at all, just push her and hold her down and restrain her from hitting me. I would tell her this is not normal. I don't believe in violence. It's not lady-like to strike out.

Q: There came a time in the course of this when you and your wife separated; isn't that right?

A: Yes, sir. It was my brother's wife's birthday and we went to Kings Dominion. I guess I wasn't paying enough attention to her [Lorena] and she felt neglected or something and then she kind of clawed my side. She got mad. And then she went out in the car and I went out there to see what was wrong, it was a big incident. But anyway, we got back home and I went to go to bed and my brother and his wife were supposed to stay over at our house. And Buddy said something to Lorena that offended her.

Q: Who is Buddy?

A: My younger brother. He [said] something like, "Why are you acting like this," or why have got to be such a, you know, something.

She got offended and said, "You leave my house now." And they packed up and left. And Lorena came back in the bedroom and she said, "You know, I did something really bad. I told Buddy and Sherry that they had to leave."

Q: How long had they been with you?

A: It seemed like all day. They came and drove all the way from Delaware to our house to stay, you know, that day, and my wife told them to leave that night because Buddy offended her by saying something.

Q: Did that cause some sort of marital problems or discord?

A: That was like at 12:00 o'clock at night she told them to leave. Right; it did. I got upset and said I said, "Well, that's it, I'm leaving." I got in my car and drove to Buddy's house. I showed up right after he did.

Q: You followed your brother back to Delaware?

A: Yeah, but he was already gone when my wife came into the bedroom.

Q: How long did you stay up there with your brother Buddy before you returned to your wife?

A: I stayed there for two weeks.

Q: Why did you go back?

A: Because I guess we worked it out on the phone and apologized to each other and then we got back.

Q: And then how long did you live together before you again left?

A: August, September, October, three months.

Q: And how did you get along during that period of time?

A: Well, not well. We weren't communicating. We weren't getting along well and we just kept to ourselves. You know, she did her thing and I did mine and we weren't really, a good couple.

Q: There came a point in time that you separated and went back to New York; is that right?

A: Yes; on two occasions.

Q: And why was it you left and went to New York on that occasion?

A: Well, our marriage had its ups and downs and we didn't get along.

Q: She had some problems at work; is that correct?

A: Yes, she had some problems at work. Soon after that, she didn't want me to leave and we talked to Barry White who is a friend of ours and anyway soon after that I left, I went home to New York for about a year or year and a half.

Q: And there was some point in time that you returned; is that right?

A: Yes.

Q: When was that?

A: In September of '92.

Q: What caused you to return, sir?

A: Me and Lorena agreed that, you know, we would work out marriage out and, you know, I had responsibilities to take care of and we wanted to try to start over again, try to work out our marriage in September of '92.

Q: And how would you communicate while you were in New York and she was here?

A: She would call a lot. She would call my mother and would try to get a hold of me numerous times. I didn't want to talk to her.

But, eventually, my mother said you've got to talk to Lorena, she's calling all the time.

Q: Did there come a time that she sent you a bus ticket?

A: Yes, that was in the summer. That was the first time I separated. I went home for like two months. She picked me up in Washington at the bus terminal.

Q: During the course of this marriage when you were with her, would it be fair to say that from time to time she would assault you?

A: Yes, yeah.

Q: Did you ever call 911?

A: Yes.

Q: And do you recall when that was and why you did that?

A: Yes, it was September. I was the first one to really initiate the 911 call. We were fighting over the TV. That was when we were playing tug of war with the blankets. She wanted me to go to bed.

This was when I was working for a cab company. I wanted to work and make money, so I stayed up and listened to the scanner so that I could pick up a call. But she would get upset because I wouldn't go to bed. And she pulled the blankets off of me and I guess we got in a fight over that. I pushed her. She kicked me in the groin. I said, "That's it, I'm calling 911." This is not the type of behavior that I, you know, I'm not used to it.

Q: And in June of '93, you and she again had a brief separation; is that correct?

A: In June of '93, yes.

Q: Do you know whether or not she was happy over that prospect?

A: No; she wasn't happy.

REDIRECT EXAMINATION

BY MR. HOWARD:

Q: As a result of what you told this jury and what Mr. Ebert has asked you about these various assaults of your wife upon you, are you telling this jury that you were a battered husband?

A: What I'm trying to tell the jury is that I didn't believe in violence and I didn't expect it out of my wife. It wasn't proper and it wasn't ladylike to strike out in that way. And that's why I left because I don't want to deal with her being like that.

Q: Then you weren't a battered husband; were you?

A: No; I wasn't. I mean, you know, she's only like 90 pounds and I'm 185 pounds and she's not, you know, she doesn't really hurt me.

The only thing is just it's just a moral value. I mean it's not proper for a lady to strike out in such a way just because things aren't going well.

KATHLEEN WILLIAMS
DIRECT EXAMINATION

BY MR. HOWARD:

Q: Yes, ma'am, would you be kind enough to give the

members of the jury your full name and what your current occupation is?

A: My name is Kathleen Ellen Williams and I am a social worker employed by the Department of Navy, Washington Anacostia Family Service Center.

Q: The month of December 1990, were you so employed at that time?

A: I was employed at the Medical Clinic at Quantico. My role and my job at the Social Work Department the Medical Clinic was to do assessments in child and spouse abuse cases and then present those cases to that committee for determinations and recommendations.

Q: Did you have an occasion to do an evaluation on John Wayne Bobbitt in December of 1990?

A: Yes; I did.

Q: Tell the members of the jury what the occasion was that you had to interview him, please, ma'am.

A: He was referred by someone within his command, Staff Sergeant Morgan on 3 December 1990 for an allegation of spouse abuse.

Q: Did you conduct an interview with him directly?

A: Yes, sir.

Q: What was the purpose of that interview?

A: The purpose of the interview was to assess whether or not abuse had occurred, was occurring and then to determine whether or not a spouse abuse case would be open.

Q: And your evaluation would be sent to whom?

A: Well, the evaluation wouldn't be sent anywhere, it would be presented to the Case Review Subcommittee. All the records were maintained as medical records within the medical clinic.

Q: Yes, ma'am, now, on the occasion that you had to

see Mr. Bobbitt, can you tell me what information you secured from him directly?

A: He talked about an incident that had occurred on Thanksgiving Day which was the reason that he was referred to my office by his command and then talked about some family history.

Q: First of all, would you tell the members of the jury the family history Mr. Bobbitt gave you?

A: He had indicated that at about the age of four, his father had left the family and he and his siblings had gone to live with an aunt and uncle.

He also indicated that he had been told that [in] his family of origin, there had been abuse directed at both him and his mother, but that he couldn't remember any of that. He also indicated that there was violence in the home that he grew up in with his aunt and uncle.

Q: Ms. Williams, did there come a time when you discussed with him whether or not he had abused his wife, just in general terms.

A: Yes, of course.

Q: And what was his position on that?

A: At that point, there was denial that any abuse had occurred, but then later on, we talked about the specific incident.

Q: Following his version of what occurred, you presented him with a questionnaire?

A: Yes.

Q: Would you tell the members of the jury what is the importance of your evaluation of the person charged with abuse of such a questionnaire?

A: I use the questionnaire as an assessment tool to—to begin to look at specific behavior not just that occurred in the incident that they were referred for, but throughout the length of the relationship.

Q: I hand you this (indicating) document and ask you if you can identify it, please?

A: Yes.

Q: What is reflected on that document?

A: There are twenty-six items that are arranged in three categories, psychological abuse, physical abuse, life-threatening violence with on the right-hand side, yes, no, is to be circled and with a comment at the top, "Ever happened."

Q: And in your presence, was that form signed by somebody?

A: Yes.

Q: And who was that individual who signed the form in your presence?

A: John W. Bobbitt.

MR. HOWARD: Your Honor, I would ask that that be admitted as Defendant's exhibit.

MR. EBERT: No objection.

THE COURT: It will be so admitted. It will Defendant's Exhibit 12.

Q: Ms. Williams, at the conclusion of the completion of that form, did he give the form back to you?

A: Yes.

Q: And you discussed these items on the form with him?

A: Yes.

Q: Did he ever make any statements to you with reference to his wife's allegations of abuse whether they were true or not?

A: The information that I have spoken to was information that he provided to me. He told me about these events of that day.

Q: Then he never denied any abuse of his wife after you had gone over the complaint?

A: No; no.

Q: After the interview itself, did you have a follow-up contact with Mr. Bobbitt?

A: Yes; I did. It was a week later when I was attempting to make contact with Mrs. Bobbitt and was not able to get through. The call would not go through, so I contacted, at that time, Lance Corporal Bobbitt to ask him if I, indeed, had the correct phone number. He assured me that the number was correct.

Q: Did he say anything else to you in that conversation?

A: He reminded me that he was due to be discharged very soon.

CROSS EXAMINATION

BY MR. EBERT:

Q: Did you ever talk to Mrs. Bobbitt at anytime?

A: No, I did not.

Q: So, really this was referred to you by the command and the rest of it basically is what he told you; right?

A: That is correct.

Q: And I think you said at first he denied having any problems and then—

A: He denied the abuse, not problems. He indicated that the reason for the referral, the reason for referral was that he was having marital problems.

Q: I think you assessed him as being very immature; is that correct?

A: Those were my words in the notes, yes.

Q: Did you—you didn't make any assessment that Mrs. Bobbitt was in immediate danger at the time; did you?

A: I always feel that clients are in danger in spouse abuse situations. There is no way to assess that based on an interview just with the individual who is the alleged perpetrator.

Q: And part of your interview was that his wife complains about his goals? His wife complains he doesn't spend enough time with her, that he's not affectionate enough?

A: Yes.

Q: He told you that; didn't he?

A: Yes.

Q: Did you get the idea when he filled out this questionnaire which has been introduced as Defense Exhibit Number 12 that he had been truthful with you?

A: I would have no way to ascertain that. I see a lot of people and I kind of assume that people in our initial visit are going to tend to want to minimize certain aspects of their behavior.

Q: Well, some of the things that he said certainly indicated that he has abused her or he's had some physical contact with his wife?

A: Absolutely.

JOHN WHITAKER
DIRECT EXAMINATION

BY MR. HOWARD:

Q: Where do you live and reside John?

A: Stafford, Virginia.

Q: Do you know a family by the name of Beltran in the Stafford area?

A: Yes, sir.

Q: On any visits to the house, did you ever meet or come in contact with a young Marine?

A: Yes, sir.

Q: Would you tell the members of the jury the name of that young Marine?

A: John Bobbitt.

Q: Did you ever engage in any kind of outside sports activity or inside sports activity with John Bobbitt?

A: Yes, sir. We use to go fishing at Lunger Reservoir on Quantico base. We went to play basketball at Quantico base, at Raimer Hall.

Q: Could you tell us, was there ever an occasion where you were present when John Bobbitt gave any feelings about forcible sex or made any statements about forcible sex?

A: Yes, sir.

Q: On the occasion that he expressed himself about forced sex, who was present in the room?

A: Jonathan Kaopua, and Rinzo Beltran and myself.

Q: Who was in the room before John entered, if you know?

A: Me, John Kaopua, and Rinzo Beltran.

Q: What were you fellows talking about before John entered into the room?

A: Girls, guy talk, girls.

Q: On the occasion that he entered the room, did he make any comments to you about his attitude towards sex?

A: Yes, sir. He said that he liked to make girls squirm and yell and make them bleed and yell for help.

THE COURT: Mr. Ebert?

CROSS EXAMINATION

BY MR. EBERT:

Q: You don't know if John was telling the truth when he made that statement or just was, shall we say, engaging in some sort [bravado]; isn't that right?

A: You could tell he was serious.

A witness, was called for examination by counsel on behalf of Defendant, and, after having been duly sworn, was examined and testified, as follows:

ELLA JONES
DIRECT EXAMINATION

BY MR. LOWE:

Q: Please state your name for the record ma'am?

A: Ella Jones.

Q: Did you know the Bobbitts?

A: Yeah, I met them.

Q: Where in relation to your apartment was their apartment?

A: Right underneath of me.

Q: Mrs. Jones, did you have occasion to hear an argument or fight between the Bobbitts sometime early this Spring?

A: Yeah, one morning, one Sunday morning, I don't know what date it was, but I heard the ruckus upstairs, running and banging and I heard her hollering, "Give me my purse, give me my purse." It didn't last very long.

Q: How long before the incident of the cutting that that happened?

A: It was less than a month.

Q: All right. Now did you see Mrs. Bobbitt the day before the cutting?

A: The day before.

Q: Would you tell us what happened on that occasion.

A: Well, she was in the parking lot, she was cleaning out her car and I was going up the sidewalk. And, she walked across to me and she was talking about, she was getting rid of everything and if I wanted anything to come up the next morning and look and see what I wanted.

And, she had said that her husband had raped her and she would rather give her things to some of her neighbors than give it to the Salvation Army.

CROSS EXAMINATION

BY MR. EBERT:

Q: Is it fair to say then that when you saw her a few days before the alleged offense which is before the court, that you knew that she was leaving and that the couple was separating; is that right?

A: Well, I figured that if she was getting rid of everything that she must be leaving.

Q: She told you that didn't she?

A: No, she didn't tell me.

Q: You just assumed from that that she was leaving. Now when you gave her the pamphlets [*Awake* Magazine, a publication of the Jehovah Witnesses] which are in evidence you ask her if she wanted to stay with you; didn't you?

A: Yes, I did tell her to come and spend the night with me that night. I don't know why, but I just asked her that.

Q: Well, you were afraid, I assume that she might be assaulted or raped, right?

A: Well, I guess so, I don't know.

Q: You didn't know that, you just assumed that?

A: Yeah, and too I was an abused wife too.

Q: I know you were. And, that is the reason that you were so concerned—

A: Yes.

Q: —And that you wanted to give her those pamphlets?

A: Yes.

Q: And, it would be fair to say that she said no.

A: She said, "No, that's all right, Ms. Ella." She didn't spend the night.

Q: Now, you knew John Bobbitt much better than you knew Mrs. Bobbitt, isn't that right?

A: Well, I had talked to him first. He came to me with some religious literature and he had some of our literature and I talked to him. I traded literature with him and they looked at my religious videos and I just thought we was going to get something going with them, bible study with them. I befriended them both.

Q: And, until June 22nd, you only had a passing acquiescenceship with Lorena, that you would nod and this was usually when you were talking to John. You had no conversation of any substance with Lorena until the 22nd day of June, isn't that right?

A: Until I talked to her, yeah.

Q: Did you ever see any bruises on her that indicated that she had been battered did you?

A: No, no I didn't.

Q: And, other than the incidents that you recall when

they were fighting over a purse, you never heard any argument or any fight come from that apartment?

A: No.

Q: You certainly heard no screaming, fighting or arguing on that night?

A: No.

BOBBIE JO LORE
DIRECT EXAMINATION

BY MS. KEMLER:

Q: Ms. Lore, do you know Lorena Bobbitt?

A: Yes, I do.

Q: Do you know John Bobbitt?

A: Yes, I do.

Q: And, how is it that you know Lorena Bobbitt?

A: I met her when I went to work at the Nail Sculptor.

Q: And, do you recall approximately when that was?

A: Summer of '89.

Q: And, when was it that you met Mr. Bobbitt?

A: Within a few weeks of meeting Lorena.

Q: And, did you have occasion to socialize with Lorena and John Bobbitt?

A: Yes, I did. We went over to their house for dinner. Went out to clubs.

Q: During those times that you were with Lorena and John, did you observe anything in particular with respect to the way that John treated Lorena?

A: He liked Lorena to be with him, only him. Didn't like her to have friends. You know one night we went out and he got upset with her in a bar because someone looked at her and he yelled and jerked her and got very angry at her and yelled at her and told her they were leaving; called her some names.

Q: All right. Did you ever have an occasion to see John become verbally abusive towards Lorena?

A: Yes. Lorena had invited us over to her apartment, her and John's first apartment together to have dinner. Lorena was cooking and we were waiting for dinner to be ready. John got very mad because she didn't cook something properly and started yelling, screaming telling her that she couldn't do anything right. He got very mad, very upset.

Q: Did there ever come a time that you became aware that John was physically injuring Lorena?

A: Yes. I believe the first time we had all went out to a bar, the same night he had gotten very angry with her, they left. He pulled her out of the bar. Because a guy looked at Lorena. They left. I went home. I was at home, at my parent's house and I got a phone call. It was Lorena. I went to pick her up, to bring her to my house to spend the night.

Q: Where did you pick her up from?

A: The Nail Sculptor.

Q: And, do you know what time of night that was?

A: Between two-thirty, three-thirty.

Q: All right. And, when you picked her up and took her home, did you observe anything about her?

A: When I first picked her up she was just very upset, hysterical crying and then I took her home to my house. I asked her what happened.

Q: Did you observe anything physically with respect to—

A: She had bruises on her arms.

Q: Did you have occasion to see Ms. Bobbitt under similar circumstances after that time?

A: Yes. A few months, the end of '89 beginning of '90, I'm not exactly sure about the dates. They all ran within a few months of one another. She called me again late at night. I went to pick her up to bring her to my house again to spend the night.

Q: And, how did she appear to you when you picked her up?

A: The same, hysterical crying, more bruises.

Q: Where was the bruising, if you recall?

A: Arms and I believe at that time she had one on her head.

Q: And, were there other occasions when you received phone calls from Ms. Bobbitt and asking you to pick her up?

A: Around that same time I think there was one or maybe two more times, after that no.

TERRI MCCUMBER
DIRECT EXAMINATION

BY MR. LOWE:

Q: Mrs. McCumber, did you at some time work with Mrs. Bobbitt?

A: Yes, sir. Late August to the last of September, maybe the beginning of October, [of] '89.

Q: Did you have occasion to go to the beach with them?

A: Yes, sir.

Q: Would you tell us what that occasion was and what happened there?

A: It was Friday evening; John came in and suggested to Lorena and I that we go to Ocean City for the weekend. And, I accepted and I went home to get my things.

I met Lorena and John and John's brother Todd at their apartment in Manassas.

We left from there in John's car and got to Ocean City late that night. We had a difficult time finding a hotel, we found one late. The next morning we got up and went to the beach and—

Q: Let me stop you before you tell the rest of the story; were you with John's brother during this or you just happened—

A: Oh, no. I went just to be with Lorena.

Q: Go ahead and tell us what happened the next day.

A: We arrived at Ocean City. We got up that morning, we went to the beach. John and Todd did their thing. They swam and me and Lorena stayed on the blanket on the beach and we decided to go up onto the boardwalk.

While we were there we were looking at key chains, buying key chains with our names on it and things like that. And, at that time, these gentlemen started whistling at—I don't know if it was at us or someone else, but at that point that is when John heard this.

He came up, grabbed Lorena by the hair, pulled her. Then I got into an argument with John about this and he pulled her back to the hotel, screaming, yelling. They were fighting. And, he said, "The weekend was over, we are going home, that's it."

Well, after screaming, yelling and going back to the motel, he threw the clothes into the car and as they were fighting in the hotel, he says that we are leaving, that's it. We got into the car and we went home.

When we drove down Lorena was allowed to sit with me. At this point he made her sit in the front seat, along side him, and I sat in the back with Todd. And, this is when the argument started he was hitting her, punching her, as she hid herself in the corner of the car. I got involved in it by screaming myself between the two front seats, telling him to stop this, you know, stop this, over and over.

He was accusing her, she was looking (Indicating) out the window, like to hide from him, from him hitting her, and he kept accusing her of her looking at other guys in the cars, because we were in traffic this weekend.

Q: Did you have an opportunity to change before you drove back?

A: No, he—the incident on the boardwalk, he drug her by her hair, straight to the hotel, and I am running behind him, to keep him from doing this and he at that point was just throwing things into the trunk, that's it, we are gone, and we were in our bathing suits and shorts.

Q: On the way back did John threaten you in some fashion?

A: Yeah, in the middle of this fighting down the highway, I'm telling him to stop it, because Lorena is so upset and he said that if I didn't shut up, he was going to put me out on I-95. And, my car was at their apartment and he refused to take me back to the house to get my vehicle.

And, he dropped me off at my parent's, about three blocks away from the house.

Q: Did you happen to see Lorena later in the day?

A: We had gotten a phone call and it was Lorena. She had called me to come and get her.

Q: Did you come and get her?

A: Yes.

Q: Did you see bruises on her when you picked her up?

A: Oh, yes.

Q: What was her emotional state when you picked her up?

A: A wreck, she was a wreck. She was a wreck in the car and at the hotel also.

Q: How long did she stay with your family?

A: I stayed with my family until October—

Q: Not you, how long did she stay with your family?

A: She spent the night there.

Q: Have you seen her bruised on other occasions?

A: Yes, before that.

Q: Did you all go to a tanning salon?

A: No, we use to—when we would close the shop, Janna allowed us to have use of the salon, to use the tanning beds or what ever. And, her and I would tan and that is when we were able to see, and I have seen many a bruises in the inside of her leg and in the backs of her arms.

Wednesday,
January 12

SUSAN INMAN
DIRECT EXAMINATION

BY MR. LOWE:

Q: When did you first meet Mrs. Bobbitt?

A: I first met her in March of last year when I saw her for an upper respiratory infection.

Q: And when did you next see her?

A: On the 12th of March. She was having cramping and diarrhea from her erythromycin. And I had sent her to the Urgent Care for evaluation because she lived so far away from the office.

And she came back for a re-check because she was still having problems with her stomach.

Q: Did you see her on occasion when her husband came with her?

A: On the 12th he brought her back because she didn't feel well enough to drive.

Q: Was there anything unusual about Mr. Bobbitt's actions in that visit?

A: I thought it was sort of unusual that he was laughing at her for being sick.

Q: When did you next see her?

A: I saw her on 4/17 for some poison ivy. And I treated her—

Q: When did you next have contact with her?

A: I saw her on 4/30 for a sinus infection, which I treated. And on 5/4 I treated her over the telephone for an apparent yeast infection. And then on 6/18 I saw her when she presented to the office for complaints of being anxious and hyperventilating.

Q: Tell us about that treatment. We're talking about the 17th or 18th of June?

A: Yes. She called the office, and we weren't busy, and she asked if she could come over. And she was having trouble doing her job as a manicurist because her hands were shaking and cramping.

Q: What did you observe when she came to visit you?

A: She was hyperventilating and she had a respiratory rate of about twenty-eight. And her hands were cramping and shaking.

Q: Did you take a history from her at that time?

A: Yes, I did. I asked her if there was anything that was going on that was causing stress that might cause her to be hyperventilating. And she said that she was having some problem with her husband and that it was making it difficult for her to sleep and pay attention to her work.

Q: Did she describe the nature of the problem with her husband?

A: I asked her had he hit her or hurt her in any way and she said, well, not really. That he had as I recall in my notes that she had told me that he had sex with her without her permission, is the way she put it. And she was very embarrassed about that and didn't want it pursued.

Q: What did you do as a result?

A: I told her that if she wanted help with that to contact Protective Services. And I gave her the phone number and gave her access to a telephone to call at that time.

Q: —and that cured the problem.

A: It resolved the symptoms.

Q: And she went back to work.

A: Yes.

Q: And because of what she told you about the history of her husband having sex with her without her permission you suspected that she should call—or at least you suggested that she call Social Services; is that correct?

A: That's correct.

Q: And she never mentioned at any time to you about any physical abuse at that time, did she? In other words, hitting, striking, did you see any bruises?

A: No, I asked her specifically did she have any injuries and she said no.

Q: And it's your custom when you see people in this— where you suspect some sort of a need for Social Services to intervene you provide the telephone for them and ask them to call; isn't that correct?

A: Yes.

MR. EBERT: That's all I have for this witness, Your Honor.

PETER WEINTZ
DIRECT EXAMINATION

BY MR. HOWARD:

Q: Detective Weintz, let me direct your attention to June 24th of this year. Did you have occasion to speak to Mr. John Bobbitt?

A: Yes, I did.

Q: Let me ask you was this the first occasion after you became involved in this investigation that you did speak to John Bobbitt?

A: Yes. Mr. Bobbitt was located at the intensive care unit in Prince William Hospital. We got permission to speak with him and Sergeant Morgan from my unit and myself responded to the hospital intensive care unit.

He was alert, didn't appear to be in any extreme pain or anything at that point in time. He stated he did wish to talk to us and was willing to answer any questions that we had at that point.

Q: When you spoke to him did you ask him whether or not he had sex with his wife that night?

A: Yes, we did.

Q: Now, any questions I'm asking you about sex with Lorena Bobbitt specifically in directing to let's say the early morning hours of June 23 when the cutting is supposed to take place.

A: Yes, sir.

Q: Did you ask him whether or not in those early morning hours just preceding the cutting whether he had sex with his wife?

A: Yes, we did.

Q: And tell the members of the jury what he told you at that time.

A: He said he had not.

Q: Did you visit the subject before you left that interview with Mr. Bobbitt about whether he had had sex with his wife that morning again before the interview terminated?

A: Yes, we did. Mr. Bobbitt said that he could not remember and that if he had had sex with his wife he must have been asleep, that he does this often and doesn't remember it.

Q: Now, on July 13th did you have occasion, sir, to interview Mr. Bobbitt a second time?

A: Yes, I did. At Mr. Bobbitt's apartment at Peakwood apartments on Maplewood Drive in Prince William County.

Q: Prior to arriving at Mr. Bobbitt's apartment on July 13th had you received some information from the forensic laboratory concerning the results of the vaginal smears and the PERK kit that was taken from Lorena Bobbitt?

A: Yes, sir, I had. Not in an official report at that time but I had called and spoke to the technician and it was confirmed that there was sperm located.

Q: When you got to the apartment did you apprise Mr. Bobbitt of anything—and I'm talking about July 13th, before the interview started—did you apprise him of anything in terms of why you were there and what his rights might have been and that sort of thing?

A: Sergeant Zinn—I was in the company of Sergeant Zinn with the County Police Department, and Sergeant Zinn and I advised Mr. Bobbitt while we were there that we had some matters that we would like to talk him about. And admonished him if he did choose to speak to us that we would like the truth, that we would like to get to the bottom of what had actually happened on the morning of the 23rd.

Q: Did you bring up the subject matter with him as to whether or not he had had sex with his wife in the early morning hours on June 23rd just before the cutting?

A: Yes, sir. His initial response again was, no, that he did not have sex with his wife.

Q: Did you ask him anything about what his wife was wearing that morning when he entered the bedroom?

A: There was a point somewhere sometime into the actual interview itself where he was asked what they normally wore to bed. And that was described.

A short time later in the sequence of events as to when he arrived home that night he stated he went directly to bed and he did not know what she was wearing because she was under the covers of the bed.

Q: That was his statement to you on July 13, 1993; is that correct?

A: Yes, sir.

Q: Did there come a time that you confronted him with your knowledge of what the forensic lab technician had told you concerning the sperm in his wife's vagina?

A: Yes, sir, we had again admonished him to please tell us the truth. And in fact, we had some lab reports that were already confirming certain information and specific mention to the PERK kit.

And at that point in time he stated he vaguely remembered several things were coming to him. He vaguely remembered touching his wife under the covers and also recalled removing his wife's panties with his feet.

Q: Did he then go from a vague recollection to some other recollection? Did he ever tell you anything specifically about what he did other than the vague recollection of removing his wife's panties?

A: Again when we questioned his response at that point and gave additional information as to what actually was specifically located on that examination, he then added that he was recalling that he had had a relation with his wife. And at the point in time where the sperm was mentioned he then went from one portion of a conversation right into the fact that he could remember penetration and that he had had an orgasm with his wife.

Q: Now, this was the first time you had heard that story, about the orgasm and the penetration.

A: That's correct.

Q: And that came after you confronted him with the information you received from the lab technician.

A: That's correct.

LYNN ACQUAVIVA
DIRECT EXAMINATION

BY MS. KEMLER:

Q: Ms. Acquaviva, do you know Lorena Bobbitt?

A: I was a client of Lorena Bobbitt's, yes.

Q: And is that a client at the Nail Salon where she worked?

A: That is correct.

Q: And when did you first meet Ms. Bobbitt?

A: Sometime in the summer of 1989 I was in the salon on a Saturday. It was a very hot day. I'm going to say it was approximately July. Ms. Bobbitt was attired in multiple layers of clothing which I found unusual for the weather, but I didn't say anything. She was wearing leggings, a tank top or t-shirt. A sort of a shirt over that under which you could see the t-shirt. And then a sweater over that.

As she worked on my hands that morning I noticed as she moved around, tossed her head back from side to side to move her hair away, and her sweater and shirts would slide to one side or the other, extensive iridescent royal blue bruising across the top of her skull, down the side of her skull, down her neck, across her chest. As her sweater would move up, and her leggings would move up as she sat at the chair, the iridescent royal bruising continued over those parts of her body as well.

Q: Did you have occasion to see Lorena Bobbitt in February of 1990?

A: Yes. Again as a client. On that occasion it was unusual that I was there during the week on an evening; however, I was. It was dark that night; approximately six o'clock.

I witnessed a vehicle pull up in front of the shop. There was one young man driving, another young man got out of the car. Came into the shop. Approached Ms. Bobbitt and asked her for money because he stated that he wanted to go and party with his friend.

Ms. Bobbitt refused to give him money. He invited her outside.

Q: Did you see what was happening outdoors?

A: Yes, I was seated much as I am right now with the glass wall of the front of the shop being in this direction. As I turned he was pulling her sharply by the arm. I did not hear a sound. I was towards the rear of the shop but did have clear vision to see out the front of the shop.

He was pulling her by her arm. Pulled her and yanking her. Pulled her around the front of the vehicle. As he did so grabbed her hair like this (indicating) and pulled her downward and I could see that he was yelling. But I did not hear a conversation.

Q: And did Ms. Bobbitt come back into the shop after that?

A: Shortly thereafter, yes, she did.

Q: How did she appear?

A: She was somewhat disheveled.

Q: Did you observe anything else about her when she came back into the shop?

A: She appeared to have been crying and seemed to be crying a small bit at that time.

Q: And did you have occasion to see Ms. Bobbitt on other occasions at the shop?

A: Yes, I did.

Q: And did you observe any other injuries at all on her?

A: Yes, I did.

Q: And would you describe what those were?

A: It was approximately three to four months after that episode of the altercation in the parking lot that I again witnessed extensive bruising over the top and sides of Ms. Bobbitt's skull into her hairline and face line and down her neck and shoulders again as before.

I did not, however, notice it all throughout the rest of her body as before.

ROMA ANASTASI
DIRECT EXAMINATION

BY MR. HOWARD:

Q: Ms. Anastasi, do you know Lorena Bobbitt?

A: Yes. In the early part of 1990. I was a customer of hers at the place of the Nail Sculpture every two weeks over three and a half months.

Q: Can you tell us if there were ever any occasions that you either came to meet her husband or see her husband there in the shop?

A: Occasionally when she was doing my nails he would just stop by to I guess visit her or whatever.

Q: Did you ever see him in there in connection with any matters dealing with her purse or money?

A: Yes.

Q: Tell us what you observed on any occasion that he might have had some connection with that purse.

A: While she was doing my nails he would walk around to the back of her where she kept it and helped himself to the money that he felt that he needed.

Q: Now, on those occasions that you observed that what kind of reaction did you see out of her?

A: She would be extremely tense, appeared nervous, and often was very sad.

Q: Was there an occasion where you received a phone call from Mrs. Bobbitt in the early morning hours?

A: In October of '91. The early part of October of '91. It was ten-thirty at night.

Q: What did you tell Lorena to do as a result of what you heard over that telephone?

A: I told her I'd pick her up. She was already at the Giant parking lot and she was pretty hysterical on the phone and it took me a few moments to decipher exactly where she was. And I told her I'd be right there to pick her, up, and I did.

Q: Ma'am, how long did it take you to get to the location where she had made that call?

A: Oh, probably two minutes.

Q: When you arrived can you describe Mrs. Bobbitt's condition as you observed her?

A: Well, where I picked her up there was lighting but it was rather dark. She was very hysterical and not too coherent. Basically I just said get in the car and let's get home and get to my house so I could help and decide what we needed to do or really find out what the problem was.

Q: When you got to your house did you make any observations about her person; that is, her body?

A: Her face was swollen. That was the first visible sign that I had that there was a problem.

Q: Did she cry at all during that period of time?

A: Very much so.

Q: As a result of whatever she told you—first of all, do you know where she was living at that time and who she was living with?

A: Her residence at that time was Pine Street.

Q: And whom was she living with?

A: With her husband John.

Q: As a result of whatever she told you did you give her any advice as to where she might stay that evening?

A: I told her that she was welcome to stay in our home. And my family encouraged her.

Q: Following this incident did you have occasion to go back to the Nail Sculpture?

A: Yes.

Q: Did you notice any difference in Lorena Bobbitt after this incident and the way she had been before the incident?

A: Her depression was very noticeable. Her sadness was very noticeable. And occasionally when she was doing my nails she would burst into tears.

There were mistakes made. At times when she was supposed to do a certain process there was confusion and she didn't do it in the proper sequence.

Q: Without telling us what you discussed is it fair to say that she confided in you a good deal after this one occasion that you just told the jury about?

A: Lorena confided in me over a three year period very consistently.

Q: During the course of sharing with you any confidences did she show any emotion?

A: Yes. She was extremely distressed, depressed, very sad, a lot of anxiety. And I had difficult times with her language barrier at times when she would describe things to me. The words that she often used were not I felt the correct words to express how she felt. So, there was confusion.

Q: Did she ever cry on any of those occasions?

A: Numerous times.

MARY JO WILLOUGHBY
DIRECT EXAMINATION

BY MR. HOWARD:

Q: Would you tell us, Ms. Willoughby, was there an occasion while you were living (on Pine Street) that you had a young couple by the name of Bobbitt move in next to you?

A: Yes. I believe it was around June of '90.

Q: Did you ever have the Bobbitts in your home?

A: Yes.

Q: On those occasions would this be for social reasons or otherwise?

A: Lorena came to our house numerous times to confide in us—confide in me.

Q: Tell the members of the jury on the many times that she would come over to your house what would be her condition? Would she appear happy and confident and settled or what?

A: No, sir. She was usually very upset. Hysterical

sometimes and crying. Sometimes she was very sad and even depressed. Often times crying and just shaking.

A: Yes.

A: Yes, she did. She was obviously distraught and upset.

Q: Did there come a time that both the Bobbitts came over to you in connection with these marital problems?

A: Yes, sir.

Q: Before that particular occasion did you often notice any marks or bruises on her?

A: Yes, Lorena had shown me one on her side, or her hip area. She turned to the side and pulled her clothing to show me a bruise.

Q: On the occasion that they were in there did they discuss with you these problems they'd been having?

A: Yes.

Q: After that discussion did you and your husband— did you advise Mr. Bobbitt or Mrs. Bobbitt of things they should do?

A: We made suggestions and recommendations.

Q: And what sort of recommendations did you make, ma'am?

A: Well, one on John's behalf is that he needed to be able to talk about these things and that it wasn't right to hit his wife and to treat her and abuse her that way.

Q: When you told John Bobbitt that did he show any reaction?

A: He didn't seem very changed by it, no.

Q: After that conference that you had with Mr. and Mrs. Bobbitt did she ever come back to your residence?

A: Oh, yes, she came often because he continued to abuse her and to—they continued to have marital problems.

BETH ANN WILSON
DIRECT EXAMINATION

BY MR. HOWARD:

Q: Yes, ma'am, would you give us your full name and your occupation?

A: Beth Ann Wilson and I'm the assistant manager at Maplewood Park Apartments.

Q: Were you so employed there in April of this year, April of 1993?

A: Yes, sir.

Q: Can you tell the members of the jury where and under what circumstances you first had contact with the Bobbitts?

A: I first met Lorena in April when she came with her application. I then met the both of them in—I'm sorry, in April, also, when I went over their lease with them for their move-in.

Q: On the occasion that you saw them together would you tell the members of the jury if you noticed anything unusual about this couple. Just from observation.

A: I did notice that Lorena seemed to be intimidated by John. She had a hard time looking towards him and had her head hung the whole time.

Q: In terms of the conversation you had with—concerning the lease itself, who did you have that conversation with?

A: Mainly with John. Lorena seemed as if she was afraid to speak.

Q: Subsequent to your initial contact with the two of them can you tell us whether or not you ever had occasion thereafter to see Lorena Bobbitt?

A: Yes.

Q: Tell us when that was, the next time after the initial lease was signed.

A: I would say I did see Lorena come in the office on two occasions. She spoke to the manager at that time. But in June, in early June, I spoke to her regarding—she had some questions regarding occupancy in the apartment.

She was very tense, very shaken, very afraid. I mean, you could see the fear in her. She was going through a terrible time and it was obvious by her actions. She would cry.

Q: Now, without telling us anything about what she said, did she begin to confide in you on that occasion?

A: Yes, she did.

Q: How often after that first occasion that she came in did she come in thereafter?

A: I would say out of a five-day work week at least three days.

Q: And would that be all the way up until June 23rd?

A: Up until two days before or a day before. I can't recollect. But it was right up until the time of the incident.

Q: On all the occasions she did come in, from the time she first confided with you up until the last time you saw her before the incident, did her appearance change—did the subject matter why she was there, was it any different?

A: She seemed to be weakening as she would come and speak to me. You could see her character was just fading. She would become more nervous. You know, she would clench her fist. She would shake when she would talk to me. The tears would just run down her face. Just by looking at her you could see the turmoil that she was going through.

Q: Let me ask you this, ma'am, did you ever have

occasion when you were confiding with her and she was confiding in you and so forth, did you ever see her husband around the area where the two of you were?

A: Yes. I'd say as far away as we are from each other right now.

Q: Did you see any reaction, physical reaction on her part?

A: She automatically began to shake. I mean, you could just see her just clam up. I mean, you could see it as soon as she knew that he was close to her.

Q: Did you ever notice any marks or bruises about this lady?

A: Yes. I saw bruises on her wrists and on her upper arms—and on her forehead.

Q: Would you tell the members of the jury the time frame that you observed these bruises, what month we're talking about?

A: This was in June of '93, within a two-week period of time before the incident.

MERCEDES CASTRO
DIRECT EXAMINATION

BY MR. LOWE:

Q: Do you know Lorena Bobbitt?

A: Yes, I do.

Q: How long have you known her?

A: I've known her since 1987.

Q: Did she live in your home for a while?

A: Yes, she did.

Q: In early October of 1991 did you have occasion to see Ms. Bobbitt in your home?

A: Yes, I did. One night she knocked on the door and when I opened the door she looked really scared. And she was crying and her hair was all messed up and everything. I told her to come inside. And then my mother got up and, you know, asked her what happened and everything and that was it.

And then my mom said for me to take some pictures of her because she said that John had hit her. And I said okay. So, I took my Polaroid camera out and we went upstairs to the bathroom, my mom's bathroom. And I told her to put some pajamas on so that it would make it easier for me to take the pictures for her.

And so she pulled up her shirt, her pajama, and she had the bruises on her; right hip here (indicating) and on her left shoulder here (indicating). And she also had some bruises on her left arm and some bruises on her right. But they haven't developed really well. It looked like somebody, like, punched her or something. We couldn't see them on the pictures.

Q: Ms. Castro, I want to show you some xerox copies of some photographs.

(Mr. Lowe handed the witness photographs for her examination.)

Q: Are those the photographs that you took?

A: Yes, they are.

Q: And you took them when?

A: October 18, 1991.

Q: Did you take them October 18th or is that the Immigration and Naturalization Service date on there?

A: No, I took them that day because I remember going downstairs after I had taken the pictures and putting the date on them. I have special marks for them.

Q: Do they show everything that was on what you saw that day?

A: No, not everything.

THE COURT: All right, sir, they'll be admitted then at this time.

CAROL PALMER
DIRECT EXAMINATION

BY MR. LOWE:

Q: Would you state your name and occupation, please.

A: My name is Carol Palmer and I'm a forensic scientist.

Q: How long have you been a forensic scientist?

A: Since 1989.

Q: Ms. Palmer, did you have occasion to examine a PERK kit in relation to the Bobbitt allegation of rape?

A: Yes, I did.

Q: And when did you do that?

A: The evidence was received in our laboratory on July 2nd.

Q: And what is a PERK kit?

A: A PERK kit is the acronym for a Physical Evidence Recovery Kit. And this is something that is supplied to the hospitals to be used for the collection of any trace evidence from alleged victims of sexual assault.

Q: What did this kit contain—involving this case?

A: Inside the PERK kit for this case included swabs and smears from the alleged body areas that were involved, which included the thighs, external genitalia, the vaginal cervical, as well as smears of those areas.

It also included a pair of underpants and a panty shield.

Q: Did you also receive the spandex shorts and the shirt that she was wearing?

A: There was clothing that was submitted to the laboratory; however, I did not examine it.

Q: And what did your examination reveal?

A: Of the PERK kit I identified spermatozoa on the thighs, external genitalia, and vaginal cervical smears, as well as in extracts of stains in the panty shield and crotch of the underpants.

Q: What conclusions, if any, would you draw from the presence of sperm in the areas that you found?

A: That it is foreign to the female and must have originated from the male.

Q: And the length of time that sperm will remain on the exterior areas is what?

A: Spermatozoa can remain on substrates exterior to the body indefinitely until some type of physical actions such as washing or cleansing of that has occurred.

Q: Would it remain after a shower?

A: Depending on how thorough the shower.

Q: And you found this in a number of different areas.

A: Yes, I did.

Q: How long will it remain on the underwear?

A: Once again, indefinitely until either washing or some other physical action removes it from the underpants.

Q: And how long will it remain interiorly?

A: On the vaginal cervical swabs it has been reported that spermatozoa can be found an average of three to five days after the alleged intercourse.

Q: Let me ask you a hypothetical question, if I may, Ms. Palmer.

Assuming that a person on Sunday had intercourse and washed on Monday morning and washed on Tuesday morning, I mean, showered in a normal fashion, put on clean clothes each time they changed; would you expect to find spermatozoa in all the places that you found it without a subsequent act of intercourse?

A: That is a possibility.

Q: What is the likelihood of it?

A: There are other variables that exist, such as if there's continual draining or drainage. You may have showered one day and then you have drainage the following day.

So I cannot testify to the likelihood but that is a possibility.

CROSS EXAMINATION

BY MR. EBERT:

Q: So, what you're telling us you don't know when it was deposited, all you know is that it was there.

A: That is correct.

Q: And spermatozoa could live inside the female body from three to five days; is that correct?

A: That is correct.

Q: And on the external place it could stay indefinitely I think you said.

A: That is correct.

LORENA LEONOR BOBBITT
DIRECT EXAMINATION

BY MR. LOWE:

Q: Ms. Bobbitt, let me start with one fairly simple set of questions.

On Monday and Tuesday in June, did you shower?

A: Yes, I did.

Q: Did you change clothes?

A: Yes, I did.

Q: Were you having any kind of a discharge?

A: No, I didn't.

Q: Where are you from, Miss?

A: I'm from South America, Ecuador.

Q: And did you move from Ecuador?

A: Yes, I did, sir.

Q: At what age?

A: At the age of five.

Q: And where did you move from there?

A: To Venezuela.

Q: For what purpose?

A: My parents want to start a better life there.

Q: What is the nature and size of your family?

A: I don't understand your question.

Q: How many people are there in your family?

A: Four—I'm sorry, five.

Q: And who are they?

A: My brother and my sister, my mother and father.

Q: How old are your brother and sister?

A: My sister is twenty and my brother is sixteen.

Q: How old are you?

A: I'm twenty-four.

Q: Ms. Bobbitt, would you describe your family?

A: Yes. I would say my mom and dad are like little kids, holding hands. There are a lot of love in my family. My brother and sister, we all, I would say together, like a regular, loving, Catholic family.

Q: What is the family view concerning premarital sex?

A: My family wouldn't allow it.

Q: What is the family view concerning unchaperoned dating?

A: My family wouldn't allow it.

Q: Did you have any unchaperoned dates before you came to America?

A: No, I didn't.

Q: What is the family view on abortion?

A: My family would not allow it.

Q: On divorce?

A: My family would not allow it.

Q: What is your understanding of the status of a divorced woman?

A: To me it's a humiliation situation; it is a shame. I would feel embarrassed.

Q: Do you believe that you have a moral right to remarry if you divorce?

A: No.

Q: To have children if you divorce?

A: No.

Q: Was there any background of violence in your family as you grew up?

A: No, no.

Q: How do you believe that difficulties should be resolved within the family?

A: My parents will close the door or just talk about the matter. Just resolve the problems talking. No yelling, no screaming, no violence.

Q: Did you expect to resolve your differences in your family the same way?

A: Yes, I did.

Q: Under what circumstances did you come to Virginia from Venezuela?

A: Right after I finished high school I wanted to

study; go to college here. And I begged my parents to let me be here in America.

Q: What was your goal in coming here?

A: I would like to go to school and have a family. Have childrens just like a regular family. Just like my family.

Q: Did you wish to marry here?

A: Marry here, yes.

Q: When you came here where did you stay?

A: First of all I stayed with my cousin. Then I met Mrs. Castro which is a family friend of my cousin's.

Q: How long did you stay with your cousin?

A: I stayed for like about two months.

Q: And what kind of a family structure did your cousin have?

A: She—it's a hard-working woman. Spanish. Almost like my family.

Q: Were you allowed to date unchaperoned?

A: Yes.

Q: Did you date at all?

A: No, I didn't.

Q: Did there come a time when you moved to the Castro family home?

A: Yes, I did. It was in 1988.

Q: Now, who lived in the Castro home?

A: Mrs. Castro, Mr. Castro, and the two daughters; Irmalene and Mercedes Castro.

Q: And how does that family function?

A: Very well. Like a normal—

Q: What religion are they?

A: Yes, very religious. Catholic.

Q: Were you going to school while you were there?

A: Yes, I went to North Community College, NOVA.

Q: Were you allowed to go out unchaperoned there?

A: Unchaperoned but with somebody else.

Q: Did you take a job at some point?

A: Yes, I did.

Q: Why?

A: So I can support myself and I can survive.

Q: With whom did you take a job?

A: I was a nanny. For Mrs. Janna Bisutti.

Q: And how long were you a nanny for Miss Janna Bisutti?

A: I would say it's about three years.

Q: Were you dating anyone during this period of time?

A: No, I wasn't.

Q: When did you meet John Bobbitt?

A: I met John Bobbitt September of 1988.

Q: How old were you then?

A: I was nineteen.

Q: Where did you meet him?

A: I met him at the Enlisted Marines Club.

Q: Why were you at the E Club?

A: I went with Mrs. Castro—one of Mrs. Castro's niece and she invited me to go. And Mrs. Castro let me go but I had to go back before twelve at night.

Q: How did you come to meet John at the E Club?

A: He came and asked me if I would like to dance and I said, sure. So, I went and danced with him. And then I came back to my table and he stayed on my table talking to me. And then he asked for my phone number and then I gave Mrs. Castro's phone numbers because I was living with Mrs. Castro.

Q: When did you next hear from John?

A: The next day he called me. We started dating. We date for like about ten months. We were getting close.

Q: What was your reaction to him?

A: I was in love with him. To me he represent everything. That was the beginning of starting my family here in the United States. And I feel that I wanted to have kids later on like a regular family. It was just like the beginning of my dream.

Q: Describe the way in which you were allowed to date John.

A: He was allowed to come home and we usually ordered pizza. And sometimes we go out but I would go out with Mrs. Castro's daughters, also. They have to come with me every time I go out with him. Mrs. Castro wouldn't allow it other way to see anybody else.

Q: Did there come a time when John proposed to you?

A: Yes, he did.

Q: Tell us about that, please.

A: Sure. We started getting more closer and I was in love with him. He was in love with me. That's the way I think it was.

He decided to give me a ring. And we went to eat ice cream and my mother came with me. So, he gave me a ring in front of my mother. So, my mother asked, well, what do you say? And I said, mom, I want to marry this person.

Q: Had John ever shown any violence towards you to this time?

A: No.

Q: Had he ever referred to you in any derogatory way to this time?

A: No.

Q: Your mother had come from Venezuela?

A: Yes. My mother couldn't stay too long because she only bought a ticket for seven days. She had to go back so she won't be lose the ticket. So, she went back.

And since he had to ask for permission from the Marines—he have to work on certain weekends, so we couldn't get married when my mother was here. So, it was, I guess—we just decide to get married like in three weeks or so. Right after.

Q: How much money were you making at this time?

A: Not too much. I just started to work for the Nail Sculptor. And I was part-time and also I was babysitting the child.

Q: What kind of money was John making then?

A: He was in the Marines. He was making I assume from five to six hundred dollars every two weeks.

Q: Would John pay for the dates that you went out on?

A: From the beginning he did. But later on he kind of always forget his wallet. And sometimes I said, well, I could pay for it because we needed money. So, I will help pay.

Q: What kind of ceremony did you have for your wedding?

A: It wasn't a ceremony. Since we didn't have any money I suggest just to go to the Justice of the Peaces. We both went there and we got married in Stafford on June 18, 1989.

Q: Did you move shortly after that?

A: Yes, we did. We moved in an efficiency. It's called Asten Park on Manassas.

Q: What furnishings did you have in the apartment?

A: We had no furniture, sir.

Q: How long was it before you had any furniture?

A: I would say like about a month later.

Q: What did you get then?

A: I just get a loveseat, very tiny. And a table.

Q: Were you sleeping on the floor during this period of time?

A: During this period of time, yes, we were.

Q: How long was it before you got other furniture?

A: I would say maybe two months later.

Q: Were you sleeping on the floor during all that time?

A: Yes, sir.

Q: Before your marriage did you ever meet John's family, the Biros?

A: Before I married? I just talked to them.

Q: When did you happen to meet the Biros?

A: When we went to Niagara Falls on July the 4th.

Q: Tell us what happened there, please.

A: Sure. We going to go to see the family. And John told me to bring my dress, the dress that I used when I went to the Justice of the Peace. And he bring his blue uniform.

And we were at Niagara Falls church and he started to get upset because nobody was at the church. So, we had to go to the campground where the people were. And they were very upset. They were very mad of—and I couldn't understand what happened. I met the parents there.

Q: What had happened?

A: Apparently John's family had told him come up to have a wedding reception because they knew that we were getting married. So, they were planning to have a church reception for us at the church. But we arrived a day later.

Q: Did you know that you were going up for a wedding reception?

A: I have no idea. I didn't know anything about that.

Q: How did the family treat you?

A: After I want an explanation why they were sad or looking at me so mad. They said you guys arrived late. And I said, excuse me, I have no idea this was going to happen.

So, obviously they said that they talked to John. That they have not talked to me. And then we have a picnic wedding at the campground. That was nice.

Q: After three days did you return to Manassas?

A: Yes.

Q: Did you come back to Manassas alone?

A: No. His brother, Todd, came along with us. I have no idea either.

Q: When did you find out that Todd was coming with you?

A: When he was unloading his clothes on the trunk of the car and then he stayed inside the car in the back seat. And I was upset. I didn't know what to do. I said, I have no idea you coming along with us.

So, I went to talk to the father and I explained the situation that we have a small apartment. We have no furniture. We can't afford to have another person there. But he come anyways and I knew that he have a drug problem.

Q: But neither you nor John ever had a drug problem, did you?

A: I never have a drug problem, sir; no.

Q: And John didn't either, did he—other than alcohol?

A: Not that I know, sir. No, I don't think so.

Q: And how long when Todd came back with you had you been married?

A: A month.

Q: How long did he stay with you?

A: He stayed at like about I would say three or three-and-a-half months.

Q: Did there come a time when you and John and Todd went to a club called Chelsea's?

A: Yes, sir. They wanted to go out. Todd liked to drink and he was suggesting that he was so bored and he wanted to do something. But when we went there we couldn't get in.

Q: How long does it take to drive from Asten Park to Chelsea's?

A: I would say an hour.

Q: What happened when you got there?

A: Well, we were wearing jeans and the person said that we cannot get in there. So, we went to another bar.

Q: What happened in that other bar?

A: We were standing at the bar and they were drinking beer and they were shooting some, I assume, Tequila because they were little tiny drinks and strong.

Q: What happened on the ride home?

A: We came back because they were about to close and we took 66. And on the way home, on the highway on 66, he was zigzagging back and forth. At that time the speed limit it was only fifty-five miles per hour. It's just recently they put it up to sixty-five. He was going like around eighty-five or ninety.

And I was really scared. There was people coming into our next right-hand side, of pushing the horn, and scare, making signals to us. And what I did was—I was scared and I told him to stop. And he couldn't—I guess he couldn't stop or something because he would not listen to me. So, I grabbed the steering wheel.

And then he punched me. He said I could not do this. I was scared not only to get in a crash but—in a car accident I mean—but I was I guess caring for the rest of the people.

Q: Did he hurt you?

A: Yes, he did, sir. He hurt me. He hit me in my left arm and I just started to cry.

Q: What did you do for the rest of the ride home?

A: First of all, I was in shock. I couldn't believe it he hit me there. His brother was in the back seat of the car and he didn't do anything. I was just crying. And he was telling me bad names; the f-words and calling me ugly names. And I just couldn't stop crying, I guess.

He told me, also, that I had to stop crying and I couldn't. I couldn't stop crying.

Q: What happened when you got home?

A: The brother came out from the car. I still in my car. He took me by my arm and he take me out of the car. He took me up to the apartment and then he kicked me. He told me that—I told you not to cry. And he slapped me on my face. He pulled my hair and he squeezed my face.

Q: At some point during that did Officer Francis show up?

A: Yes, he did, sir.

Q: What happened when Officer Francis showed up?

A: Well, we have no curtains so I thought somebody must have saw what happened. So, he knock at the door and I thought it was Todd. And John opened the door.

As soon as John opened the door and it was somebody else he quickly, I will said, calm down. But he immediately changed from that attitude.

Q: Do you remember what Officer Francis and you and Todd talked about?

A: Yes, I remember.

Q: As a result of what you talked about what did you do?

A: The officer said if I had a place to go, and I said, no. But I leave anyways. So, I left the apartment. I was crying and I was hysterical. So, I took my car and I went and I stayed in the parking lot of my work in Centreville.

Q: Where did you sleep that night?

A: I sleep in my car.

Q: Did you go home the next day?

A: I went home like maybe four hours later, yes.

Q: Was John there when you got home?

A: No, he wasn't.

Q: What did you do?

A: I took a shower, and I put my work clothes, and I went to work.

Q: Did you tell anybody about this?

A: No, I didn't. No, I couldn't.

Q: Why not?

A: Because I was—I couldn't understand why the person that I love had react that way. I couldn't understand why my husband hit me. I couldn't understand many things. I was in shock. I was—I couldn't believe that. I was embarrassed to tell people, also. And I thought he might change, he never going to do it again.

Q: Did he ever apologize to you?

A: He kind of apologized, yes. I wanted to talk to him and I said just don't do it again. You hurt me. And to me I thought he understood. I thought he understood.

Q: Did there come a time a little later in the summer when you went to the beach?

A: Yes.

Q: Who did you go with?

A: We went with Todd and Terri—Terri McCumber.

Q: How did you end up going to the beach?

A: John suggested we do something on Memorial weekend. And we decide—we all decide to go to Ocean City. It was going to be like a long weekend.

Q: Did something happen while you were at the beach?

A: Yes. We went to the beach and Terri and I we have our bathing suits on, like a beach suits, shorts. And we started walking around the beach and looking for something; we were thirsty and also we were looking for like key chains with our own names. Something like a souvenir.

And these two gentlemen started I guess looking at us and he started to—they started whistled to—actually we didn't know exactly what was going on because as soon as we hear that whistle we just kind of moved. But I saw John came towards me. And he grabbed me. He pulled up my hair and he grabbed me by the arm.

And he said to me what are you doing. And I didn't know what to do. There was a lot of people watching and there was also my friend. And I expect I think I thought at the time he was going to do something but he didn't.

Then he was very upset, very mad, and he suggested to go back to the hotel. And we went to the hotel. And, of course, Terri came along with me, and also Todd, because they didn't even know what was going on.

So, we went to the hotel and he started taking his clothes out of the hotel and put it in the trunk. And, also, he was taking my clothes and putting it in the car. And he says, we are leaving now.

So, I was just crying and I said—I guess I didn't want to have any more yells. And I just said, okay, but I wanted him to stop. And I just did whatever he told me to.

Q: Did he give you an opportunity to change out of your bathing suit?

A: No, I just went with my bathing suits.

Q: What happened on the ride back?

A: I was in the back seat first because I didn't want to stay with him. So he stayed with his brother, Todd. Then we had to stop for drinks and gasoline. So, then I went to get some drinks. And then I came back. And then he told me to sit next to him in front. And I just sat next to him in front.

And when we were in traffic, I guess, there's a lot of young people around. And he was always telling me where I was looking. I was just looking through the window, the side. And he thought I was looking at guys. And I guess these other gentlemen were kind of like saying hello to us but I was crying. And he started to grabbing my hair. And Terri came in the middle of this and said, stop John, don't do anything. Stop it. You can't treat her like that.

Todd never do anything. Never. So, John get really aggressive with Terri and he suggested that he was going to stop it. He called her names and he suggest her to go on 95. He was going to leave her in the highway because she told him to stop.

Q: What happened after that?

A: I just keep on crying.

Q: Were you leaning up against him or leaning up against the door?

A: I was leaning against the door like this (indicating) holding my hands up so he would not touch me and he would not pull my hair.

Q: Did John eventually drop Terri at home or where did he drop her?

A: Eventually we went to the apartment and she returned to her place. Then I just keep on crying and then he continued hitting me when we were in the apartment. He punched me. He slapped me again. He squeezed my face with his hand and he tortured me with the Marine techniques.

Q: What do you mean by the Marine techniques?

A: He had to learn some defense in the Marine Corps. They have to defend themselves and they have to teach some techniques in order to defend themselves. Some sort of like karate-type of thing—techniques, I think.

Q: Where was Todd during all this?

A: He was always smoking. He was always would be outside smoking because I don't smoke and I don't like smoke in my place.

Q: Did you leave the apartment that evening?

A: I called Terri and I mentioned what was happening. And I just said I'm going to go to my place and I going to stay there. So, I went to the Nail Sculptor, my work. And I guess she knew that I was there and she came with her sister, Bobbie, and came and picked me up.

Q: What did you tell Terri and Bobbie had happened to you?

A: I told them what happened.

Q: Did there come a time shortly after that when there was a problem with being late in going to Janna and Nazar's place?

A: Yes, we were going to a reunion. We were running late and I was in the car. And then I said we were running late. And so he grabbed my hand and my wrist and twisted me, twisted my wrist, and said, we're not late, it is your fault.

And I said, why are you doing this? I was jumping up

and I said, I cannot—like it was—scared, because of he twist my arm, too. So I thought he was going to hit me there, too, or do something. I was scared.

Q: During this period of time did John at some point get sick in the closet?

A: Yes. He was going out drinking with his brother, Todd, and sometimes they come back later at night. And I guess he had too much to drink so he had to vomitate. And so he did it in the closet. And he expected me to clean. So, I said, no, I don't want to clean that because it's so dirty.

And I just took my shoes. He vomitated on my shoes and I had to clean my own shoes; but I didn't clean the rest. So, he grabbed me by the hair. He punched me again. He kicked me and slapped me.

Q: How often were John and Todd going out drinking at night without you?

A: I will say a lot. Most of the time Todd was the one who was saying that he is bored and he wanted to do something.

Q: Did there come a time when you found some drug paraphernalia in the apartment?

A: Yes, I did. I was scared. I found some syringes and I didn't know what they were. So, I called Terri and I said, Terri, I found some syringes here and she suggested that I had to take it to the police.

And I said, okay. I put it in the plastic bag and I was going to take it to—as a matter of fact, I drove to the police station and I said—I freak out. I thought that the police were going to think that I was the one who was doing the drugs.

Q: So what did you do with it?

A: I throw them away.

Q: Did you even know what kind of drugs they were?

A: No. After later that I found burning spoons.

Q: When did you find out what burning spoons meant?

A: Well, I have to use my spoons, so I think it was the same night when I needed to use a spoon.

Q: When did you find out what burning spoons and a hypodermic needle meant, what kind of a drug it meant?

A: When I came to your place and you asked me about the burning spoon. I didn't know anything until that time.

Q: Did you do something to get rid of Todd?

A: I called the mother and I explained what happened. I was scared because I didn't know how to deal with a person that they have drug problem. And his mother was crying and she told me to give him another opportunity.

So, I said, okay, ma'am, that's fine. He can stay with us. But you have to talk to him. He's not going to do drugs anymore.

When he did it again, the drug problem . . . I told John that I don't know how to deal with this problem. So, he called his parents, I think, and then he kicked his own brother out.

Q: Were you frightened of this situation?

A: Yes, I was.

Q: Did John's parents come to visit at some point?

A: Yes, they did. They came for Thanksgiving.

Q: How much furniture did you have by then?

A: Just the couch. And we—by the time we already have the bed. That's it.

Q: When did you find out that John's parents were coming to visit?

A: They surprised me. I wasn't prepared. I have no turkey. I have no nothing.

Q: Where did John's parents expect to stay?

A: They stayed in the apartment.

Q: Were you comfortable to stay with that many people in the apartment?

A: No, sir. It was the mother, the father, John, me, Todd, and the little brother, Joshua. So there were six people in the tiny, teeny, apartment with no furniture.

Q: So, what did you do?

A: I told them they can have my bed and I will sleep with my friend. And I just went to sleep at my friend's house.

Q: Did you have some discussion with John about their showing up without any notice?

A: Yes, I said it cannot be unplanned especially if it's your parents. I would not treat your parents like that because I wasn't prepared.

Q: How did he respond to that?

A: He was upset. He was pushing me. As a matter of fact, we have an incident in the car because I was explaining the situation. It can't be done like that. I was pretty uncomfortable.

Q: Lorena, in December of 1989 did you move from Asten Park?

A: We moved to Lakewood in Stafford.

Q: Why?

A: Because he wanted to be closer to the base. It was only five minutes far away.

Q: Was John having some problems in the Marine Corps at that point?

A: He was late.

Q: Why was he late?

A: Because he will go out and drink.

Q: When did you have your first fight at Lakewood?

A: We were having a discussion about a Christmas tree.

Q: Tell us about that, please.

A: Well, he wanted a real Christmas tree. I wanted a plastic Christmas tree. And I was suggesting that I wanted a plastic Christmas tree because I would only spend one time and I can reuse the next year.

And he would not agree with me because I think he like real trees. So, to me plastic tree is just a tradition because in South America you can't have pines. It's not cold weather. So, I guess it mean a lot to me the plastic tree because I grew up with a plastic Christmas tree.

So, I suggest it and he told me not to tell him what to do. He grabbed my face—I was in the kitchen. Again, he squeezed my face really tight and he said not to tell me what to do right in front of my face. And he pushed me around. And I came out from the kitchen towards the living room and I said, what are you doing this to me? And you can't just strangle me like that.

And I guess I wanted an explanation. And he just told me again, you don't tell me what to do. He kicked me. I fell to the ground. He punched me—he punched me also in my chest. And he slapped me and then he pulled my skirt up.

Q: Did that put you in the mood to have sex?

A: No, I escape. I ran away from him.

Q: Did you threaten to call the police that time?

A: No, we didn't have no phone.

Q: Did some people come and live with you at this apartment?

A: Yes, my two friends from Venezuela.

Q: Who were they?

A: They were two brothers, Miguel and Jose Baserva.

Q: And do you remember when they came to live with you?

A: After Christmas I would say.

Q: At Christmas time did John's parents show up again?

A: Yes, they did again, sir. Again, I wasn't prepared. I have no idea they were going to come over.

So, they came and that was before Jose and Miguel moved. We decided to go and have a Christmas party on Mrs. Castro's mother. So, we all went there.

Q: Did the Biros' coming also put you out of the apartment again?

A: No. This time we had two bedrooms, two bathroom apartment. So, it was more comfortable.

Q: Were there a number of incidents in the spring of 1990 that were physical between you and your husband?

A: Yes.

Q: Tell us about that, please.

A: Well, he wanted to have a computer. And I said, I don't know anything about computers. I really don't know anything about computers and I don't understand why we have to have a computer when we don't use one.

But he always wanted one. So, we purchased a computer and I had to pay for that.

Q: What happened on March 25, 1990?

A: Actually, I didn't want the computer and I was going to get stuck with the payments and I didn't want that. And I suggest not to get the computer. And he was so upset because he wanted that computer and he told me that I had to pay. And I said, no, I don't want to pay.

So, he—he twist my arm, my wrist, and he did the Marine tortures again. He twist my foot.

Q: Did you end up going to the hospital?

A: Yes, I did. Because my wrist hurt and I thought it

was broken because it really hurt. It was kind of swelling. And my foot was swelling, also. I thought it was broken or something. So, I went to the hospital.

Q: How did you get to the hospital?

A: I drove my own car.

Q: And did John go to the hospital?

A: He followed me in his car.

Q: Did you want him to follow you?

A: No. I was crying. I didn't even know he was following me.

Q: Did he offer to drive you to the hospital?

A: No, he was just following because I left the apartment crying.

Q: What did you tell the people happened to you at the hospital?

A: I went to the emergency room. I was in the emergency room and I was just crying. And then he was right next to me and I was scared. I didn't want to tell anybody that he did this to me. So, I told the lady that I fell and I'm hurt.

Q: Why wouldn't you want to tell the lady at the hospital that he did it to you?

A: No, I didn't want to say anything to anybody.

Q: Why?

A: Because I was scared that he will hit me again.

Q: How did John arrange to pay for the computer?

A: He was taking money from the bank without telling me anything.

Q: Did you all have two accounts or one account or what?

A: We only had one account together.

Q: Did his paycheck go automatically into the account?

A: Automatically it will go into the account.

Q: And you were depositing yours?

A: The same account, yeah.

Q: Who was paying the bills during that time?

A: Me.

Q: You were paying or he was paying?

A: It was both of our money. So, we used the same checking account.

Q: Was it sometime in February or March of 1990 that the first incident of forced sex between you all occurred?

A: Yes, sir.

Q: Describe that for us, please.

A: The first time you mean he raped me; you want me to describe that?

Q: Yes, ma'am.

A: Okay; we were living at the time on Pine Street. We had a house and—

Q: Did that happen after you moved to Pine Street?

A: Yes.

Q: All right, let me stop you then. We'll get to that in a few minutes then.

When you were living in Lakewood, when John would get mad, what would you do to try to avoid getting into fights with him?

A: I would run to my room, or to the bathroom, and I will just stay in there. I will just try to lock myself.

Q: And what did he do?

A: He will take a screwdriver and unscrew the knobs of the doors.

Q: In July of 1990 did you move again?

A: Yes, that's when we buy the house.

Q: Where is that house?

A: It's located in Manassas; Pine Street.

Q: Was the house important to you?

A: It was because it was the beginning of starting a family. I wanted to have like a dream house, family, children.

Q: When did you move into the house?

A: We moved like two days later.

Q: How did you happen to select this house?

A: He drove it. And he told me that he saw the house. The dream house that he wanted. And he drove me there.

Q: And what kind of a house did you want?

A: I wanted either a condominium or a townhouse.

Q: Why?

A: Why? Because when you start you start from the very beginning, I guess. We didn't have no money. We didn't have enough money to support that kind of house.

Q: Did you tell John that?

A: Yes, I did.

Q: What did he say to that?

A: Nothing. He just fell in love with the garage. He wanted a bigger garage he said. And the townhouse that I saw didn't have no garage.

Q: How much was the payment on this house?

A: It was fourteen hundred dollars.

Q: And John was taking home five or six hundred dollars every two weeks?

A: Yes.

Q: Could you all afford this house?

A: No, we couldn't.

Q: Now, on Thanksgiving, did you have a visitor at Pine Street?

A: Yes, we did.

Q: Who was the visitor? I'm talking Thanksgiving, 1990. Did your mother come to visit?

A: My mother came to visit, yes.

Q: How long did your mother stay?

A: My mother stayed for like about a month and a half. I don't really remember.

Q: Did something happen between you all on Thanksgiving Day in 1990?

A: Yes. My mother came from Venezuela on Thanksgiving Day. I have to cook dinner and that was our first Thanksgiving dinner, I guess, since my mother was in Venezuela. So, we cooked dinner. And on Thanksgiving Day we have the parade day. My mother wanted to watch TV Thanksgiving parade. And John wanted to watch a football game.

So, I asked John, I said, you know, my mother is here. She's in Venezuela and I will have her to have the opportunity to please her. And he didn't really seem very happy because I guess to him the football game was more important. But to me my mother at that time was a lot important. And so I want to make her happy and so she will see this parade. And he was very upset because I changed the channel to the parade.

And he went up to the roof of the house. He break the antennae of the house and then he came down. When he came down, of course, I was cooking with my mother in the kitchen. He forgot to unlock the door and the door was closed because it was windy.

So, he knock at the door. I look at my mother and I was going to open the front door. But then by the same time that I was going to open the front door he ran to the back door. And, of course, the back door was also locked, and at that same time he was knocking very strongly in the back door.

And so my mom wanted to open the door. Obviously it wasn't fast enough so he kicked the door down. He almost hit my mother.

He came in and he just put the door kind of back and he was very upset. And I said, what did you did to the TV? It's static. So, he said nothing and we just turned the TV off. Dinner was ready. We were serving the table. And I just putting the drinks and everything.

And he went to the room and he stayed in the room with his music loud. And my mother said, what happened to John. So, I said, I don't know. So, I went over there and knock at the door to see what's going on and he wouldn't answer to me. My mother also went there and knock at the door and she can't speak English, so she always saying, John, John.

And I tell her how to say come on. And she's just repeating what I was saying. And she was saying, John, come on. And John wouldn't answer to either of us. And we went back to the table and eat when we saw John come into the kitchen. And I guess he—I don't know exactly what he was doing. And then he come back to the room and listened to his music.

And when we finished dinner I asked my mother just to come with me because I wanted to watch something. Since we didn't have no TV, since he broke the antennae, I invited my mother to the movies. So, he came down with an empty dish to the kitchen. And I was putting my jackets on and my mother was putting also her jacket and he said, what are you guys doing? And I said, I'm just going to the movies.

And he took my car keys. And he went outside, opened the front of the door where the engine of the car is. He took something out of the car so I would not start my own car. Then he will keep my own car keys and he will go to his car and I would just follow him. I said, what did you do to my car? Give me my car keys back. And he would not listen to me.

So, he went into the car and I was asking him in the window, in the car, I said, give me my car keys, I need to go with my mother. And he just grabbed my arm, twist it, hold onto me and dragged me. He was backing out. He dragged me with his car and he pushed his car door and he hit me. He knocked me down to ground and I stayed there.

So, my mother come back and she said, what happened, why he's doing this to you?

Q: What did you do after that?

A: I was crying. I was just crying. And I called my neighbor, Mr. and Mrs. Willoughby, and I explained the situation.

Q: What did you tell the Willoughbys?

A: I told them exactly the same what happened. And I told them that John kicked the door, almost hit my mother, and he dragged me with the car. He twist my arm and he knocked me down to the ground. That's what I told them.

Q: Is this the time that you called the Marine Corps?

A: I didn't know who I was calling. I thought I was calling the police. Obviously it was the Marine.

Q: Why would you get the numbers mixed up?

A: I've got a list of numbers on the refrigerator and one of the numbers that I saw it was the Marine Corps, I guess, and I just called.

Q: What, if anything, do you know that the Marine Corps did to assist you with this situation?

A: I just explained what happened and I told them what happened. They didn't do nothing to me.

Q: Did they do anything with John that you knew of?

A: I didn't know it.

Q: Lorena, when you were still living at Lakewood did you go to a Christmas party with John?

A: Yes, sir, I did. I went to the Christmas party at Mrs. Beltran's, Mrs. Castro's mother.

Q: Did an incident involving John and Amelia Hoyt occur at that party?

A: Yes, sir

Q: Would you describe the incident, please, and tell us what happened?

A: My husband had got me a present, a Christmas present, in which I had to open. It was a Christmas, little tiny thing, a box. So, I opened it up. I had no idea what it was. So, when I opened it was a lot of gentlemen around me and it was also his family.

I was real embarrassed when I took the little tiny underwear. It was color red color and I was embarrassed. I tried to hide it. I tried to hide it on my back. And I went towards the entrance of the house and he followed me. I had no idea he was following me. He grabbed me and he said, what do you think you're doing, you didn't like it? And I said, no, well, that wasn't nice.

And he grabbed me by my chest and he struck me towards the wall and he keep me there. And it was like I was up (indicating). And I just told him to put me down. And he did put me down. So, he let me go there.

Q: Were you afraid of him?

A: Yes, sir, I was afraid of him.

Q: At the Pine Street house there was damage to the rear door that you told us about.

A: Yes, he kicked the door down.

Q: Was there any other damage to that house?

A: Yes, there was damage in the bathroom. There was

a hole in the bathroom. There was a hole in the bathroom door and there was a hole in the bedroom door, one of the bedroom's door.

Q: Would you tell us how those incidents of damage occurred?

A: There were so many incidents on which—different times I called 911.

Q: How did the door get damaged?

A: He punched the doors. Every time I locked myself in the bathroom or in the bedroom he will punch the door and come with a screwdriver. And I would not lock the door.

Q: Did there come a time when Brett [John's older brother] moved in with you?

A: Yes, sir, he came from Niagara Falls, New York.

Q: Did your husband discuss with you Brett's moving down?

A: No, sir; no. It took me by surprise.

Q: Did you and your husband agree that he would live there?

A: Yes—yes, sir.

Q: When did you become aware that he was coming?

A: Once again he showed up. He showed up at my house.

Q: Now, how long did Brett stay with you?

A: I would say like about almost two months. I can't recall exactly, sir.

Q: Was Brett working while he was there?

A: No, sir, he came—he moved from New York eventually to have a job in Virginia. That's why he came.

Q: By the time Brett came was John still in the military?

A: I can't remember.

Q: Did he leave the military in the end of December, 1990, or the first of January, 1991?

A: I would say 1991, yes; the first of January.

Q: When Brett came down was John working a taxi cab?

A: Yes, sir, he was.

Q: Was Brett contributing to the food budget?

A: No, sir, nothing. He did not have no work, no job.

Q: [John's] military pay wasn't coming into [the] account anymore, was it?

A: Oh, no, sir. He stopped the military. So there's no more paychecks.

Q: In the March/April of '91 when Brett was down here, was John putting any money in the family account?

A: No, sir.

Q: Was he eating there?

A: Yes, sir.

Q: Who was doing the cleaning?

A: I was doing the cleaning. I was doing the cooking. I was doing it.

Q: Did either John or Brett assist in that?

A: No, sir, none of them.

Q: Now, did there come a time when you asked Brett to leave?

A: Yes. Well, first of all, because he was very messy. He didn't clean. He didn't have a job. I supplied a list of jobs and he didn't want to start until the work that he would have will pay him fourteen dollars an hour.

And I suggest the constructions and he would not work in constructions. He wanted some different jobs that would pay him fourteen dollars an hour.

Q: What was John's reaction to your getting Brett out of the house?

A: He was very mad. He hit me there, too.

Q: What happened in that fight?

A: Brett wasn't around. I think he went out to a bar. And John also wanted to go with Brett and I guess I told him the consequences. I said, you know, you are always going out and also your brother is here making a mess of my house. It's not fair.

And he just slapped me in my face. And I went to the room and that's one of the incidents of the hole—the room, the door—and the hole in the door happened. He put a hole in the door. And I was just scared.

Q: Was there any sex involved in that incident?

A: No, just hitting and beating.

Q: Did you end up calling 911 in that incident?

A: Yes, I tried to call 911.

Q: What happened when you tried to call 911?

A: He would disconnect the phone, sir. He will hide the phone on top of the refrigerator because I could not reach it. I'm not tall enough to reach the cabinet on top of the refrigerator. So, he will put it in that way.

Q: Did you tell Janna about this beating?

A: I think I told her.

Q: Did you tell her essentially what you told these people?

A: I can't recall if I told Janna, but, yes, this is what happened about that time. There were so many incidents.

Q: Did you have bruises from this beating?

A: Yes, I did, I had bruises. I have in my arm and in my back.

Q: Did you succeed in getting through to 911 this time?

A: No, I couldn't.

Q: Now, about two weeks later was there a food-related incident?

A: Yes, sir.

Q: Would you describe that for us, please?

A: Brett wasn't at the house anymore. I had to cook. Every time I work until eight o'clock I had to go back and prepare dinner. So, I was in there and John only wanted to watch TV. And I served the dinner and he would not come and eat it.

So, I will suggest to come to the table and eat. And he will not eat. So, I said, well, think about the people who doesn't have food and things like that. And, again, he will come to me and squeeze my face and tell me that I don't have to tell him what to do.

Q: Did you get any rug burn on this incident?

A: Yes, I did. He kicked me. He kicked me and then I went towards the wall. And I fell on the floor. He choked me and I tried to stand up but I couldn't because he came and pulled my hair and grabbed my arm and dragged me. That's when I had my rug burn in my elbow and in my knees.

Q: Did he choke you?

A: Yes, he did.

Q: Would you show us how he would choke you?

A: Sure. He would put his hands around my neck and he will choke my—this part of my neck (indicating). He will put his two thumbs pushing me very down, low (indicating).

Q: How did you feel when he did that?

A: I feel like I needed my air and I have no air. I feel desperate. I need a desperate breathe. I couldn't breathe. There was no air. I only saw like white and I guess my face was turning red and purple—I don't know, just—it was horrible.

Q: Did you try to call 911 this time?

A: I think I did, sir, yes.

Q: Did you succeed?

A: I think so, yes. The police called back and the lady wanted to find out if I was the one who called. And I said, yes, I did. And she asked if I was all right. And I said, yeah, I think so.

That was one of the many incidents that I called 911, sir.

Q: Did they take him out of there or anything of that sort?

A: No, he left. He wasn't at the house.

Q: Did you all have sex before he left?

A: Not at that time.

Q: Did there come a time in the spring of 1991 when you purchased a satellite dish?

A: Yes.

Q: How much did that cost?

A: I don't know how much that cost but it was expensive.

Q: Is that something you wanted?

A: No.

Q: Who paid for it?

A: I did.

Q: Why did you pay for it?

A: Because he wanted the satellite dish and I was the only one who was working.

Q: John wasn't working?

A: He was working as a taxi cab and—he was working in so many jobs, sir, I couldn't even remember.

Q: With the satellite dish, did John stay up late early on, when you knew he had the dish, watching TV.

A: Yes, sir.

Q: Were you working during this time frame?

A: Yes, sir.

Q: Was he working during this time frame?

A: No.

Q: How did he like to listen to the television?

A: Very loud.

Q: Did that affect your ability to sleep?

A: Yes, sir, it did.

Q: Did it affect your ability to work?

A: Yes, sir, it did.

Q: Did there come an occasion in which you woke up and objected to the set being so loud?

A: Yes, sir, it did.

Q: Tell us what happened when that happened.

A: It was very late, maybe three or four o'clock in the morning. I couldn't really go to sleep. I couldn't sleep. And I wake up and I turned the TV off. And I said, it's really loud; plus, it's really too late and I want to go to work tomorrow.

And he immediately get upset because I did that and he followed me. He beat me up there—here (indicating).

Q: This is one of the instances in which you told Janna and Nazar about the incident?

A: Yes, sir, I did.

Q: Did something happen to the house in this incident?

A: Yes, sir. I went to the bathroom and he punched the bathroom doors and he also—I went into the bedroom and locked myself. And he opened it with a screwdriver.

Q: Did you and John ever engage in anything other than vaginal sex?

A: He did it, sir. I didn't.

Q: When did it happen?

A: Some of the nights that he used to watch the TV.

I was come to him and said, please turn it down. So we went to bed and he grabbed me and he turned me and I was with my stomach down. And he—he—he—he have anal sex on me.

Q: Did he ask you if he could?

A: No, no. No, no.

Q: Did you give him permission to?

A: No, no, no.

Q: Did he use any lubricant?

A: No, no, no.

Q: Was it forced?

A: Yes, yes, yes, he did.

Q: Were you injured?

A: Yes, I was.

Q: What injuries did you sustain?

A: I was bleeding, sir.

Q: Did he ever threaten to do it again?

A: Yes, sir. Yes, he did.

Q: How frequently?

A: Every time we would have sex he would threaten me.

Q: How would he threaten you?

A: He would say he would like to have that kind of sex. And I wouldn't—I wouldn't let him. I tried not to let him happen again.

Q: Did he give you choices between types of sex?

A: I don't understand.

Q: Did he give you a choice; giving him the regular sex or getting anal sex?

A: That wasn't my choice, sir.

Q: Lorena, let's go on a little bit. Did there come a time in the summer of 1991 when Janna and Nazar arranged an interview for John for a decent job?

A: Yes—yes, sir, they did.

Q: Will you tell us what happened in that incident?

A: It was a Sears job. He wouldn't take it.

Q: Did you get a call from the man who he was supposed to go to interview with?

A: Yes, sir. He was asking my friend Janna why John didn't take the job.

Q: Was there an incident in which the man was shouting at John about not missing the job interview?

A: That was another person, sir. That was somebody else who called the house asking because he was very late for an appointment.

Q: What happened to you after that incident?

A: The man called the house and was yelling at him very loud. I could hear it from the phone. And I was concerned what happened to this person. And he was screaming at him. He was very mad at him. He was saying bad words to him. He was insulting him.

And when he hang up the phone I asked him what happened. I said, why this man is insulting you? Why he's talking that way to you? I was concerning. He was my husband. I needed to know what was wrong with him, this man that insult my husband.

So, I asked him that and then he was very upset. He come and grabbed my face and he told me again not to—I don't have to tell him what to do. He called me bad names, bad words. And he kicked me. He punched me. He slapped me in my face. He pulled my hair and he tortured me and he raped me.

Q: Was there an incident when John was on punishment from the Marines that you're taking food to him?

A: Yes, sir. It was very late so I had to bring him food to the Marine Corps.

Q: Did that situation get to be physical at any time?

A: Yes, sir.

Q: Would you tell us how and when?

A: I was late and I went to the Marine Corps. I just get him a steak and sandwich because he was there, he didn't have anything to eat. And he just wanted me to be on time but I couldn't because I was working in Centreville and the Marine Corps place is forty-five minutes away from the base through my work. So, he was mad.

Q: What happened?

A: He hit me again. He tortured me with the Marine techniques that he knows. He twist my arm really bad and he punched me and slapped me.

Q: Were you telling the Willoughbys about this as this was going on, about these different incidents?

A: Yes, I told them, my neighbors.

Q: Did something happen on February 21, 1991?

A: Yes, sir, he was arrested. I called 911.

Q: Tell me what led you to call 911.

A: It was one of the incidents at the house. That he abused me; he hit me; he punched me in the face. He make my lip bleed and he used the techniques to twist my arm and my foot. And he hit me in my back and in my arms.

Q: Did you see the picture of the injury to your foot?

A: Yes, I did.

Q: Who caused that injury?

A: John did.

Q: Did you attack him that night?

A: No, sir, I did not.

Q: He got you arrested the next day, didn't he?

A: Yes, sir, he did.

Q: Did John swear out a warrant against you the next day?

A: Yes, sir, he did.

Q: Is this John's handwriting (indicating)?

(Mr. Lowe handed the witness a document for her examination.)

A: It is his handwrited.

Q: Read that, please.

A: (The witness complied with the request.)

"I base my belief on the following facts." His handwrited said, "That my wife, Lorena Bobbitt, caused argument, then kicked me and punched to the groin. Then,"—I can't understand his handwrited—"I lost my balance and cut my foot, left, on a nail that was sticking out of the wall. When I went into a separate room to avoid any more violent engagement."

Q: And that's sworn to, isn't it?

A: Yes, sir.

Q: Is there any truth to it?

A: No, sir. No.

Q: Now, when John was arrested that night he was ordered, according to the file, not to come back to your home. What did he do when he got out?

A: He was there. He was there but I had no idea that they told him not to go home.

Q: What happened to the case against you?

A: Nothing.

Q: Lorena, did there come a time in 1991 in which you went to visit your mother?

A: Yes, I did, sir. It was in May. For only one week. In Venezuela.

Q: Did you come back from the visit?

A: Yes, I did.

Q: Who was supposed to pick you up?

A: John was supposed to pick me up.

Q: Did he pick you up?

A: No, he was like two hours late.

Q: What explanation, if any, did he give?

A: I don't know, sir. I have no idea.

Q: Did he tell you—did you find out about somebody named Rhonda?

A: Yes.

Q: How did you find out about Rhonda?

A: Well, the lady called the house and she was asking for John while he was in the shower. And I just said, he's taking a shower. And I asked her name and she said this is Rhonda.

And I said, I'll take a message. And she said, that's okay, I'll call back. And she hang up the phone and I hang up the phone.

Q: Now, when you called back what happened?

A: I talk to my friend Janna about what happened and we couldn't believe it because of we were going to go to the boat—to the Potomac River. And the lady was invited. The lady, Rhonda, was invited, too.

Q: To go out with both you and Janna on the boat?

A: Yes, sir, with me, also.

Q: Lorena, later did John show you a list?

A: Yes, sir, he did.

(Mr. Lowe handed the witness a document for her examination.)

Q: And it's a list of what?

A: A list of ladies.

Q: And what did he tell you about that list?

A: He only told me that this is the ladies that he used to sleep with him in New York. And this is the list of ladies who love him and that I don't deserve him because he's too much for me. That's what he told me, sir.

Q: Is Rhonda's name on that list?

(The witness reviewed the document.)

A: Yes, sir.

Q: What did he use this list with you for?

A: Every time when he was in this first separation; and then the second separation he will name list of ladies that sleep with him.

Q: Where did that list come from?

A: He used to write it on different papers, different times. And that particular list was written from a book that he liked about how to make my family happy. It's a green book.

Q: I want to show you that green book—

A: Yes, sir. That's it.

Q: Where did you find the book?

A: I don't know. I guess the church give it to us, I think—I'm not sure.

Q: Now, the original of that piece of paper has got some torn edges on it, doesn't it?

A: Yes, it is.

Q: I'm going to show you the front page of this book.

A: Yes.

Q: Is that the missing edge of that page—of that xerox copy?

A: Yes, sir, that's it.

Q: Now, this book has got some things underlined in it, doesn't it?

A: Yes, sir.

Q: And whose book was it?

A: It was John's.

Q: Did you make any of the underlinings in the book?

A: No, sir, I did not.

Q: In about the beginning of October of 1991, did John leave and go back to New York?

A: Yes, sir, he did.

Q: Prior to leaving were you and John in any kind of a physical situation?

A: Yes, sir, he beat me up before he left. Yes, sir.

Q: I want to show you an exhibit that's been admitted that's number 17 and ask you what that is.

(Mr. Lowe handed the witness photographs for her examination.)

A: Yes, this is the pictures that Mercedes Castro took. I have a bruise right here (indicating), and in my hips, and in my leg.

Q: When were these pictures taken?

A: On 10/18 of 1991.

Q: Where are the original pictures now?

A: I don't know, sir. We sent it to Immigration when Immigration send me back. I don't know where they are.

Q: You said you sent it to Immigration. You are not an American citizen, are you?

A: No, sir, I'm not.

Q: And you weren't born here.

A: No, I wasn't born here.

Q: In October of 1991 what was your status here, immigration status?

A: I have an alien card, a green card. But it was temporary, a temporary green card.

Q: Did it expire sometime in '91?

A: Yes, sir, it was supposed to expire like—I don't remember exactly but this 1991, sir.

Q: Did you make an application in October of 1991 for a permanent green card?

A: Yes, sir, I did.

Q: Did John do something to interfere with that application?

A: Yes, sir, he took it with him when he went to New York.

Q: Did he take anything else?

A: He took all the bills of the house.

Q: Did he pay them?

A: No, he didn't.

Q: When he took the application did he take any of the papers that go with it?

A: Yes, sir, he did.

Q: Did he sign your application to—a substitute or a replacement application to obtain a green card?

A: No, sir.

Q: What did you have to do in order to obtain a permanent green card?

A: I call Immigration place and Mrs. Castro helped me with this. She said that I have to ask for an Immigration application in order to prove that I wasn't with my husband since I wasn't—I was married to an American but I wasn't with my husband. I have to show and prove that my husband is separated and my husband beat me up.

Q: What did you use these photographs to do?

A: To show the Immigration people that my husband beat me up and I have my bruises here, sir.

Q: I'd like you to look through the rest of that file. Does it look familiar to you?

A: Yes, sir. This is the papers that he took from my application. He took it with him so I could not obtain my Immigration green card.

Q: Did you get substitute papers?

A: I had to ask—request Immigration for the applications.

Q: Did you have to submit supporting documents with the papers?

A: Yes, sir, I had to show the pictures. I had to send letters. I had to send how my husband hit me. A lot of people have signed—the priest and my neighbors have sent letters to Immigration.

Q: And is this the Immigration file?

A: Yes, sir, it is.

Q: After your husband left you did you move?

A: Yes, sir, the house was going to be foreclosed and I had to move, yes. I moved with Mrs. Castro in Stafford.

Q: Did you tell Mrs. Castro how your husband had been treating you?

A: Yes, sir, I did.

Q: Did you—with respect to anal sex, did you mention that to anyone?

A: To Mrs. Castro and her daughter.

Q: Which daughter?

A: Irmalene Castro.

Q: What did you tell them about that?

A: I asked if couple—if it's okay to have it. I didn't know.

Q: Did you tell Irmalene what had happened to you?

A: No, I just asked her about it.

Q: And while you were staying at Mrs. Castro's did you stay in contact with John?

A: Yes, sir, he called different times. Yes, he did.

Q: Did you call him, too?

A: I followed Mrs. Castro's advice to ask for some money because since he took the papers from the house the collector were calling my work and calling every time. They also called Mrs. Castro's house asking for money.

So, I have to call. Part of my responsibility is part of his responsibility. I didn't want to take the responsibility of paying everything.

Q: Did John come and visit while you were at Mrs. Castro's?

A: Yes, sir, he came in May.

Q: Were you glad or sad or how did you feel about his absence?

A: I always wanted to make my marriage work out. I was glad to see him because I thought he was going to be a good husband.

Q: Did he make you some promises?

A: Yes, sir, he did. He told me that he's never going to hit me again. That he will be a nice guy and he will respect me like a wife. And he will never hit me. He also told me that he loved me and I believe him.

Q: When did John come back?

A: John came in May.

Q: How long did he stay in May?

A: It was only like a couple of days.

Q: And when did he next come back?

A: He came back in September.

Q: When he came back in September did you know he was coming?

A: No, he surprised me again. In May he surprised me. He stay at Mrs. Castro and asked Mrs. Castro if he could sleep there in her house. Mrs. Castro did not want to let him sleep. And he came back in September and he bring some money. And he promised me that he's going to work hard and everything. So, I accept my husband back.

Q: When you accepted him back where did he live for the first bit of time that he was here?

A: He stayed at Mrs. Castro's house until we found a place for us together.

Q: Mrs. Castro or Mrs. Castro's mother?

A: Mrs. Castro's mother.

Q: You were still at Mrs. Castro's?

A: I was still at Mrs. Castro's, sir; yes.

Friday,
January 14

LORENA LEONOR BOBBITT
DIRECT EXAMINATION

BY MR. LOWE:

Q: Ms. Bobbitt, shortly after the two arrest warrants were served in February of 1991, did it come to your attention that your husband applied to become a police officer?

A: Yes, it did.

Q: What happened, between the two of you, as a result of that?

A: He couldn't qualify for the police work that he applied because they have to check on his record, and I told him also that it doesn't make sense to apply because they going to check on his records, since he had a file for battery husband, so the police record could check that, and they denied the job for him. They didn't accept. As a result of that he beat me up again.

Q: Can you put that at a point in time? I know you don't know the dates perfectly, but do the best you can.

A: Right after he came to the Court.

Q: During the course of the time that all of this was going on, did you talk to Mrs. Castro and her daughter, about the abuse that you were receiving?

A: Yes, I did, sir. I went to their house and her daughter—her oldest daughter, Mercedes, took some pictures with her camera, and she send the pictures to Immigration Office.

I told them that my husband had hit me and slapped me, and pulled my hair, and beat me up.

Q: Did you tell them about having had an abortion?

A: Yes, I did.

Q: And what did you tell them about that?

A: I said I feel guilty, so I started talking to them. I told them how sad I was; I told them that I didn't want to have an abortion.

Q: June the 15th, 1990 is the day the abortion was performed?

A: Yes, sir.

Q: When did you first become aware that you were pregnant?

A: When we were used to live in Lakewood Apartments, on 1990.

Q: How did it happen that you got pregnant?

A: I stopped taking the birth control, and—so I can become pregnant.

Q: Why did you want to become pregnant?

A: Because I wanted to become a mother, and because I wanted—I wanted to have his child.

Q: Had you talked to John, before you got married, about having children?

A: Yes, I did.

Q: How many children did you want to have?

A: I wanted to have three children.

Q: Why three?

A: Because I grew up—my mom and dad have three children.

Q: What was your reaction to getting pregnant, to finding out that you were pregnant?

A: My reaction was very happy. I wanted to just do what my mom did when she got married, and right after I got married, I wanted to become pregnant.

Q: How did you tell John about that?

A: I bought a little bib, and I went to the house, and I wanted to surprise him, so I put the little bib in his chest, and he—he took it off.

Q: What did he do? What did he say?

A: He—he told me that why did I get "F" pregnant, and I was sad. He was saying that the baby would look ugly, and he also was saying that I'm not going to be a good mother.

Q: What did he do next?

A: I went to my room and cried. He was very upset because I was pregnant, and he said that he doesn't want to have a child. He also said that he doesn't want me to have a baby, so he said to do whatever the rest of the girls in trouble do.

So, he showed me a Yellow Pages on which he opened it up and showed me some clinics, that do the abortion, I guess abortion centers.

Q: Did you consider yourself to be a girl in trouble?

A: No, I was married to him.

Q: When you were shown these abortion clinics what did you feel that your choices were?

A: He also told me that if I don't have the—that if I had the baby—'cause I told him that I would have it without him anyway, he said that he would leave me, so

I said, "How could you do this? I don't want to have a child without a father, because I didn't grow up without a father." And then I couldn't even support the baby.

Q: Did you have more than one choice in what you could do at this time?

A: Yes. I felt the pressure of having an abortion, and also, my husband would leave me.

Q: Did you, eventually, go some place with your husband?

A: Yes. We went to the—he—he took me to the abortion clinic.

Q: How did he treat you at the abortion clinic?

A: I was very nervous, and I was never in that kind of place before, and we were waiting in the waiting room and he was saying to me that I going to die, the needles were going to be so big and they're going to go through my bones, and that I was going to die.

He was laughing about me and I was crying. The nurse have to come up and—and ask what happened to me, what was wrong, because I was crying. I just tell her that I want my husband to be away from me, and she took me to another room.

Q: How did you feel after you had the abortion?

A: I—I didn't want to have an abortion. I feel very sad. I was guilty. I feel really guilty. That's how I feel.

Q: Were you willing to sleep with your husband after that?

A: No, no. I didn't want to sleep with him. I didn't want to see him.

Q: Did it affect your appetite?

A: Yes, it did. I couldn't eat. I was—I feel very weak. I feel sick. I feel, also, sleepy, tired. I feel like nothing—

like the life is over. I feel—I feel like I was falling apart. I don't know.

Q: Did you tell Mrs. Castro all about this?

A: Yes, yes I did.

Q: Let me change subjects with you, for a minute, if I may. Did your husband ever talk to you about your immigration status?

A: Yes, he did. He told me that he was going to—I don't deserve to be in this country, and that I was from another country, and I told him that this is a free country, and I would like to stay here if it's okay.

He always threatened me to kick me out, to tell Immigration that they can kick me out. That what he said.

Q: Did he tell you anything about talking to the police?

A: Yeah, he said that the police would not believe me, that they would believe him because he speak better English than I do, and they don't understand me.

Q: Do you remember a pregnant customer that came to visit you, in May or June of 1991, who you talked to?

A: Yes, I do. I did her nails.

Q: In this period of May or June of 1991 tell us what your sensations were concerning your marriage.

A: Yes. I don't understand the question. I'm sorry.

Q: What sensations were you having concerning the marriage and having children, when you saw this pregnant woman and talked to her?

A: I feel glad because she was going to have her own baby, and I was happy for that lady. I—I was talking about what happened to me, and I told her that my husband beat me up, and I told her that I was very sad.

Q: How did you feel about religion, and your marriage, at that point?

A: I didn't want to get a divorce because I'm Catholic,

and I was still married, so I—I really—I really feel that it wasn't correct. I feel like it wasn't right. I always tried to work out my marriage.

Q: Ms. Bobbitt, you moved into the Beltran home in the end of September of 1992. Under what circumstances did you move in there?

A: We were going to rent a basement, and also a room, in Mrs. Beltran's home, for John and I to live together.

Q: Did John make any promises to you, and Mrs. Beltran, and Mrs. Castro, concerning his conduct toward you?

A: Yes, he did.

Q: What promises did he make to you, and to them?

A: He promised Mrs. Castro and Mrs. Beltran that he was never going to hit me again; that he will be a nice guy and he will be a hard working man.

Q: Did there come an incident when he came home late, from the Red Lobster, sometime before the end of the year?

A: Yes. He came back late. I don't know exactly what time in the morning it was, but I was asleep, and he came and I think he was drunk.

He pulled my pajamas off and he forced me—he forced me into sex, and I told him I don't want to have sex, but he did it anyways, and my head was hitting the wall, and that hurt me. I had bumps in my head the day after. I told him that if he doesn't let me go I were going to scream, and the people in the house will hear me. He wouldn't care, and he just close my mouth, with his hand (indicating).

Q: Where was he and how was he making love to you? Having sex with you; not making love to you, I'm sure.

A: Yeah. He forced me.

Q: What position were you doing it in, if you remember?

A: Just regular position.

Q: Was there another incident, on New Year's Eve?

A: Yes.

Q: Who was in the house for New Year's Eve?

A: Mrs. Beltran, her family, and some friends of hers, and I.

Q: Were there friends of John's there, as well?

A: No, they went out, and they came back late.

Q: What were you supposed to do New Year's Eve?

A: I thought we were going to be together, because I thought New Year's Eve you are with the people that you love, for New Year's Eve, and I guess, for me, New Year's Eve has a lot of meaning because in South America you are with the person who you love, like your family and friends, and so you can hug everybody at twelve o'clock.

Q: Did you go out with your husband that night?

A: No, he didn't take me. He went with—he went with his friends and his cousins. I stayed home. With Mrs. Beltran and friends.

Q: When did you go to bed?

A: I don't remember. I was just staying in my room.

Q: What happened later?

A: He came back, later on.

Q: Do you have any idea of the time?

A: Probably three or four.

Q: What was his condition?

A: He was drunk.

Q: What happened?

A: He grabbed me. He wanted to have sex and I was pushing him away, and I ran out. I look at him. I knew he was going to follow me, so I ran out from the—from the bedroom, and I went down to the basement of the house.

He pulled me hair, he slapped me, he kicked me, and he punched me in my chest.

Q: Did anybody get up?

A: Yes, the cousin and the friend, Robert, was there and they turned the light on to see what's going on, because I fell next to Robert's bed, and they were sitting there, watching, and he was ready to punch me again, and I scream.

So, Mrs. Beltran and her husband come down, to the basement, and they stop him.

Q: Did John say something about what was happening, to the Beltrans?

A: No, he was immediately change. He stop his reaction when he saw Mrs. Beltran and her husband, and I was just crying.

Q: Did he claim that you had hit him?

A: Yeah, he did. Yes, he did.

Q: During this period of time, did you and John spend any time at Janna and Nizzar's house?

A: Yes.

Q: Was there an incident at Janna and Nizzar's house?

A: Yes, he came late from the Red Lobster work—that he used to work, and he—he kind of like was drunk, and he wanted to have sex again, and I just say no.

He pulled my hair and he slapped me, and he called me names. He called me bad words.

Q: When did you find out that John wanted to have somebody else move in to this apartment on Maplewood?

A: When we moved to Maplewood, the apartments in Manassas, he maybe—like a month later, he started talking about having his friend, Robert, move with us.

Q: What did you think about having Robert move in with you?

A: From the beginning I didn't know he was going to live with us. I thought he was just going to come for two weeks of visiting, which is okay. Two weeks, people does it every time, for a vacation.

But, he said that he want his friend to move back to Manassas, from New York, and so we have a discussion because of that. We only have one-bedroom apartment, and we didn't have enough space for—for more people, plus it was illegal to have three people in a one-bedroom apartment.

Q: Did John propose any changes to the apartment?

A: Yes; he wanted to build up a wall in the middle of the living room, and I went and told the manager what he wanted to do, and the manager disagreed. He say he can't do that.

Q: Were there any fights over that?

A: Yes. He said that I have to leave the apartment. He said that if I don't leave he will kick me out, so that's when I started packing my things, and he hit me too, that time.

Q: Was John coming home on time from work each night, as you lived at Maplewood, the last couple of months?

A: Sometimes, but not often. He used to come back drunk.

Q: What time did he come home?

A: Sometimes he would come home very late at night, like maybe two, three, maybe four o'clock in the morning the next day.

Q: That last month, before the incident, did John get involved in any fights that you were aware of?

A: Yes. One time he came with a bloody shirt, and I was asleep. Then, he turned the lights on, and I wake up, and then I look at his shirt. It was all bloody, and I say, "What happened to you?" and he was very happy because he had beat up some guys at the Chelsea's Restaurant. He was very proud of himself.

Q: During that time frame was there another incident of anal sex?

A: Yes. In the apartment he—we were having—we were having sex, and then he immediately turned to me the other way, and I just push him away, and I was just crying. Then, he promise me not to do it again because I was crying, so he did it in the regular way again, but he have anal sex that time, sir.

Q: Did you agree to that?

A: No, sir; it took me by surprise, and that's why I was crying.

Q: Was John interested in any particular type of Kung Fu, or anything of that sort?

A: He took Karate.

Q: Were you aware of any training he had in the military?

A: Yeah, the techniques that he had trained on, I guess it's the military techniques. They look like Karate.

Q: Was there a particular name that he assumed, in that regard?

A: Well, he watched a lot of movies, like the Karate guys, like, for example, Jean-Claude Van Damme, the Steven Segall, and Bruce Lee.

Q: Did he use one of those names, as if it was his name?

A: Yeah, he thought he was John Claude Van Damme.

Q: I want to show you a book that Mr. Ebert admitted

as Commonwealth's Exhibit Number 2. Are you familiar with that?

A: Yes.

Q: What is it?

A: It's—the lady write a book about how to satisfy a woman.

Q: Did he ever read parts of it to you?

A: Yes, he did.

Q: Did you want to hear it?

A: No. No, I didn't want to hear it, no.

Q: Now, did John use foreplay in your marriage?

A: No.

Q: This book is about foreplay, isn't it?

A: I don't know, sir; I never read it.

Q: What occupation did John have when he was in New York, to your knowledge?

A: He was a bouncer on a Marine club. I'm sorry, the person who owned that bar was a Marine, or something like that.

Q: Did he discuss with you what he did as a bouncer?

A: Yes. He beat up people.

Q: How frequently?

A: I don't know, maybe almost every other night, he said.

Q: Did John like to demonstrate these Marine moves that he would use on you, to other people?

A: Yes, sir.

Q: Did you have discussions with Margaret McGary concerning these problems that you were having?

A: Yes, I did.

Q: Did there come a time when your husband's automobile was repossessed?

A: Yes, it happened. I believe it was May.

Q: What happened to you after his car was repossessed?

A: His car was repossessed. He didn't have transportation, so he wanted to use my car. I [had] to go to work, but he still wanted to use my car, and he feels frustrated because I would not let him use my car, because I have to go to work.

And, he would not drive me to work, and also, he told me that I need to buy him a truck.

Q: Were you willing to buy him a truck?

A: No, he—he beat me up because I didn't buy her a truck from the neighbor.

Q: During this time frame was he telling you about sexual relations with somebody named Scott?

A: Yes, he did. He said that he used to watch his friend Scott and his girlfriend have sex, and then his girlfriend would switch to John, and then Scott would watch it. That's what he told me, sir.

Q: Did he want you to participate in things like that?

A: I was scared when his friend, Robert, would come, and then he would suggest something like that.

Q: Did John ever suggest anything of that sort?

A: No, he would just say that. He just told me that.

Q: During the May, June period of time, were there occasions when he took money out of your purse?

A: Yes, he always took money out of my purse.

Q: What would he tell you when he did that?

A: He would just grab my purse and then he will take some money from my purse.

Q: In early June, was there an incident involving a tape recorder?

A: Yes, sir.

Q: Why did you have the tape recorder?

A: I wanted to have a divorce, and I told him in May

that I wanted to have a divorce, because his friend was going to come down, and I started pack my things.

So, he told me that if I don't leave he will kick me out of the house, but I had no money, so I had to—I remember listen to this attorney, and I guess, she wanted—I wanted to give her some evidence, and I didn't know how to get it, so I have to get—I got myself a tape recorder, and I recorded the insults and the put-downs that he did to me, so I can show it to the divorce lawyer.

Q: What kind of insults and put-downs was he giving you?

A: He was saying—he was saying bad words to me, and he—

Q: Did he talk about your figure?

A: Yes, he said that I'm Spanish, that I don't have blond hair, I don't have blue eyes, and I'm too small and skinny, and he want a bigger woman. And he told me that I was Spanish, and I didn't deserve him. All this was with bad words, together.

For example, he would say, "F" Spanish—I'm sorry. I can't say it.

Q: Did he say those sorts of things about Janna and Nizzar, as well?

A: Yes, he would say those things of my friends.

Q: What happened the night that he found the tape recorder? What did he do?

A: Well, he wanted to grab money from my purse, and instead of money he find the little tape recorder, so he took the tape recorder and he played the tape. It was his voice coming out from the tape recorder, and I said, "Give me that," and then he said, "What is this?" Bad words. He used bad words all the time.

I said, "Nothing." He hit me, and slapped me. He pulled my hair.

Q: Did he play some of it so he knew what was on it?

A: Yes, he knew it was him, it was his voice on it he was hearing.

Q: What happened next?

A: He wanted an explanation and he came to me, and I didn't give him any explanation, and he beat me up there. He also raped me there.

Q: Now, would you describe the kicks that he used?

A: He would kick me in my stomach and he would throw me to the wall.

Q: Were you afraid of him?

A: Yes, I was really scared. I was really afraid.

Q: Is this the incident that Ms. Jones heard?

A: Yes, I was screaming, and I was screaming, "Give me my purse." He would not give me my purse, either.

Q: At the end of May, was there an incident when you were going to a movie and Denny's?

A: Yes. We went to the movies and then we came back, and he took his shirt off, and we were going to this restaurant, and some restaurants would not let you eat without shoes or without a shirt, so he only have a little tiny shirt, and I suggested that, please put the shirt back on because we were going to go to this restaurant, and he said, "You don't have to tell me what to do." He grabbed my face, and he slapped me, and he punched me in my arm. I was driving.

Q: Did you tell your co-workers how you got these bruises?

A: Yes, sir; I went to the nail place and I told one my co-worker.

Q: In June, did your husband get involved in an altercation that you refused to watch?

A: Yes, sir. I came back from work and I saw a lot of people around, and this person was yelling from the car, and John was around, ready to fight with this person, or to defend his friend's neighbor.

I just went straight up to my apartment, and he came up follow me, and he was really upset because I didn't stay there, watching him, because he was ready to fight with this person.

Q: Did he do anything to you afterwards?

A: Yes, he beat me up.

Q: Did you talk to Mrs. Anastasi about what was going on during this time frame?

A: I talked to Mrs. Anastasi, yes.

Q: Did she give you some advice, or did Mrs. Castro give you some advice, not to cook for him?

A: Mrs. Castro. Mrs. Castro was the one who told me not to cook anymore, because she knew I was going every time to her office, and her work, and I was explaining what's going on. I told her I didn't know what to do, I have no idea, I'm scared.

And she would say, "Don't do anything. If he kick you out of the house you don't have to cook for him anymore."

Q: When you refused to cook what would your husband do?

A: He beat me up.

Q: Were you afraid of him at that point?

A: Of course I was afraid, yes.

Q: Now, there came a time when you went to see Dr. Inman?

A: Yes. I couldn't work. I couldn't do my work right,

so people started complaining, and I would say, no, I don't understand what happened to me.

I called Mrs. Castro, and she told me to go to the bathroom and drink some water. I did what she told me to do and then I called her back, and I said, "I think I need to go to the doctor, because I can't do my work right."

So, I make an appointment—I didn't really make an appointment, I just show up, and I told Dr. Inman, I said, "Give me something for this shake. I can't work." And so she tried to calm me down, and she asked me what was wrong.

I just cried, and then she said, "Is there something to do with your husband?" I said, "Yes."

My hands were cramped, and I was just shaking. I didn't know what was wrong with me.

(Whereupon, the witness is in tears.)

Q: Did you tell her what your husband was doing to you?

A: Yes. I told her, I said, "My husband raped me."

Q: What did Dr. Inman advise you to do?

A: Dr. Inman called the woman center, some place, and that person called back and she talked to me.

Q: Who was that person?

A: The person from the woman's center. I really can't remember who she was, but she told me that I had to get some Protective Order.

Q: You saw Dr. Inman on Friday, the 18th of June?

A: Yes, I did.

Q: Did you have occasion to come to this Courthouse.

A: Yes, I did.

Q: And was that on the following Monday?

A: Yes, sir; it was.

Q: I'm going to show you a petition for a Protective Order. And ask if you can identify it?

(Whereupon, counsel approached the witness.)

THE WITNESS: Yes this is it. Yes, it is.

Q: The parts of it that are in handwriting, is that your handwriting.

A: No, it's not.

Q: Whose handwriting is it in?

A: It's the gentleman who helped me for the Protective Order, sir.

Q: Was he writing down what you were telling him?

A: Yes.

Q: Now, what time of the day did you go in to get the Protective Order?

A: I think it was in the morning.

Q: Did you ever get the order issued?

A: No, he told me to come three or four hours later, or Wednesday, because his secretary was at lunch time, or something.

Q: Wednesday was after the incident, isn't it? This happened Tuesday night, and Wednesday morning?

A: Yes.

Q: Had you—why did you leave? Why didn't you stay and wait for the Protective Order to be issued?

A: First of all, I was scared. I didn't know what was going to happen. I was embarrassed to be there. I never was in the Courthouse, and I was embarrassed to talk about it with a stranger, and especially a man.

I didn't know this gentleman, and I was real embarrassed to tell—to tell him what was going on in my life. I was uncomfortable. I didn't want to be there.

Q: You've had some experience in the past with your

husband being ordered to stay away from you, after the June—the February 21st hearing?

A: Yes, yes.

Q: Did you really think he would live up to this one?

A: No, I don't think so. I don't think so.

Q: Were you afraid of him at this time?

A: Yes, sir; I was.

Q: And he threatened to do something to you when you left?

A: Yes, sir; he did. He also say he will, if I have a divorce, that he will follow me, and I said, "I don't need to give you an address. I don't need to see you anymore. You're not going to follow me."

He said that he will follow me because he will know, he will stay outside of my work. He know where I work and he will follow me, no matter what, and he can have any kind of sex, anywhere, anyhow, no matter what. That's what he told me.

Q: When you would resist sex, what kinds of sex would he threaten you with?

A: He will have anal sex, and he will force me into sex.

Q: On the Monday—I guess it was Tuesday, Tuesday afternoon did you see Mrs. Jones?

A: Yes, I did. I told Mrs. Jones that he raped me, and she said that she will like to talk to me, and I said, "I have to go to work," and she said, "Okay, I hear you scream the other day," and I say, "Yes," but I had to go to work.

So, I went to work, and I finished my work, and I went to eat something at Kentucky Fried Chicken, and then I came back to work. It was like about ten at night, and Mrs. Ella was outside in the balcony, and she—

Q: Does she live near you?

A: Below the apartment, yes.

Q: Tell us what happened when you saw her that evening.

A: She said, "I need to talk to you because I hear your scream the other night, and I wonder what happened to you."

I told her, again, what happened, so she give me those little books, and—

Q: I show you an Exhibit that has been admitted, and ask if you can identify it.

A: Yes.

Q: What is it?

A: That's about the spousal abuse, husband that hit the wife and rape, and force sex.

Q: Is this the book that she gave you?

A: Yes, there is two books.

Q: What did you do with the literature that night?

A: I went back to the apartment and I tried to just look at it, but I didn't want to look at it because I saw ugly pictures. I didn't feel comfortable looking at it, so I put it—I just put them away.

Q: What time did you go to bed?

A: Maybe it was 11:30.

Q: How were you dressed when you went to bed?

A: When I came to work I put my comfortable clothes. I have a cotton T-shirt and my spandex short.

Q: Did you have any underwear on?

A: Yes, sir; I did have underwear on.

Q: Now, a pair of underwear has been admitted in evidence in this case. Was that the underwear that you had on?

A: That's the underwear I had, yes.

Q: Did you stay awake in bed for a while? Did you go to sleep? What did you do then?

A: I turned the TV on, but nothing was on, nothing interesting was on, so I just turn it off, and I have to go to work the next day.

Q: Why did you stay in the apartment that night?

A: Nobody was at home, and I didn't have no money to go anywhere.

Q: Couldn't you have gone to stay with Janna, or Mrs. Castro, or something of that sort?

A: No, I didn't want my friends to know that he was hitting me again.

Q: Could you have gone and stayed with Mrs. Jones?

A: No, I was scared because I was scared that something might happen to her.

Q: Did the fact that Robbie was with John make any difference in your decision to stay there?

A: I thought that he was going to have a friend there, and that he's going to be entertained by [his] friend, and he's not going to do anything to me.

Q: What is the next thing that you are aware of?

A: I went to bed, and I—I was awaked by the strong closing—the slam door, so I wake up.

Q: What time was it?

A: I look at the clock; it was maybe from 3:15, 3:30.

Q: Are you sure?

A: Not really, I was just awake.

Q: So you woke up when he came in?

A: Yes.

Q: Did you talk to him?

A: Yes.

Q: What did you talk about?

A: I said if he have work today, and he said, "No, I went to bar." So I just tried to go back to bed again.

Q: What do you next remember?

A: I went to bed, and then he slip by my side, and I just tried to go back to bed.

Q: Did you go back to sleep?

A: Yes, yes, I did.

Q: Did there come a time that he woke you up?

A: I feel like a pull down to my underwears, and then he was on top of me again, and I wake up. I was like try to—try to find out what is going on, and he grabbed my wrists and press it down to my hips.

Then he—I felt like I couldn't breathe, and he was— his chest and his right shoulder, was on my face and my mouth. And then he—I asked him, "What are you doing?" and he didn't say anything. I said, "I don't want to have sex," and he wouldn't listen to me. He wouldn't let me go, and he started to pull down my underwears with his foot.

Q: How did he get your pants off?

A: It was down on my knees first, but then he realized it didn't took my underwear off, so he tried to take it off with his foot.

Q: Did you try to fight him?

A: Yes, I tried to keep my legs closed, and I tried to keep my underwear on, but I couldn't. I only grabbed my right side with my three fingers (indicating), and I hear a rip on my right-hand side of my underwear.

He took it off. He pulled my underwears down, and he force himself into me again. I was just crying. I tried to cry loud, but I couldn't breathe. I couldn't breathe. It was hurting me. He hurt me.

Q: Were you afraid of him then?

A: Yeah, yeah, he was hurting me.

(Whereupon, the witness is in tears.)

THE WITNESS: I feel like, I don't know, like my vagina was ripping up or something. I couldn't say this—I can't describe. Maybe you don't understand because you are a man, or he didn't understand because he's a man, but it hurt me! It hurt!

I don't want to think about it.

(Pause)

THE WITNESS: I'm sorry. I'm sorry.

(Pause)

Q: What happened when he finished?

A: I looked for my underwears, and I was—I was looking in the bed, and I put my—I put my underwear on again.

I was sitting by—in the bed, and I told him why he do this to me again, and again, and again?

Q: What did he say to you?

A: Nothing, he push me away, say he doesn't care, he doesn't care for my feelings. That's what he say.

Q: What did you do?

A: I just tried to calm myself down. I went to the kitchen for a glass of water.

Q: What happened next?

A: I get the glass of water—I get the glass from the cabinet, and I pour some water from the refrigerator, and I—I was drinking the water, trying to calm myself down, and I—the only light that was on was the refrigerator light, and I saw the knife.

(The witness remains in tears.)

THE WITNESS: I remember many things, things that—I remember a lot of things he had said to me; I remember the first time he raped me; I remember when he told me about the syringes to go through my bones and I was going to die.

I remember the put-downs that he told me. There was just so many pictures on my head. And they were just pictures—there were just pictures there, in my head.

I remember the insults and the bad words that he told me. I remember every time that he had anal sex—anal sex with me. It hurt me, it hurt.

I remember everything, everything. I remember when he told me about the abortion. I remember everything.

Q: Do you remember cutting him?

A: No, I don't remember that. No, sir; I don't remember that.

Q: What did you do after that?

A: I was driving. I couldn't make a turn. I couldn't make a turn and I—I couldn't make a turn, my hands were busy, and I—I tried to turn but I couldn't because my—my hands were busy, and I just scream and I saw it, and I throw it out.

Q: Where did you go from there?

A: I want to see my friend, Janna. I thought the people that I work is going to be there. I thought the clients are going to be there, and I—I just want to tell them what happened, what he did to me, so I went to the shop.

Q: Did you expect to see Janna at the shop, at three or four o'clock in the morning?

A: Yeah, yeah.

Q: What happened when you got to the shop?

A: Nobody was there. Nobody was there, so I—I just keep on crying and screaming, and I felt—I—

Q: How did you get into the shop?

A: I don't know, but I—I couldn't open the door. My—my—I saw my hand had the knife, and I scream and I throw it away, I throw it in the trash can. That's what I did.

I get into it and I try to call my friend, and I couldn't. I saw my hand with just a little blood, and my left hand, and I went and wash it, and I fell, and I wash it real quick, and so I came back and called her, but the answering machine was on, so I went back and I just drove to her house.

Q: What did you do when you got to her house?

A: Nobody was open the doors, so I just stand up in the front door and I just—I was knocking at the door, and her husband came down the stairs, and I was looking—I said, "Where is Janna, where is Janna?"

And he came and get her, and I was in the corner.

I couldn't tell her what happened. I didn't know, I didn't know what happened. Then I tried to explain it to her, and she couldn't understand me. She couldn't understand what happened. I couldn't explain it to her, so eventually I—I told her what happened.

She—she said that she needs to call the police, and she needs to call the ambulance, so I said, "Okay." So she did call the people that she need to call, and she called Mrs. Castro, and she told her what happened.

Q: Did she call the ambulance and then the police, and then Mrs. Castro?

A: Yes, yes.

Q: What happened next, if you know?

A: I have to go to the Prince William Police. They asked me—they asked me where the body part was, and I told them where I think it was, and so I had to see Detective Weintz, and I needed to talk to her—to him.

I tried to explain what happened. I want to tell him what he did to me.

Q: Were you taken to the hospital?

A: I went to the hospital for an examination after.

Q: After the examination, what happened?

A: I went back home.

Q: Did they take you back to the police station?

A: No, that was before.

Q: Before the examination?

A: Yeah, I think so. I don't remember.

Q: Did you have a conversation with Detective Weintz?

A: Yes, I did.

Q: How was he treating you?

A: Very nice.

Q: Was Janna present for the conversation?

A: Yes, she was, sir.

Q: How were you feeling when you talked to him?

A: I was confused. I tried to tell him many things, but I—I couldn't tell me what—I couldn't—I just, I was talking. I don't even remember what I was talking, but I did talk to him.

Q: After you talked to him for a while did he turn on a tape recorder?

A: Yes, it was a tape recorder there.

Q: Did he then ask you some questions again?

A: No, he only asked once, I think.

Q: When you talked to Detective Weintz, were you trying to tell him the truth?

A: Yes, yes.

Q: Had you told the other police the truth, to the best you knew it?

A: Yes, I did, sir.

Q: Did you tell him it happened about three o'clock in the morning?

A: Like about that time; yes, sir.

Q: Did you tell him that your husband had raped you?

A: Yes, I did, sir; yes, I did.

Q: Did you tell him that you were afraid of him?

A: Yes, I did; yes, sir.

Q: Were you afraid of him that night?

A: Yes, I was, sir. I was very afraid. I was very afraid. I feel trapped. I don't know where to go. I don't know what to do. I was very scared of him. I didn't want him to rape me anymore. I didn't want him to hit me anymore. I did not want him to follow me and rape me.

Q: You made some statements in your statement, that sex should be mutual. What do you mean by that?

A: Well, I don't like when my husband take me and grab me, and rape me. That's what I mean. I don't want to be forced into sex, like he did to me. That's what I mean.

Q: Did you tell him that you were angry at your husband?

A: Those words were one of the words that I tried to explain to him, yes, but there were so many of them together, my feelings and emotions were all mixed up, and I couldn't really explain. It was that, and much more. There were so many things that I couldn't—I couldn't explain.

Q: Do you remember Detective Weintz telling you, "All right, you didn't know what you were doing?"

A: Right, yes. I didn't know.

Q: How did you feel about that statement?

A: I didn't know what I was doing. I—I tell him how I feel.

Q: Was he right when he said that?

A: Right; yes, sir.

THE BOBBITT CASE

MR. LOWE: Your Honor, that's all the questions I have of this witness.

CROSS EXAMINATION

BY MS. O'BRIEN:

Q: Mrs. Bobbitt, was it your testimony this morning that you don't remember cutting your husband's penis off, on June the 23rd?

A: No, ma'am; I don't.

Q: It's your testimony that the last thing that you remember was being in the kitchen, holding a knife?

A: Yes, ma'am; I was in the kitchen holding the knife; yes, ma'am.

Q: And the next thing you remember after that, was when you were in the car driving to your friend Janna's house?

A: Yes, ma'am.

Q: And this is your knife, right? (Counsel is holding up the knife.)

A: Yes, ma'am; it is.

Q: Do you remember getting to Janna's house?

A: I was driving to the work, first, ma'am.

Q: After you went to work you went to her house?

A: Yes, ma'am.

Q: And when you saw Janna you told her what happened, didn't you?

A: Yes, I tried to explain, ma'am, what happened; yes.

Q: And you told her that your husband raped you, and you told her that you cut him, didn't you?

A: I tried to explain to her what I assume happened,

when I found myself—my hands busy, after he raped me;
yes, ma'am.

Q: And, certainly, you told her the truth, didn't you?

A: Yes, ma'am.

Q: And she made some phone calls, and then you went
to the police station, and then you went to the hospital,
right?

A: Yes, ma'am.

Q: And you saw Detective Weintz at the hospital?

A: Yes, I did saw Detective Weintz, ma'am.

Q: And he was very kind to you, wasn't he?

A: Yes, ma'am; he was.

Q: He didn't scare you, Mrs. Bobbitt?

A: He didn't scare me, but I was very nervous and I
was very, very emotional.

Q: Sure, and you talked to him a little bit, informally,
before he turned on the tape recorder and asked you
questions, right?

A: Yes, ma'am.

Q: What you told Detective Weintz was the truth,
wasn't it?

A: Yes, ma'am; I tried.

Q: You did not lie to him?

A: No, I tried to tell the truth, ma'am; I tried.

Q: And then he turned on the tape recorder, didn't he,
back at the police station and both of you talked into the
tape recorder, and he asked you questions and you answered the questions?

A: Yes, ma'am.

Q: To the best that you could?

A: Yes, ma'am; yes.

Q: You weren't making anything up or anything?

A: No, I wasn't. No, no.

(Whereupon, counsel approached the witness.)

Q: After—in the months since this has happened, after you gave him the statement, you have seen typewritten copies of this statement, haven't you?

A: Yes, I saw some.

Q: Does this appear to be the statement that you've seen before?

A: Yes.

Q: Mrs. Bobbitt, would you turn to page five of the document?

At the top of that page you were talking about your car being repossessed; isn't that right?

A: Yes, ma'am.

Q: And then, do you remember him saying, "After you and John—after he forced you to have sex this morning, can you tell me what happened then?"

Do you remember him asking you that?

A: Yes, ma'am.

Q: And do you remember saying, "He pushed me away, like when he finished, like he did it before, sometimes pushed me away. Like make me feel really bad, 'cause that's not fair, that's not nice. I don't feel good when he does it."

Do you remember saying that?

A: Yes, ma'am.

Q: And do you remember saying, "Uh, I come back to pick up my clothes, looking for my underwears, and I didn't even have my shirt off, and I put my underwear back."

Do you remember saying that?

A: Yes, ma'am.

Q: And that was the truth?

A: Yes, ma'am.

Q: Do you remember saying to him, "My other shirt—my spandex shirt on, and I was hurt. I went to the kitchen to drink water."

Do you remember saying that?

A: Yes, ma'am.

Q: And that was the truth, too?

A: Yes, ma'am.

Q: You remember going to the kitchen and drinking water?

A: Yes, ma'am; yes.

Q: And then you said, "I opened the refrigerator, and I got a—a cup of water?"

Do you remember saying that?

A: Yes, ma'am; I do.

Q: And again, that was the truth?

A: Yes, ma'am; yes.

Q: And then you said, "Then I was angry already, and I turned my back, and the first thing I saw was the knife."

Do you remember saying that to him?

A: I remember; yes, ma'am.

Q: And that was the truth, too; right?

A: Yes, ma'am; it was the truth.

Q: And then he said, "Okay, you need to go on." And you said, "Then I took it, and I was just angry."

Do you remember telling him that?

A: Yes, ma'am; I do.

Q: And that was the truth, too; right?

A: Yes, ma'am; it was.

Q: You were very angry?

A: I don't know how angry I was, ma'am, but I remember saying that, ma'am, and it was so many feelings at the same time, ma'am.

Q: And then you said, "Then I took it, and went—I

went to the bedroom, and I told him he shouldn't do this to me. Why he did it? Then I asked him if he was satisfied with what he did, and then he was half asleep or something. I was just mad and"—

Do you remember saying that?

A: Yes, ma'am.

Q: And that was the truth, too?

A: Yes, ma'am; it was the truth.

Q: You told Detective Weintz the truth?

A: Yes, ma'am; I was.

Q: And then Detective Weintz started to ask you a question, and he said, "What is"—and you said, "Then he said he doesn't care about my feelings, he did say that, and I asked him if he had orgasm inside me, 'cause it hurt me when he made me do that before."

Do you remember saying that?

A: Yes, ma'am, I do.

Q: And that was the truth, too?

A: Yes, ma'am. I tried to explain what really happened to me. I said the word, "orgasm," because I wanted him to explain that he did something sexually to me, ma'am.

Q: Sure, and you were explaining to him, too, why you were so angry when you took the knife, right?

A: Yes, ma'am; I used the word, "angry," but I—if I could just tell you in one word, I could not find a word. There was so many feelings at the same time, ma'am. There were so many feelings.

Q: You were somewhere even beyond angry? Furious?

A: There was so many feelings, ma'am. I did not use that word.

Q: Well, you used a couple of different words. You said, "angry," once—

A: Yes, ma'am.

Q: —and you said, "mad," another time.

A: Yes, ma'am.

Q: And those are the types of words that you would use to describe how you felt, right?

A: Those are the words that I thought I could use to describe, yes, ma'am, all my feelings.

Q: And then you said, "He always have orgasm and he doesn't wait for me to have—to have orgasm. He's selfish. I don't think it's fair."

Do you remember saying that?

A: Yes, ma'am; I did.

Q: You were explaining to him why you were so angry. Isn't that right?

A: I didn't explain to him what I was so angry. I tried to explain how were my feelings were. I was sad. I was mad. I was hurt. I was remember all these feelings. I was very hurt, my feelings and physically hurt.

Q: Sure, and you didn't think it was fair, did you?

A: No, ma'am. I don't think that a man should rape a woman; no ma'am.

Q: And then you told Detective Weintz, "I pulled back the shirt—ah, the sheet, and then I did it."

Do you remember saying that?

A: Yes, ma'am; I do remember saying that.

Q: And Detective Weintz was trying, apparently, to get you to explain what you did, and he said to you, "All right, you cut him?" And you said, "I—yes."

Is that right?

A: Yes, ma'am; yes.

Q: And then, a little later on, he asked you if you were talking to him, and he was talking to you, when you cut him, and you explained to him that your husband was asleep at the time you cut him, didn't you?

A: That's what I thought it was, ma'am. I thought he was.

Q: You thought he was asleep? Did you think he was asleep because of the way he was lying on the bed?

A: I don't remember, ma'am. I really don't remember. That's what I thought, and I say that, yes.

Q: He wasn't moving, at all, when you came back into the bedroom, was he?

A: I really don't remember, ma'am. I just thought that, and I said to Detective Weintz that.

Q: You thought that he was asleep?

A: Yes.

Q: And you told Detective Weintz the same thing you told Janna, isn't that right?

A: I don't remember exactly what I told Janna.

Q: But you told both of them about the rape, and about going to the kitchen?

A: Yes.

Q: And about getting the knife?

A: Yes, ma'am; yes, I did.

Q: And you told both of them you went back into the bedroom, and lifted up the sheet, and cut him?

A: Yes, ma'am; I did. Yes.

Q: And that was the truth?

A: That's what I think I did, ma'am. That's what I—I tried to explain.

Q: My question to you is, you didn't make anything up, did you?

A: No, no. I didn't, ma'am, no.

Q: And you didn't tell them you weren't sure what you did?

A: Right. Yes, ma'am; I wasn't sure.

Q: But you didn't tell them that you weren't sure what you did, did you?

A: No, I guess not. I didn't say anything, I guess. I can't remember, ma'am.

Q: When this happened—

(Whereupon, counsel approached a diagram next to the witness.)

BY MS. O'BRIEN:

Q: This was your bedroom (indicating)?

A: Uh-huh (affirmative).

Q: And this was where Robbie was, in the living room (indicating)?

A: Yes, ma'am.

Q: And then this was the kitchen (indicating)?

A: Yes, ma'am.

Q: And the knives were over here (indicating); right? Where you keep the knives is over here?

A: I—

Q: I this corner?

A: No. I—we always keep in that space, but I'm not sure if it was in the corner.

Q: Do you know where you got the knife from? Was it in the corner, or next to the sink?

A: I think it was next to the sink, ma'am.

Q: Do you remember that or are you just guessing?

A: I think I remember.

Q: You think you remember the knife was next to the sink?

A: Yes.

Q: And then you walked out into the dining room, right?

A: Yes.

Q: And then you walked through the living room?

A: Yes.

Q: And then you walked over to the bedroom—

A: I didn't walk through the living room. I went from the dining room through the bedroom, I think. I'm not sure. I'm not sure. I'm not sure, but I don't think I went—I don't—I don't remember, ma'am. I really don't remember if I went to the living room.

Q: Well, why would you tell me just now that you didn't go in the living room?

A: I'm telling you I don't remember if I went to the living room, or if I am going to the bedroom. I don't remember. You are putting two, two lines. I don't really remember what I did.

Q: But then you walked into the bedroom. Do you remember that?

A: I think so, yes; I think. I think I do that, ma'am.

Q: Do you remember doing that?

A: I don't remember doing—walking into the bedroom. I don't.

Q: Do you remember, after you pulled the sheet back, and cut your husband's penis off, do you remember being in the kitchen, and picking up your purse, and leaving?

A: I don't remember that, ma'am. I really don't remember.

Q: Have you been able to remember it, at all, since it happened?

A: I assume I did that, because I took a Nintendo in my purse, and when I found—in my hand, I assumed I did what I did. I tried to explain myself, and I tried to answer myself what I did do it.

Q: After this happened, did you ever tell Detective Weintz, when you were talking to him informally, or on the statement, that there were things that you just didn't remember?

A: He never asked me that, ma'am; no.

Q: I understand that, but what I'm asking you is, did you ever tell him you didn't remember things? There were things you didn't remember?

A: I think I did, ma'am; yes, I think.

Q: Did you tell him that when he had the tape recorder off?

A: I don't remember that. I'm not sure.

Q: When do you think you told him that there were things that you don't remember?

A: I don't know if I—if he asked me that question.

Q: I know you said that he didn't ask you that question. I'm asking you, did you ever tell him that there were some things that you just didn't remember; and you just told me that, yeah, you think you did.

A: I don't think I said that. I'm not sure.

Q: You're not sure whether you ever told him there were things that you don't remember?

A: Right. I'm not sure.

Q: Now, when you came here you were seventeen years old?

A: Yes.

Q: And when you came—you said that you grew up in a very strict, Catholic family?

A: Yes, ma'am.

Q: And that was part of the reason why you didn't want a divorce?

A: Right, yes.

Q: And that was part of the reason why you wanted to have children?

A: Yes, I wanted to have children; yes, ma'am.

Q: And that was part of the reason why you felt so bad about the abortion. Is that right?

A: Yes, ma'am; yes.

Q: So, when you grew up in a strict Catholic family, you went to Mass every Sunday, right?

A: Yes, ma'am; yes.

Q: And when you came here and you lived with Mrs. Castro, you went to Mass every Sunday?

A: Yes, ma'am; yes, I did.

Q: And you certainly recognize, that in the Catholic Church, marriage is a sacrum; right?

A: Yes, ma'am; yes.

Q: And that, to be considered married, in the eyes of the church, you have to go to a church, right?

A: Yes, ma'am.

Q: You got married by a Justice of the Peace. Is that right?

A: Yes, ma'am.

Q: And that was your idea?

A: No, ma'am; it was his idea. He give me the ring and then we have to get married.

Q: I know it was his idea to get married, but it was your idea to go to the Justice of the Peace?

A: Yeah, we have to get married, yeah, yes.

Q: Now, you were living with Mrs. Castro at that time?

A: I was living with Mrs. Bisutti.

Q: Janna Bisutti?

A: Janna Bisutti, and Mrs. Castro.

Q: But you were still friendly with Mrs. Castro? You were living with Janna Bisutti during the week, and with Mrs. Castro, on the weekends?

A: Yes, yes.

Q: And Mrs. Castro didn't want you and John to get married, did she?

A: She has her opinions, yes.

Q: And those opinions were that you were too young, or that, for whatever reason, you should not be getting married right then. Is that right?

A: I think so, yes.

Q: She conveyed those opinions to you, didn't she? She told you that?

A: She said that, yes. She told me that, yes.

Q: And you said that after your marriage you went to Niagara Falls.

A: Yes.

Q: You were a day late for a party that John's parents were going to have?

A: Yes, ma'am; yes.

Q: But they still had the party, anyway? Isn't that right?

A: Yes, ma'am; they did.

Q: And they were very welcoming to you, weren't they?

A: No, they were mad because we came late for the church. It was going to be at the church. We were going to get married at the church, and they weren't—they weren't very nice to me because they were—we came late for that.

Q: Did something happen when you were up there, where you got upset with John because he was talking to a cousin and left you out?

A: No, ma'am; I don't remember that. No, ma'am.

Q: You don't remember that, at all?

A: No, ma'am.

Q: You weren't jealous of his talking to someone else?

A: No, ma'am. I don't think that happened. No.

Q: Now, when you came back, Todd came back with you, didn't he?

A: Yes, ma'am; he did, yes.

Q: And you weren't very happy about that, were you?

A: No, I wasn't very happy about that, ma'am; no.

Q: In fact, you were fairly angry about that. Wouldn't that be fair to say?

A: No, I was—I was disappointed. I would say disappointed, ma'am.

Q: "Disappointed," is the word that you would use?

A: Yes, I would use, "disappointed," yes, ma'am; I would.

Q: And when Todd came back, Todd and John would go out by themselves at night. Is that right? When the three of you were living together, sometimes Todd and John would go out and leave you?

A: Yes, yes, ma'am; yes.

Q: And you didn't really like that, and you didn't think that was right, did you?

A: No, ma'am. I was working and then I used to come back to work—from work, and I just stay at home.

Q: My question to you is, you didn't think that it was right that your husband and his brother would be going out to a bar, every night, did you?

A: Once in a while, okay; but not every night. I knew he have to work the next morning, and I don't want him to be late for the Marines, ma'am.

Q: And you told John that, didn't you?

A: I said, "Please don't be late for the Marines, because they keep some money from you, and you have to work extra hours." Yes.

Q: And you told him that you didn't think he should be going out with his cousin every night, or his brother?

A: No, ma'am. I did not say that, no; no, ma'am.

Q: The only thing you expressed any concern about was whether he was going to be late for work?

A: Yes, ma'am; I did.

Q: When you went to the Spanish club, in Washington, you said, Chelsea Joe's?

A: Something like that, yes.

Q: You and Todd and John went; isn't that right?

A: Yes, ma'am.

Q: And you drove in your car?

A: I didn't drove, ma'am; he drove.

Q: Did you and John just have one car at that time?

A: No, we have three.

Q: You had three cars?

A: Yes, we give the one to Todd.

Q: So each one of you had a car?

A: Yes.

Q: And you couldn't get in to the club because John was wearing sneakers. Isn't that right?

A: Everybody were wearing jeans, ma'am.

Q: You were wearing jeans?

A: I was wearing jeans, ma'am.

Q: And you said that he was—that he had had a lot to drink, and he was driving crazy on the road?

A: Yes, ma'am; after we decide to go to another club, after the Chelsea.

Q: And when he was driving crazy, you said he was driving fast and weaving in and out of traffic?

A: He was going back and forth from the side to side, and the people right next to us were making signals and they were pushing their horn, saying that slow down, and insulting us.

Q: And you were pretty upset about that, weren't you?

A: I was scared ma'am. I was really scared.

Lorena Leonor Bobbitt, 24, and Lisa Kemler, one of her attorneys, entering the Prince William Circuit Courthouse in Manassas, Virginia. (*AP/Wide World Photos*)

Listening to her attorney during the jury selection.
(*AP/Wide World Photos*)

Pensive and alone, Lorena awaits the beginning of her trial for the malicious wounding of her husband, John Wayne Bobbitt. (*AP/Wide World Photos*)

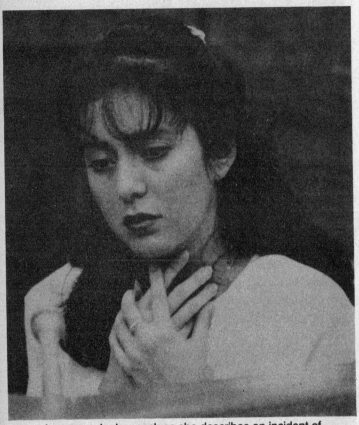
Lorena grabs her neck as she describes an incident of abuse by her husband. (*AP/Wide World Photos*)

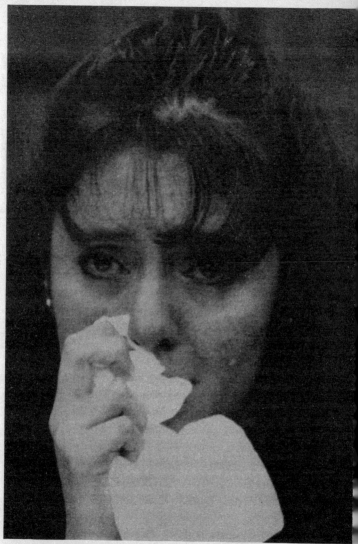
Tearfully, Lorena testifies about the night in question.
(*AP/Wide World Photos*)

As she continued to relate the events of that night, Lorena became increasingly emotional. (*AP/Wide World Photos*)

Prosecutor Mary Grace O'Brien shows Lorena a passage
from the transcript of evidence during cross examination.
(*AP/Wide World Photos*)

Leaving the courthouse after the fourth day of her trial,
Lorena waves to her supporters. (*AP/Wide World Photos*)

John Wayne Bobbitt, 26, and his aunt Marylyn Biro leave the courthouse after his acquittal for sexual assault against his wife Lorena. (*AP/Wide World Photos*)

Bobbitt swears to tell the truth as he prepares to testify during Lorena's trial. (*AP/Wide World Photos*)

In the witness box, John ponders a question during his testimony. (*AP/Wide World Photos*)

Using a diagram, John relates events in the apartment he shared with his wife. (*AP/Wide World Photos*)

Bobbitt walks past the ranks of the press as he arrives for the fourth day of Lorena's trial. (*AP/Wide World Photos*)

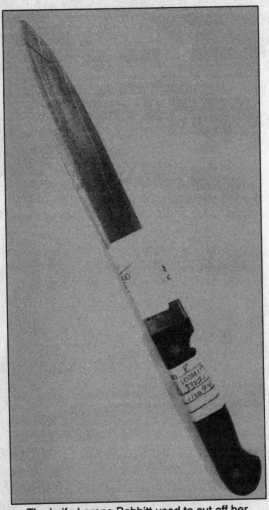

The knife Lorena Bobbitt used to cut off her husband's penis. (*AP/Wide World Photos*)

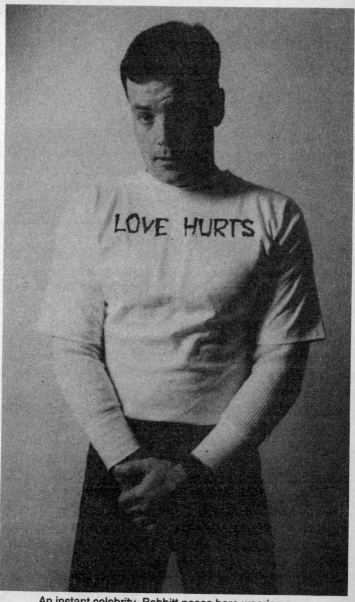

An instant celebrity, Bobbitt poses here wearing a souvenir T-shirt. (*Detroit News Photo by Donna Terek*)

Forensic scientist Myron Scholberg displays a pair of Lorena's panties similar to those she says her husband tore off her body on the night in question. (*AP/Wide World Photos*)

Satellite TV trucks and scores of photographers crowd the streets outside of the Prince William Circuit Court-house to cover Lorena's trial. (*AP/Wide World Photos*)

The blood stained bed where Lorena cut off John Bobbitt's penis. (*Sygma Photo News*)

Urologist James Sehn testifies about John Babbitt's wound, displaying a photo of the severed penis. (*Sygma Photo News*)

Lisa Cushing and Jeff Fairman from Manassas sell
Bobbitt trial souvenir T-shirts. (*AP/Wide World Photos*)

Supporters of Lorena Bobbitt hold signs and shout their
support outside the courthouse. (*AP/Wide World Photos*)

Q: And you were angry with the way your husband was driving, right?

A: I would not use, "angry," ma'am; no, I wouldn't.

Q: You said, at that point he had started hitting you in the car?

A: Yes, ma'am; he did.

Q: Isn't it a fact that, actually, you hit his arm in the car, and tried to grab his arm?

A: No, ma'am; he did it.

Q: And then you came back to the apartment, and you said that when he got to the apartment, I think you said that he kicked you and slapped you in the face?

A: Yes, ma'am; he did.

Q: Was Todd there then?

A: He was outside smoking.

Q: And you were yelling, weren't you?

A: I was screaming, "Stop, stop," ma'am; yes.

Q: And he was yelling, as well, right?

A: Yes, ma'am; yes.

Q: And Officer Francis came to the door?

A: Yes, ma'am.

Q: And did you tell Officer Francis what your husband was doing?

A: Yeah, I told him that he was beating me up.

Q: You told him that he was beating you up?

A: Yes.

Q: Did you tell him how he was beating you up?

A: No, I was crying. I couldn't tell any more. I was crying.

Q: Did you use those words, do you remember? Did you say, he is beating me up?

A: I quite don't remember, ma'am; I really don't. I

think I told him that, yes. That's what he ask me, if I
have a place to go.

Q: Well, this is important. That's why you just said
that you told him that John was beating you up. Then,
you said you don't remember whether you told him that?

A: I—

Q: Did you tell him that, or didn't you tell him that,
or don't you know what you said?

A: I was crying, ma'am. I was—I couldn't remember
right now, it was so long ago. I could not—I'm really
have a bad memory of my recollections of the dates, and
also, what I said at that time. I'm sorry.

Q: This was a long time ago, and so you don't remember it very clearly.

A: I—I think I said something to him, that's what he
asked me, if I have a place to live, but I don't really
quite remember exactly why—

Q: Well, just generally, do you remember generally
what you said to him? A minute ago you said that you
told him your husband was beating you up. Do you remember, generally, what you said to him?

A: Yeah, I think I told him that—that he hit me. I
think; I'm not sure, ma'am. One more time, I'm sorry I
cannot remember exactly.

Q: You remember exactly what he did, but you don't
remember what you told someone about it?

A: I told him that he hit me.

Q: You're sure about that?

A: I—I think so, ma'am. I quite cannot tell you if I
say that, or not, or if I put it in another words, or if he
beat me up, or if he hit me, or if he slap me, or if he
kick me. I cannot remember.

Q: I'll just move on. Now, you said that that same

summer, you and a friend of yours, and Todd, and John, went to the beach?

A: Yes, ma'am.

Q: You said that John got very upset because someone whistled at you and your friend?

A: Yes, ma'am.

Q: So he pulled you by the hair and made you come back home?

A: Yes, ma'am.

Q: And he beat you up in the car?

A: Yes, ma'am; yes.

Q: Isn't it true, Mrs. Bobbitt, that what actually happened was you ran out of money Saturday afternoon, so the four of you decided to come back early?

A: No, ma'am; no. We have money enough to spend for the weekend. Because it was a long weekend we have enough money, ma'am.

Q: In November of 1989 you said that his parents came for Thanksgiving.

A: Yes, ma'am, they did; yes.

Q: And you said that you were taken by surprise. You did not know they were coming?

A: Right, yes, ma'am; that happened.

Q: You had not talked to his mother on the phone, beforehand, about them coming?

A: No, ma'am, no; they surprised me.

Q: And you said, I think on direct examination, that you felt bad because you didn't have a turkey?

A: No, ma'am. I wasn't prepare. I was not prepare, and I have no food in the house.

Q: Mrs. Bobbitt, didn't you talk to John's mother beforehand, about them coming down for Thanksgiving?

A: No, ma'am, I do not talk to her, no ma'am. No.

Q: Didn't they bring a turkey and all the other Thanksgiving food with them, when they came?

A: I think they went and buy the turkey at the supermarket, yes, because I wasn't prepare, ma'am.

Q: You don't remember them coming in with the food?

A: No, ma'am; I don't remember that, no.

Q: Now, in 1990 you moved to Pine Street. Is that right?

A: Yes, ma'am. Yes.

Q: You said you had some concerns about the house because you thought the house was too expensive? Isn't that right?

A: Yes, ma'am; yes, yes.

Q: And you said that you were working six days a week.

A: I was trying to work more than that, ma'am, yes, but I was working Monday through Saturday.

A: And, in fact, you said that you were working to try to make sure that you could make the mortgage payment, since you were bringing in most of the money. Is that right?

A: Yes, ma'am, yes, I did, yes.

Q: And that was the time when some of this physical abuse happened. Isn't that right?

A: Yes, yes, ma'am, yes.

Q: That is also the time when you were taking some supplies from your employer, that you stole from her, weren't you?

A: Yes, ma'am. I did that; yes, ma'am.

Q: You did, and John found out about that, didn't he?

A: No, I show it to him, ma'am.

Q: And he was very upset about that, wasn't he?

A: Yes.

Q: And he insisted that you take that back to Mrs. Bisutti, didn't he?

A: No, he did not insist, but I told him that I was going to take this to Mrs. Bisutti because—because it belonged to her.

Q: You knew it belonged to her when you took it, didn't you, ma'am?

A: Yes, yes, ma'am; I did know that, yes.

Q: And he said that he thought you should return it to Mrs. Bisutti, didn't he?

A: He did not say that, ma'am. I took it—me. It was me who took it.

Q: He went with you when you took it back, didn't he?

A: Yeah, he went with me. Yes, ma'am.

Q: You talked a lot yesterday about a Thanksgiving fight that you had when your mother was here, visiting.

A: Yes, ma'am.

Q: And that was the fight about whether you were going to watch the parade or the football game?

A: Yes, ma'am; it was, yes.

Q: Did you think—were they on at the same time?

A: Yes, ma'am; it was.

Q: And you switched the TV from the football game to the parade?

A: Yes, ma'am.

Q: And that made John angry, didn't it?

A: Yeah, he wanted to watch the football game, ma'am.

Q: And you were angry that he wouldn't let your mother watch the parade, weren't you?

A: I didn't understand why he did that to my mom, that's what I thought.

Q: And that made you mad, didn't it?

A: That made me feel uncomfortable for my mother, 'cause she was the guest.

Q: You were embarrassed about your husband, weren't you?

A: I didn't know. I had no idea how the way he was acting, ma'am.

Q: And you weren't very happy about it, were you?

A: No, I wasn't very happy because he disconnect—he took the antenna.

Q: So he maybe unscrewed a cable on the back of the—

A: No, ma'am, he took—he broke the antenna and the TV was a static.

Q: When he went outside, did you know he was going to do that?

A: He just went outside. I have no idea what he was doing, what he was going to do, ma'am.

Q: And after he went outside you locked the door in back of him?

A: No, ma'am. I was cooking with my mother, in the kitchen.

Q: Well, the door was locked in back of him, wasn't it?

A: The door was lock in the back, yes, ma'am, but he leave from the front door.

Q: And then you locked the front door, right?

A: No, ma'am, I did not lock any doors.

Q: So he could have come back in the front door, but instead, he went and broke down the back door?

A: Ma'am, we always keep our back door lock—lock, and the wind—the wind, I think, was the one who close the door, and sometimes we have a knob that is—you can open, but if it close, the door is locked, so you can't—

Q: You didn't lock him out because you were angry with him?

A: No, ma'am; I did not lock him out, no.

Q: And then, he did not have Thanksgiving dinner with you, right?

A: He kicked the door, and he did not have the Thanksgiving dinner with us because the TV was static, and he would not watch the football game.

Q: And then you went to leave with your mother. Is that right?

A: I was having dinner with my mother and we call him for dinner, but he would not come out, and he did something from the kitchen, and then he went back to the bedroom.

Q: And then there was a fight about the car. Isn't that right?

A: We wanted to leave. We wanted to watch a movie, so I invite my mother to go and see the movie because since we didn't have TV, we—I wanted to do something with her, and he saw us, the two of us, putting our jackets, and we were ready to leave.

Q: Let me make the question a little more narrow, please.

A: Okay.

Q: He got into his car, and you tried to grab his arm, didn't you?

A: No, ma'am. I was looking for my car key. He took my car key. He would not let me and my mother go to the movies.

Q: You never grabbed his arm as he was trying to back out?

A: No, ma'am. He grabbed my arm and twist it.

Q: He grabbed your arm as he was driving?

A: Yes.

Q: Weren't you, in fact, trying to grab him, and he drove across the neighbor's lawn?

A: No, ma'am.

Q: He never drove across the neighbor's lawn?

A: I think he drove, but not across. I don't know how long he drove at the neighbor's.

Q: And you called his supervisor at the Marine Corps, and you called the Marine Corps, and you told them about this, didn't you?

A: I called some number, but I didn't have no idea who I was calling. I was crying after he knocked me down, and I was just crying.

Q: You were upset and angered, weren't you?

A: I didn't understand why my husband did this to me on front my mother.

Q: And so you called and you told the supervisor about that?

A: I called somebody, and I tell what happened.

Q: Because you were thinking you wanted some help, right?

A: Yeah, I think so; yes.

Q: And then there was another fight at the Beltrans' you said about a Christmas present?

A: Yes, ma'am; yes. My Christmas present.

Q: You said, I think, in answer to one of your lawyer's questions, that he gave you a present and there were a lot of gentlemen around?

A: Yes, it was everybody, even his family and people.

Q: Well, who was there from his family, Mrs. Bobbitt?

A: From his family it was his cousin, Todd; his cousin, Joshua; his mother and father.

Q: And they all saw you open this present?

A: No, I—that wasn't with them. They were talking to somebody else, but in the living room—in the dining room, there were more different people.

Q: Were any of these people in the kitchen where you opened the present?

A: No his family. His family was in the living room. We were in the dining room.

Q: You said that his brother, Brett, came to stay with you?

A: Yes; yes, ma'am.

Q: How long did he stay with you?

A: I have no idea, ma'am.

Q: I thought you said that he stayed for about two months, on your direct examination.

A: I thought he was maybe a month and a half, or two months. That's what I thought. I'm not sure.

Q: You have no idea, or do you think it might be two months?

A: I couldn't remember exactly long he was.

Q: If I told you that he was there for less than two weeks, would that surprise you? Does that refresh your recollection?

A: No, he was more than two weeks. I knew he was more than two weeks, ma'am.

Q: He saw you and John having some fights, didn't he?

A: I don't know. I don't remember he saw us having some fights, no.

Q: You didn't fight, at all, in front of his brother?

A: No, no.

Q: You didn't take the phone jack out of the wall when you thought he was talking to—

A: No, ma'am; no, I did not do that.

Q: Let me finish my question before you deny it.

A: Okay.

Q: You never took the phone jack out of the wall, when you thought he was talking to his mother for too long?

A: No, ma'am. No, I did not do that, no.

Q: Now, in February of 1991, you and John had another fight, and you called 911; right?

A: There are so many incidents that we call 911.

Q: That was the one where John was arrested.

A: Yes, ma'am.

Q: And then, you were arrested the next day? Is that right?

A: Yes, yes.

Q: And then you went to Court together, didn't you?

A: Yes, yes.

Q: And it was in this Courthouse, right?

A: I don't remember if it's this room, but I think it was downstairs.

Q: This building, though?

A: This building.

Q: And you and John came to Court together?

A: Yes.

Q: Because you had made up after your fight?

A: I don't understand your question, ma'am.

Q: You weren't in a fight when you came to Court, were you?

A: No, they told me today I have to come to the Court, ma'am.

Q: Right. You and John came to Court together. You were living together then, right?

A: Yes, yes.

Q: And you were getting along pretty well?

A: No, I was—I was sleeping in the other room. He was sleeping in another room.

Q: And when you came to Court, you thought those charges were dropped, didn't you?

A: I have no idea what was going on, but I came to Court because I was—I was told that I have to come to Court.

Q: And after you got to Court, you don't know what happened?

A: Not really, no. I have no idea what happened. I think they—they told us that my charge was drop.

Q: And did you think you had decided to drop his charge, too?

A: I don't remember that. The Judge was the one who drop it.

Q: I'm sorry?

A: The Judge was the one who decide that, I think. (Whereupon, counsel approached the witness.)

Q: Do you remember the Protective Order that you got on Monday?

A: Yes, yes.

Q: And is this your handwriting?

A: Yes.

Q: Would you read, starting with, "Have"—right here (indicating) "Have any other cases"?

A: "Have any other cases involving the defendant been filed in a Virginia Court? If so, explain. On 1991 we went to Court and I decide to drop the case."—I think—

Q: You think what?

A: I think that's what I thought it happened.

Q: Start with, "Have," if you would, please.

Q: So you thought you had decided to drop the case? Is that right?

A: That's what I thought it happens, ma'am; yes.

Q: You just told us, though, that you didn't know what happened. Is that right?

A: I'm not sure. I am not sure if I have to do it, or the Judge have to do it, but I said that, yes.

Q: In the summer of 1991, you and Bunny, and Sherry and John, went to Kings Dominion, didn't you?

A: We went to Kings Dominion, yes.

Q: And that was with his brother and sister-in-law?

A: Yes, ma'am.

Q: And you and John had a fight there, didn't you? You became angry with him, weren't you?

A: No, ma'am. I don't remember the fight; no ma'am, no.

Q: You don't remember being angry with John and going back to the parking lot?

A: We were ready to leave. That's why we came back to the parking lot, but we weren't fighting. No, ma'am.

Q: You didn't go back to the parking lot earlier?

A: No, ma'am, we didn't. I didn't.

Q: You didn't have any fight with John, at all, that day?

A: No, we didn't. I don't recall that.

Q: You never—you never slapped him, or hit him?

A: No, ma'am; no.

Q: You weren't jealous of him, at all, that day?

A: No, ma'am. We have a good time, ma'am, at Kings Dominion. It was fine.

Q: You remember a very good time that day?

A: Yes, it was very fun.

Q: And his brother and sister-in-law, they came down from Delaware, right?

A: Yes, ma'am; yes.

Q: And you always got along, particularly with Sherry?

A: Yes.

Q: You and Sherry were friends?

A: Yes, yes.

Q: And they were staying at your house that night, weren't they?

A: Yes; yes, ma'am.

Q: And you became angry about the fact that they were there, and told them they should leave, didn't you?

A: No, ma'am; no.

Q: You never did that?

A: No, they decide to leave because Sherry's husband is in the Navy, and they have to—he have to go to work the next day, and he have to wake up early.

Q: So, what time did they leave?

A: I don't remember, but it was—I really don't remember what time they left. I think it was dark.

Q: But they didn't leave because you told them to leave?

A: No, ma'am. I never told them to leave; never.

Q: And you never told John that you did something awful by telling them to leave?

A: No, ma'am; no. I did not tell them to leave, no.

Q: Well, that's when John left you, isn't it?

A: No. He didn't left me. He was still there.

Q: He didn't leave and go up to Delaware, right after his brother?

A: No, no; he did not.

Q: That summer he left for a couple of weeks, after a fight. Isn't that right?

A: I think he leave only for a week.

Q: And he went back to Niagara Falls?

A: No, that was a month and a half that he left me to go to Niagara Falls.

Q: And that was after a fight?

A: That was after a confrontation that he—he—I told him that he was going out with somebody, and we still marry, and I think he just left because I say that, yes.

Q: He went up to Niagara Falls?

A: Yes.

Q: And you called up there a lot, didn't you?

A: I called; yes, ma'am.

Q: And you called, not just called, but you called a lot, didn't you?

A: I don't quite remember how much I called, but I did call.

Q: If I told you you called about sixty times in a couple week period, does that sound like it might be right?

A: I'm not sure, ma'am. I never count the calls. I'm sorry. I don't remember that many calls.

Q: You don't remember that many?

A: No, I don't remember.

Q: And when you would call, you would talk to people in John's family, and ask them to send him back, wouldn't you?

A: No, ma'am. I was asking the family to please send money back; and how—he also called collect to my work.

Q: You never asked his mother to send him back, saying, you are his mother, you can send him back?

A: No, ma'am. I don't remember that. What I told his mother was, that I can't handle so many bills because my house were about to be repossessed, and I told them to please send me some money, because I couldn't pay the bill payments, and collectors are calling me.

Q: So you didn't want him to come back, you just wanted some money? Is that right?

A: I—I talked to him, and I said, "If you want to come back to help—to fix our marriage, then you know where I am." I talked to him, yes.

Q: And you didn't have very much money at all?

A: No, ma'am; no.

Q: But you sent him a bus ticket to come back?

A: I don't remember the bus ticket.

Q: How did he get back? Do you know? Do you remember that?

A: He came with the bus, but I don't remember the bus ticket.

Q: You don't remember whether you bought the bus ticket?

A: No, and he called me from the bus station to come and pick him up, because he was there. As a matter of fact, he surprised me.

Q: During that time that he was gone, after he had been gone for about a month, you called 911 again, didn't you?

A: I don't remember when I called, but I think I called.

Q: You called 911, at some time when he had been gone for a while, didn't you?

A: I'm not sure about that, ma'am. I did so many calls to 911.

Q: Did you ever call 911 when he wasn't living with you, Mrs. Bobbitt?

A: I—I'm not sure.

Q: You wouldn't have had any reason to call 911 when he wasn't living with you, would you?

A: I might feel sick or something. I don't know why—

Q: Sure, but I mean you would not have any reason to call 911, with a complaint about him, if he wasn't there, would you?

A: I—I'm not sure, ma'am. I might call 911 because I was feeling so sick.

Q: Did you ever call 911 because you were "feeling so sick"?

A: I might.

Q: Do you remember doing that?

A: I don't quite remember doing it. I'm not sure, ma'am. I couldn't tell you.

Q: Do you remember calling 911 the summer of 1991, after he had been gone for a month, and complaining about him?

A: No, I don't remember that; no.

Q: You don't remember that?

A: No, I don't remember. I might call 911, but I really don't remember the date of the calls.

Q: Now, after he came back, you separated in October of 1991. Is that right?

A: We were separated—

Q: That was your separation for a year?

A: Yes, yes, ma'am; yes.

Q: And that was the separation that you said that you went to your friends and showed them some bruises on you, so you could get pictures taken so you could get your Immigration status changed, or get reclassified?

A: No, he beat me up, ma'am, and I didn't know what to do, so I—I called my—

Q: And that is why you separated for a year?

A: Yeah, he—he hit me, and then he left.

Q: Didn't you separate for a year because he found

out you had stolen $7,200 from your employer and he was tired of you stealing?

A: No, ma'am. I confronted him because he was seeing a lady, and I said, "This is going again. I don't think you should be here, so please"—

Q: You thought that he was having an affair, or that he was seeing a lady?

A: Yeah, he was seeing a lady. The lady came to my shop.

Q: And that's why you were upset, or angry?

A: I was disappointed, and I—I told him to—

Q: Come on, Mrs. Bobbitt; you were more than just "disappointed," weren't you?

A: I probably was mad, yes.

Q: You're saying that's the reason that you separated for the year?

A: I confronted him and then he—he said that I don't have to tell him what to do, and then he beat me up, and then he left.

Q: Do you remember talking to him, at all, about the $7,200 you stole from Janna?

A: Yes, he knew. As a matter of fact, I told Janna to please, bring my husband, because I want to tell him that in front of her.

Q: He wasn't very happy about that, was he?

A: No, I guess not.

Q: He wasn't very happy about your stealing, was he?

A: No, I guess not. I wasn't either.

Q: And he wasn't happy about another incident in which you stole, was he?

A: (No response.)

Q: At Nordstrom's?

A: Right, right.

Q: And he told you he wasn't happy about that stealing?

A: No, I told him that.

Q: And after he left for the year, you would call his parents, up in Niagara Falls, wouldn't you?

A: I don't remember that.

Q: You don't remember calling them?

A: I probably remember calling him.

Q: You don't remember talking to his mother?

A: I talked to his mother, yes, asking for money.

Q: Did you tell his mother if he would come back you would stop the stealing?

A: No, I do not remember that, ma'am; no.

Q: Did you ever talk to his mother about your stealing?

A: Yes, I told him—I told her that.

Q: And you told her you were sorry about the stealing, and you were going to stop, didn't you?

A: Yes, ma'am. I was so sorry. I knew I did wrong.

Q: And you told John that you were sorry about the stealing, and you were going to stop, didn't you?

A: Yeah, I did say that.

Q: He told you if you would stop stealing he would be willing to give your marriage another try, didn't he?

A: No, that wasn't like that, ma'am. I—I stole because I have a lot—a lot of payments to do, and I couldn't handle by myself, the payments. And I—I was desperate for money, but I knew it was wrong, and I just needed to pay the bills, to keep my marriage together.

Q: But what you stole from Nordstrom's didn't have anything to do with paying the bills, did it?

A: I stole from Nordstrom because he didn't like my dresses, and he always tell me that I was ugly, and I wanted to be pretty for him.

Q: So it was sort of his fault that you stole?

A: I felt guilty. I know I never do that. That's what I

get caught. That was my first time in stealing. I never do that and—

Q: Well, it wasn't really your first time stealing, that was your first time stealing from a store.

A: Yes.

Q: You had stolen from Janna?

A: Yes, yes.

Q: It was the first time you got caught stealing from a store?

A: Yes. I know I did wrong.

Q: After he came back—for the year that he was gone, you lived with Mrs. Castro?

A: Yes.

Q: And John came back at one point, and surprised you for your birthday. Is that right? But he was late for your birthday?

A: I don't know, but he came back in May.

Q: In May?

A: Yes.

Q: Your birthday is in May?

A: Yes.

Q: And it was a little bit after your birthday?

A: I don't remember, but he came in May.

Q: And you talked about getting back together, right?

A: He wanted to live in Mrs. Castro's house, and yes, we did talk about going back together, yes.

Q: Both of you wanted the marriage to work, didn't you?

A: Yeah, I don't [know] how much he wanted it, and I believe him he wanted to get my marriage work—our marriage work.

Q: And you had talked to a minister, Barry White. About counseling, and making your marriage work, didn't you?

A: Yes, yes.

Q: You and John, both?

A: Yes, we both; yes.

Q: And you had told Barry White about the stealing problems?

A: Yes, I did, because it was a confession because I knew I did wrong. My mother never taught me that, and I did it. I was desperate to pay the bills. I didn't have no food in the refrigerator, and I was—I was desperate, and I was so lucky I have a boss like that, because she understood my situation.

Q: She's been very good to you, hasn't she?

A: She has been very good to me; yes, ma'am.

Q: In May of this year, when you and John were having problems, and you told her that things were bad with John she said she would open her home to you?

A: Yes, ma'am; she has.

Q: And you knew she would because you had lived with her before, right?

A: Yes, ma'am; yes.

Q: And you've also lived with Mrs. Castro? You lived with Mrs. Castro for the year you were separated?

A: Yes, yes.

Q: And she's also been very good to you?

A: Yes, very good, ma'am; yes.

Q: When John first came back, you were happy to see him, weren't you?

A: Yes, I was happy to see him, yes.

Q: And you moved in with the Beltrans?

A: Yes.

Q: And now you talked some about a fight that you had this past New Year's Eve.

A: Yes.

Q: John and his friends came to visit?

A: Yes.

Q: And they were staying in the basement, weren't they?

A: Yes, yes.

Q: And you and John had a room upstairs, didn't you?

A: Yes.

Q: And they went out New Year's Eve, and you had to work?

A: Yes.

Q: And they stayed out until the early morning hours?

A: Yes.

Q: And you weren't very happy about that, were you?

A: I was sad because, like I said, I wanted to—to have the loved one next to me for twelve o'clock, so I can hug.

Q: And you were a little angry that your husband was out with his friends, instead of with you, weren't you?

A: I would be say more sad, because I was also crying.

Q: And you were sad when he came home?

A: I was—I didn't want to see him, because he promised me to pick me up from the work, and he never did it.

Q: And you said that was one—that was the time that he raped you?

A: No, he wanted to have sex, and I didn't let him, so I push him back, and so he—he fell to the bed, and I could see his face, and I knew he was going to do something, so I left the room and I went to the basement.

Q: And that's where his friends were, right?

A: That's where his friends were.

Q: And you say that he followed you into the basement?

A: Yes.

Q: He pulled your hair and slapped you, and hit you, and punched you in the chest?

A: Yes, ma'am; yes, he did.

Q: And they all saw that?

A: Yes, ma'am; yes, they did.

Q: And you were yelling?

A: Yes, ma'am. That's when I wake up Mrs. Beltran and Mr. Beltran.

Q: And Mr. and Mrs. Beltran came down, and she separated you and John, didn't she?

A: Yes, she—she said, "Stop."

Q: Mrs. Bobbitt, didn't you go downstairs to tell his friends that they should leave, they shouldn't be here?

A: No, ma'am; no. They hear my scream when John kick me and I fell to the bed of Robert.

Q: And they didn't do anything?

A: No, ma'am; they were sitting there. They turned the light on and they were looking at—

Q: They were just sitting there, watching him beat you up?

(Whereupon, the witness is in tears.)

THE WITNESS: Yes, ma'am; they did not do anything.

Q: Now, this April you moved to your own apartment—you and John moved to your own apartment. That apartment, right there (indicating). Is that right?

A: Yes, ma'am.

Q: And it was in May that you learned that Robbie was going to come for a visit?

A: Yes.

Q: And you weren't very happy about Robbie coming down to stay, were you?

A: I thought he was only going to come for two weeks.

It's okay if he come and visit for two weeks, but not to live with us.

Q: Well, you had talked about getting a divorce before, didn't you?

A: No, ma'am; we talk when I found out that Robert is going to be here, to live with us.

Q: And when was that?

A: I think that was in May.

Q: In May?

A: Yes, I think so.

Q: Were things very bad, all through May and June, with you and John?

A: No, it wasn't. No, it wasn't that bad. I felt we were going to have a nice place, think we have our own place, a nice family and a nice marriage.

Q: After you heard Robbie was coming down, were you angry with John, or upset with John, or sad with John?

A: I was upset with Robert, not with John.

Q: And you and John had talked about getting a divorce in May, and in June?

A: No.

Q: Off and on?

A: I said if your friend—if your friend wanted to stay here to live, then I think it's time for me to—for you to get away, to be separate, and have a divorce. Yes, I say that.

Q: And you went to see a lawyer about how to do that, didn't you?

A: Yeah, yes.

Q: And you were thinking pretty seriously about getting a divorce and going somewhere else, or having him go somewhere else?

A: Yes.

Q: And your lawyer told you that if you could get some of John's statements on tape, that would be a good thing to do?

A: Actually, he was asking—I asked if I could take my husband for mental cruelty, because I explained to her that he was insulting me, and he was putting me down all the time, and he was hurting me, and so he said, "Did you see anything? I mean, do you have anybody that heard those things?" I say, "No."

Q: You didn't tell her about the pictures that Mrs. Castro had taken?

A: No, it's hard for me just to come and say that.

Q: So then—so you decided on your own to get a tape recorder, and—

A: I decided on my own, yes.

Q: So you thought that would be a good way to get some of this mental cruelty on tape?

A: Yes, and I wanted to show Mrs. Castro and my friend, Janna, that, too.

Q: Well, Mrs. Castro and your friend, Janna, believed you, didn't they?

A: I think so, but I wanted to show them to them. I just want to show that.

Q: In fact, when you talked to Janna in June, she suggested that you move out, and get a place—get an apartment with a couple of other women, didn't she?

A: Yes.

Q: She was giving you some good suggestions, wasn't she?

A: Yes.

Q: The end of May you and John went to Luray Caverns for a day, didn't you?

A: Yes.

Q: And you had a good time?

A: Yeah, I wanted to go there; yes, ma'am.

Q: You wanted to go, and so he said he would take you?

A: No, he would follow me. He went with me. He didn't want to go. I want to go.

Q: But he went with you?

A: But he came with me, yes. I didn't want to take him, but he came anyway.

Q: And then you went out to dinner afterward?

A: No, I don't remember that, ma'am.

Q: You don't remember doing that?

A: No, no.

Q: When you would have fights with John, when you were married, you told this jury about a number of times when he would hit you, and kick—and beat you, and rape you?

A: Yes.

Q: And he used Marine torture techniques on you?

A: Yes, yes.

Q: You hit him some, too, didn't you, Mrs. Bobbitt?

A: No, ma'am; I did not.

Q: And you scratched him?

A: No, I tried, but I couldn't because I was so—my—my arms were twisted, where he applied the Marine techniques on, and I couldn't move.

Q: And you never scratched him?

A: I did scratch him, yes. Only one time, yes.

Q: Only one time you scratched him?

A: Yes, in his face; yes, I did.

Q: And that was down the side of his face; isn't that right?

A: I think so, yes. The side of the face, yes.

Q: And you pretty angry the time you did that, weren't you?

A: I wanted him to stop raping me, ma'am, because he was raping me that time. I wanted him out of my body, out of—away from me. I scratch him, yes, because I didn't want him to rape me any more.

(Whereupon, the witness is in tears.)

BY MS. O'BRIEN:

Q: When you had this tape recorder in your purse and he found the tape, he was mad about that, wasn't he?

A: Yeah, that's the time that he raped me and I scratch him.

Q: And you were mad because he went in your purse, weren't you?

A: Yes, yes.

Q: And he took the tape, and you came after him, trying to get the tape back from him?

A: No, he wanted to money. Every time he want to go to my purse for money, and he found the tape in the purse, and he play and it's his own voice. And then he asked me what was that, and I said, "Nothing." And then,

Q: Then you said—give me my purse, right?

A: Yes, I think—

Q: And then he took the tape, right?

A: Yes.

Q: And you came after him, trying to get that tape back from him, didn't you?

A: Yeah, yes. I didn't want him to see. That was my only thing to show the attorney.

Q: And you were pulling at him, trying to get the tape back from him, and he flushed the tape down the toilet, didn't he?

A: He break the tape and flush it down the toilet, yes.

Q: And that was when you scratched him?

A: No, he raped me.

Q: He raped you and then you scratched him?

A: And then I scratch him, yes. I didn't know I was scratching, I just pull him away, and then I grab his face, obviously, and I scratch him. I just wanted him to be away from me.

(Whereupon, the witness is in tears.)

(Pause)

BY MS. O'BRIEN:

Q: Mrs. Bobbitt, the Friday before you cut off your husband's penis you were at work, and you couldn't work because your hands were—you said your hands were cramping, right?

A: Yes, I couldn't open my hand.

Q: And you were very upset, so you called Mrs. Castro, and then, after you talked to Mrs. Castro, you went to see Dr. Inman?

A: Yes.

Q: And why did you go see Dr. Inman?

A: Because I could not work, ma'am. I—my hands were shaking, and I felt like I was going to faint or something. I really feel sick.

Q: You went to her for some help, didn't you?

A: Yes, I did.

Q: And did Mrs. Castro suggest that you go to Dr. Inman, or were you thinking that on your own?

A: No, I was just—I needed the help so I went to the doctor.

A: Did you know when Robbie was coming at that time?

A: No, not exactly. I didn't know.

Q: When did you find out when Robbie was coming?

A: He surprise us, he just knock at the door.

Q: You didn't know that he was coming on Sunday?

A: No, no, ma'am. I had no idea he was coming on Sunday.

Q: When you went to see Dr. Inman, she helped take care of your physical problems, didn't she?

A: Yes.

Q: She showed you how to breathe into a bag?

A: Yes.

Q: And you told her that you were having problems with your husband, too; didn't you?

A: Yes.

Q: And did you say that she called the Protective Service?

A: Yes.

Q: Didn't she give you the number, and you called?

A: She called somebody, and then she give me the number, and then she make me call. Somebody call. I can't remember how it happened, but I talk to the lady that the service, some center, woman center, or something.

Q: And she explained to you about getting a Protective Order?

A: Yes, she did.

Q: And that seemed like a good idea to you?

A: Yes, I didn't want my husband to rape me any more, and to follow me.

Q: And you wanted him out of your house, didn't you?

A: Yes.

Q: After she told you about getting a Protective Order, did Dr. Inman make sure that you felt safe going home that night?

A: I don't know, ma'am. I just—

Q: Did she ask you any questions about that?

A: No, she didn't. I—she just give me that Protective Order, and—the phone number, and I called.

Q: And you were—after you went to see Dr. Inman, you were able to go back to work, that day. Is that right?

A: No, I still shake, ma'am.

Q: You didn't go back to work, at all, on Friday?

A: She never give me any pills or something for the shake.

Q: So what did you do on Friday?

A: I—I was at work.

Q: After you went to see Dr. Inman?

A: I came back to work.

Q: And then Friday night you went home?

A: Yes.

Q: And was your husband home at that time?

A: No, I don't know where he was.

Q: Did something happen Friday night?

A: Yes.

Q: What happened Friday night?

A: He wanted to have sex, and he grabbed me. He forced me into sex. That happened in the hall.

Q: Did he say anything to you then?

A: He just wanted to have sex, and I told him, "No."

Q: You told him you didn't want to?

A: Right, I told him, "I don't want to have sex, no."

Q: Did he say anything about forced sex?

A: Yes, he told me, like he also said, the forced sex excites him.

Q: Were those the words he used, Mrs. Bobbitt? "Forced sex excites me"?

A: Yes, ma'am; those are his words, yes.

Q: And that was Friday night?

A: And he only didn't say those words, he said it before, too. He said that the forced sex excites me—excites him and it was his foreplay, that's what he said.

Q: He said that Friday night?

A: He said forced sex excites him, on Friday night.

Q: And after that, did you sleep in the same bed together?

A: No, I didn't want to see him.

Q: Did you get up Saturday and go to work?

A: Yeah.

Q: Were you able to work on Saturday?

A: No, I was still shake and stuff. I—I—it wasn't that bad, but I was still shaking.

Q: So you did work?

A: Yes, I did work. I have to work. I needed money.

Q: And you were making plans to leave then, weren't you?

A: My bags—my—my clothes were packed in boxes.

Q: You were packing your clothes up to leave?

A: Yeah, but that was back in May, too.

Q: You were doing some of that that weekend, too; weren't you, Mrs. Bobbitt?

A: No, I wasn't. I wasn't. They were already packed. I wasn't that weekend; no, I did not.

Q: You know some of the neighbors around you, don't you? A lady named Diane Hall, right?

A: Yes, yes.

Q: And you talked to Diane Hall that weekend, and you told [her] that you were moving out, didn't you?

A: I don't remember exactly when I told Diane, but I said, "I need to find a place."

Q: And she told you you were welcome to store your boxes at her house, didn't she?

A: Yes, ma'am; she offered me her house, yes.

Q: In fact, you had dinner with her. Was it Saturday night?

A: I don't remember, but I had dinner with her, ma'am.

Q: Over that weekend?

A: I don't remember exactly, but I had dinner with her.

Q: And when you and John were happier, did you socialize some with Diane Hall? Did you do some things with her; have dinner up in your apartment, or dinner down in her apartment?

A: Yes, we were talking, yes.

Q: You were fairly good friends?

A: No, we were just neighbors, ma'am.

Q: She offered you a place to stay, didn't she, Mrs. Bobbitt?

A: Yes, ma'am, I think—yes.

Q: And that weekend that Robbie came, she offered you a place to stay, didn't she?

A: Yes. She wasn't there. She was not there, ma'am. She wasn't there, no.

Q: You had dinner with her right around that time, and you told her you were leaving, and she told you you could put some boxes in her apartment?

A: Yes, she said that; yes.

Q: And she also said you could stay in her apartment, didn't she?

A: I think so, yes; but her apartment—she was living with a lot of people, ma'am.

Q: I understand that. Do you remember her telling you that you could come and stay with her, if you needed to?

A: I think so. I don't quite remember that, but maybe she offer me—yes, maybe. Yes, I—

Q: You don't remember it?

A: Not quite, but maybe she did. She's a good woman. She's a very nice lady, so I assume she did offer me that.

Q: But you don't have any specific memory?

A: No specific, ma'am.

Q: Saturday night, you and John slept in the same bed?

A: I came Saturday night from Father's Day with Mrs. Castro, we have at church, and I came back at one o'clock. Since the church party was finished at that time, I came back at one o'clock, and I—John was in the couch outside the living room, and I went to bed.

Q: And then he came and got into bed, didn't he?

A: Yeah, he came and got into bed, yes.

Q: And then Sunday morning you had sex, didn't you?

A: Yes, yes.

Q: And that was consensual, wasn't it?

A: Yes, it was, ma'am; yes.

Q: He did not rape you Sunday morning?

A: No, he did not, ma'am. No.

Q: And his friend, Robbie, came early Sunday afternoon, didn't he?

A: Yes, ma'am; yes.

Q: And you and John were still in bed, weren't you?

A: No, ma'am. I was fixing breakfast.

Q: You were fixing breakfast when Robbie got there?

A: Yes, I was fixing breakfast.

Q: You said that you were scared of Robbie, because you thought that John might say that the three of you should have sex together?

A: Yeah, he—John mentioned that before, before Robert came.

Q: Robert never made any advances to you, did he?

A: No, ma'am; he did not.

Q: Robert never did anything improper to you, did he?

A: No, ma'am; he did not.

Q: He was quiet, but he was courteous, wasn't he?

A: Yes.

Q: Now, when he got there—when Robert got there on Sunday, did you say to John, I need my privacy, or it's my house, too. I have the right to ask him for some privacy?

A: No, ma'am. I did not say that to him; no.

Q: Were you happy that Robert was there?

A: No.

Q: You did not want him to be there?

A: No, because he was going to live with us.

Q: You did not want him to live with you?

A: Have a vacation is not the same than live there permanently. Yes.

Q: I understand. You didn't want him there?

A: No more than two weeks, or three weeks. It's okay.

Q: John and Robert went down to the pool, didn't they?

A: I don't know where they go, ma'am. I have no idea.

Q: Later that afternoon you went down to the pool to get John, didn't you?

A: Yes, I was looking for my car keys, and I was thinking that maybe he—he hide my car keys, or something.

Q: Do you remember that clearly?

A: Yeah, yeah, I remember. I was looking for my keys; yes, ma'am, yes.

Q: You've thought a lot about what happened that

weekend, that Friday, Saturday, Sunday, Monday, Tuesday, the five days. You've thought a lot about it, haven't you?

A: I think so. I tried so hard, ma'am. Yes.

Q: And you've talked to a lot of people about that, haven't you?

A: I talked to my neighbors, yeah, ma'am; yes.

Q: You talked to your neighbors, you talked to your lawyer?

A: Yes.

Q: You've talked to me about it, haven't you?

A: Yes, I talked to you.

Q: And you talked to Police Officers about it, haven't you?

A: Yes.

Q: Detective Weintz and Sergeant Zinn?

A: Yes, I think so. I never talked to Sergeant Zinn; no, ma'am, but—

Q: But you talked to Detective Weintz?

A: Yes.

Q: And you testified about what happened that weekend, didn't you?

A: Yeah, I think so. Yeah.

Q: Sure, in Court.

A: Yes, yes.

Q: And you testified, specifically, about what happened Saturday, Sunday, Monday, and Tuesday; didn't you?

A: I think so, yes. I tried my best, ma'am. Yes.

Q: And you told the truth, right?

A: Yes, ma'am; yes.

Q: Do you remember testifying about two months ago?

A: Not quite, but I remember testifying; yes, ma'am,

but I don't remember exactly—exactly what I said, ma'am.

Q: Do you remember being asked about whether or not you went down to the pool, at all, on Sunday?

A: I think so.

Q: You were asked a lot of questions about that, weren't you?

A: I was asked a lot of questions; yes, ma'am.

Q: I asked you about whether you went to the pool, and another lawyer asked you about whether you went to the pool.

A: I think so, ma'am; yes. You asked me, yes. Yes.

Q: Do you remember what you said?

A: I—I went to the pool, yes.

Q: Do you remember saying you didn't go out to the pool, at all, on Sunday?

A: I didn't remember at that time.

Q: Oh, you remember now, but you didn't remember two months ago, that back in June you went down to the pool?

A: I was looking for my car keys, ma'am. That's what I—

Q: My question is, you remember it now, but you didn't remember two months ago, what you did in June?

A: No, I—it's hard for me to remember specific things, ma'am. So many things happened.

Q: You've done a wonderful job of remembering specific things for a day and half. I'm asking you about what happened in June, that Sunday in June, and you're saying, now, that you went down to the pool in the afternoon?

A: That's what I think I did. Yes, I did. Yes.

Q: You're sure about that?

A: Yes, I went and ask John for my car keys, yes.

Q: And two months ago you said you didn't go down to the pool.

A: No, ma'am. I—I didn't remember at that time, ma'am. I'm sorry. I'm so sorry.

Q: Do you remember John coming back upstairs to the apartment with you, ma'am?

A: He help me look the keys; yes, ma'am.

Q: He came back up to the apartment with you?

A: Yes, ma'am.

Q: And you remember having sex with him, again, when he came back to the apartment?

A: No, ma'am. Then he went back—right back, because his friend was in the pool, he said.

Q: So you deny that you had sex a second time, on Sunday?

A: Yes, ma'am. We only have one time on Sunday, yes, yes.

Q: Where did you go on Sunday evening?

A: I was with my friend.

Q: Or did you stay in the apartment?

A: No, I was with my friend, Diane, I think. I think I was with her.

Q: And that was when Diane said to you that you could stay in her apartment if you needed to?

A: I think so, yes. I think we also have dinner.

Q: Monday was your day off, right?

A: Yes; yes, ma'am.

Q: And Monday morning you decided to go and get a Protective Order, didn't you?

A: Yes, ma'am; yes.

Q: And you came to this Courthouse at this area, to get a Protective Order, didn't you?

A: Not to this building, but the other building; yes, ma'am.

Q: And you talked with Stephen Rouke?

A: I don't know his name, but I talked to a gentleman; yes, ma'am.

Q: And he was very kind and you felt that you could tell him the truth?

A: He was very kind, ma'am. Yes.

Q: And he helped you fill out the paperwork that is in evidence?

A: Yes, ma'am; yes.

(Whereupon, counsel approached the witness.)

BY MS. O'BRIEN:

Q: Is this your writing, or his?

A: This is his handwriting.

Q: Is that what you told him, though? Go ahead and take a look at it.

A: Yes, ma'am. Yes, yes.

Q: And then you filled out this part down here, right (indicating)?

A: Yes.

Q: Now, he asked you to tell him about what your husband had done to you; isn't that right?

A: Yes, yes.

Q: He asked you to tell him about what he had done to you most recently. Is that right?

A: Yeah, I think so, yes. Yes.

Q: And then you told him and then he wrote down on those papers, that you said was his handwriting, what you told him?

A: Right, yes.

Q: And this is on Monday, Monday morning, right?

A: Yes, yes.

Q: This is after your husband had raped you Friday night?

A: Yes, ma'am; yes.

Q: There is nothing in any of those papers about him raping you Friday night, is there?

A: No, ma'am. I was very embarrassed to tell him that.

Q: Mrs. Bobbitt, you weren't embarrassed at the end of it, to tell him that he had raped you in the past, were you?

A: Yes, but it's really hard. Even I have a hard time with you. Remember when we were asking—when you asking me a long time ago about the anal sex, it was really, really hard for me to explain, even to you, ma'am.

Q: So you didn't think that you could explain it to him?

A: No, ma'am; no. No. He was—I'm really scared of gentlemen. No. It's so difficult for me to—

Q: But you explained that he had raped you, you just got the day wrong?

A: No, ma'am. He did it. He did it, but I did not tell anybody else what he did, ma'am. I'm sorry.

Q: And he asked you whether you felt safe going back there. Is that right?

A: I think so; yes, ma'am.

Q: And you told him you felt safe because John's friend Robbie was there. Is that right?

A: Yes, ma'am; I did say that. Yes, ma'am.

Q: But you understood that if this Protective Order was entered, then they would have to leave, and you would have the apartment. Isn't that right?

A: I quite don't understand. I just following the advice of Mrs. Castro and Dr. Inman, ma'am.

Q: What did you think was going to happen with the Protective Order?

A: I have no idea. I just want my husband not to follow me, because he threatened me to follow me, and have any kind of sex.

Q: This was the day after you had consensual sex with him once?

A: Yes, ma'am. I was still scared. Yes. I did let him do consensual sex because I did not want to feel like he was raping me again, no.

Q: But you didn't tell Mr. Rouke that you were scared. You told him you were not scared, right?

A: I said, "His friend is going to be there. Maybe his friend is going to entertain him."

Q: And he told you that you just had to wait for that to be typed up, and then it could be entered, didn't he?

A: Yes, yes.

Q: And you told him that you had lunch plans, didn't you?

A: Yes, I said that I did not want to be there anymore, ma'am. I was scared to be there, also.

Q: Well, did he do something to scare you?

A: No, ma'am, but I was so—He was very kind, a very nice person.

Q: And you had already told him all the hard things. But you decided that you didn't want to wait for that document to be typed up?

A: No, ma'am; because I was—I was very uncomfortable in there. I did not want to be there anymore.

Q: You thought that that document was going to help you, though, right; from what Dr. Inman and Mrs. Castro had said?

A: I think so. I didn't know what was going to happen. I just follow advices, ma'am. I'm sorry. I follow advices.

Q: And then you told him that you had to go to lunch, and he said that you could come back that afternoon. Is that right?

A: Yes, ma'am. He told me that I can come back that afternoon. Yes.

Q: And you said you couldn't come back, or you suggested you could come back that afternoon, or Tuesday?

A: Yes, I was—I didn't want to go back. I wasn't comfortable going back to him. I did not want to go back.

Q: But what you told him was that you had to work on Tuesday, and maybe you would come back on Wednesday?

A: Yes, I said that. I did say that.

Q: Tuesday morning you went to work, didn't you?

A: Yes, I did.

Q: And you were able to work all right on Tuesday?

A: I was—I feel—the shakes weren't there anymore, I think. It was okay.

Q: And you saw Mrs. Ella Jones in the morning?

A: Yes, ma'am; yes.

Q: And you told her Tuesday morning that your husband had raped you?

A: She told me that she hear scream, and she asked me why you were screaming, and I—I told her what happened. I said, "My husband beat me up and he raped me." That's what I said.

Q: You didn't know her very well, did you?

A: No, ma'am; I did not know her.

Q: But you felt like you could tell her that?

A: I felt like—yes, because she was worried for me, ma'am.

Q: And then, Tuesday night you came home, and you saw Ella Jones again, didn't you?

A: Yes, she was waiting for me in the balcony, or something.

Q: And her apartment is right underneath yours?

A: Yes, ma'am; yes.

Q: And you went up and talked to her for a fairly long time, right?

A: She invited me to her apartment, yes.

Q: And she was a very kind lady. Is that right?

A: A very kind lady; yes, ma'am.

Q: And you felt comfortable with her?

A: Yes, ma'am. I feel comfortable with her.

Q: And she told you, Mrs. Bobbitt, that you could stay there Tuesday night, didn't she?

A: Yes, but she's—with respect to her, I thought she was going to have something, because she carry a little oxygen, and I was afraid that she was going to do something, and I didn't want to feel responsible.

Q: Well, you said that you were scared that something might happen to her?

A: To her, yes.

Q: Well, you didn't think John was going to do anything to her, did you?

A: Maybe I thought that, too, ma'am, yes. I was scared more for the oxygen, for the state of Mrs. Ella.

Q: John had never hurt her before?

A: No.

Q: John didn't give you any reason to think that he would do anything to Mrs. Jones?

A: No, but he would hurt me, I thought.

Q: Tuesday morning, before you went to work, did you

go out into the living room and see a lot of clothes that were on the floor in the living room?

A: No, ma'am.

Q: Robbie was staying in the living room, wasn't he?

A: Tuesday morning?

Q: Yes, ma'am.

A: Oh, yes. I went—I went to work and I saw a lot of clothes in the living room.

Q: And you picked up some of those clothes because you didn't want to have all those clothes in your living room, didn't you?

A: It was all messy, ma'am, and I just pick up. Underwears, they were around, and socks, and everything was a mess, so I started picking things up, yes.

Q: And you picked up Robbie Johnston's wallet, too, didn't you?

A: The wallet was out there, too. Yes.

Q: And you took $100 from his wallet, didn't you?

A: The $100 was in there, too, so I saw the $100 and I took it, yes.

Q: It was inside the wallet?

A: No, it was outside the wallet. It was—I could look at it. I could look the $100.

Q: It was hanging out of the wallet?

A: Yes, ma'am; I could see that, yes.

Q: That was Tuesday morning before you went to work?

A: Yes, he had like 300. I only took 100.

Q: Was the rest of it in tens or twenties?

A: I quite don't remember. I think it was twenties, fifties, and another one hundred. Two one hundred, and the rest in—

Q: Do you remember or are you guessing?

A: I guess—I'm guessing.

Q: Have you ever said anything different?

A: I don't remember.

Q: If I told you that you said that there were three one hundred dollar bills, would that sound right?

A: I—I assume so. I didn't really—

Q: And you took $100 from Robert Johnston's wallet?

A: Yes, ma'am; I did. I am so sorry. I shouldn't took it, but I took it. I needed money. My husband have no work, and I thought he was—I felt when he was starting working he was giving the money to his friend, and I thought he owe me money.

Q: You didn't think Robert owed you money?

A: No, I thought John owed me money.

Q: You took the money from Robert's wallet, and you knew that wasn't your money?

A: Right; yes, ma'am.

Q: And you knew you didn't have the right to that money?

A: No, that's true. I feel ashamed. I shouldn't take that money.

Q: Did you feel ashamed like you felt ashamed when you stole before?

A: Yes, ma'am.

Q: And when you stole from Janna?

A: Yes, ma'am.

Q: And when you stole from Nordstrom's?

A: That was wrong. Yes, ma'am.

Q: When you saw Ella Jones Tuesday night, you came back upstairs afterwards?

A: Yes, ma'am.

Q: Where was the $100 at that time?

A: I don't know. I think it was in my purse. I keep it in my purse.

Q: You didn't take the hundred dollars after John and Robbie had gone out?

A: No, I took it before, when I went to work, and I think I used it for lunch.

Q: You think you used a hundred dollars for lunch?

A: Yes, I didn't have no money, ma'am.

Q: Where did you go for lunch and spend a hundred dollars, or break the hundred dollar bill?

A: We order from any deli that is around the shopping center. We order.

Q: And who did you give the hundred dollar bill to?

A: I—to the place, to buy the sandwich, I guess.

Q: Ella Jones gave you those pamphlets you've identified?

A: Yes, ma'am; yes.

Q: You said you looked through them, but you didn't like the pictures in them?

A: No, I didn't want to read through the pictures because I feel that was a horrible book. I mean, that was horrible pictures.

Q: And you took the book and you set it on your dresser, didn't you; the two books, and set them on your dresser?

A: My dresser is right next to the TV, yes.

Q: It's your testimony that then you went to bed, and you were wearing your spandex shorts?

A: Yes.

Q: And your underpants?

A: Yes.

Q: And a T-shirt?

A: Yes, yes.

Q: Now, this is something special that you have talked to a lot of people about, haven't you?

A: Yes.

Q: About what happened after you went to bed Tuesday night?

A: Yes, ma'am; yes.

Q: It's your testimony, from what you told your lawyer, that you were asleep, and you woke up and your husband was on top of you, or he was getting on top of you?

A: Yes.

Q: And that you told him that you didn't want to have sex?

A: Yes.

Q: Incidentally, you never screamed, did you?

A: I told him what he's doing to me, and then he—I couldn't scream, I was just crying.

Q: You couldn't scream because his shoulder was in your mouth?

A: Yeah, he's bigger, and his chest is in my face.

Q: You said he took off your panties with his foot?

A: Yes, ma'am; he did.

Q: And you said—I think twice—on direct examination that you heard them rip.

A: I think so, but I'm not sure, ma'am. I'm not sure.

Q: Well, you were sure about twenty minutes ago, or an hour ago, weren't you, Mrs. Bobbitt?

A: Yeah, I heard them rip.

Q: It's pretty important whether they ripped, or whether they were cut, isn't it?

A: Yes. Yes, ma'am; I heard them ripped.

Q: Did you tell Detective Weintz anything about hearing your underpants rip?

A: I think so, but I'm not sure, ma'am. There are so many questions.

Q: You've got your statement in front of you?

A: Yes, ma'am.

Q: Go ahead and take a minute. Look through it and see if you can tell me where you think you told him that you heard the underpants rip.

(Whereupon, the witness is reviewing the document.)

(Pause)

THE WITNESS: I'm not sure if I tell him, or not.

BY MS. O'BRIEN:

Q: There is nothing in there about your underpants, is there?

A: I don't know. I haven't read it too much.

(Pause)

THE WITNESS: There is so many questions, ma'am. There is so many things that I wanted to tell him, but sometimes I could not explain myself, and I couldn't explain exactly what happened to me that night.

You have to understand, please. There are so many questions.

Q: And in all those questions, and all those feelings, you never said until today that you heard them rip, did you?

A: No, ma'am. I mention it to my friend, Janna, and I mention it to somebody else, I think.

Q: After you heard the underpants rip, what was the next thing that happened?

A: He push it down with the foot, and he—he force me. I couldn't keep my legs closed. He opened it, and he have intercourse with me. He force me into it, and I—I couldn't scream. I just tried to shake my head, and tried to move, but I couldn't.

He's so strong, and then he keep on pressing my hands down to my hips.

Q: What did he do after that?

A: I just keep on crying. He was just keep on raping me, and—and I was just crying, and I keep on saying, "no," moving side to side, and he would not let me go. I couldn't breathe. It was uncomfortable. It hurt.

Q: After he did that, what did he do?

A: He push me away.

Q: What did he do after he pushed you away?

A: I was just look for my underwear and my spandex short, and I put it on. I was in bed, in the side of the bed, and I said, "Why are you doing this to me over and again, and again, and again, and again?"

Q: You were pretty angry with him, weren't you?

A: It was everything, Miss. It was everything.

Q: Did he say anything to you when you said, why do you do this to me again, and again, and again?

A: He say he doesn't care. He doesn't care for my feelings.

Q: Do you remember saying those words?

A: He push me away.

Q: Do you remember saying those words to him, "How can you do this to me again, and again, and again?"

A: Yeah, I tried to ask him, yes.

Q: He said he doesn't care for your feelings?

A: Yes.

Q: Was that all that he said?

A: He said, "Leave me alone," and then he pushed me away, and I couldn't understand that. I feel guilty.

Q: And then he rolled over?

A: No, I don't know. I didn't see him. I just—I was just crying, and I was just everything inside me. I can't explain this, ma'am. I'm sorry I can't explain it, it's just so many things together.

Q: And then you put your shirt on and you finished getting dressed?

A: I just put my underwear on.

Q: Your underwear and your spandex shorts?

A: And my spandex shorts.

Q: And then you put your shirt on, after that, didn't you?

A: No, my T-shirt was never off.

Q: Your T-shirt was on while this happened?

A: When he raped me, yes. He just interested for my body part of my body.

Q: And you put those clothes back on because you were going to go out in the kitchen. Is that right? You didn't want to walk out in the kitchen, because Robbie was asleep in the living room, and you didn't want to walk out in the kitchen with just a T-shirt on. Is that right?

A: I don't know, ma'am. I have no idea, but I just—I just went for a glass of water.

Q: Okay, but my question is, why did you put your underpants and your spandex shorts back on?

A: Because I never want my pants to be off. I never wanted them off. I need it to be on.

Q: Then you walked out to the kitchen for a glass of water?

A: Yes, ma'am; I did.

(Whereupon, counsel approached a diagram next to the witness.)

BY MS. O'BRIEN:

Q: And you were on this side of the bed, right (indicating)?

A: Yes; yes, ma'am.

Q: And you walked this way (indicating). Is that right?

A: Yes, I walk that way, I think. Yes, to go to the kitchen, yes. I have to.

Q: Well, you remember that part, don't you?

A: I have to. The only way there is the kitchen, I have to go that way; yes, ma'am.

Q: You went—do you remember walking through the living room?

A: I went to the kitchen. I needed water. Yes.

Q: And when you got to the kitchen you opened a cabinet door to get a glass?

A: Yes, the glasses are in my cabinet—in the cabinet of the kitchen, yes.

Q: And you decided that you wanted cold water from the refrigerator, you didn't just want water from the sink. Is that right?

A: No, ma'am; we always keep our water in the refrigerator. I'm used to drink water from the refrigerator, ma'am.

Q: So then you walked over to the refrigerator to get the water from it?

A: Yes.

Q: And you poured a glass of water from your refrigerator?

A: Yes, from the—yes, to the cup, yes.

Q: Did you drink any of the water?

A: Yes, I was drinking the water, yes.

Q: And was it at this time that you said you were thinking about the abortion, and you were thinking about the times that he had raped you before?

A: Yes; yes, ma'am. Yes.

Q: Do you remember what you were thinking about after that?

A: No, ma'am. No, I just thought so many things together. The first time he raped me, when he raped me, how he raped me, how he torture me, how he hit me, the abortion, and when he laugh about me and saying all those ugly things to me.

I remember—there were pictures—there were like pictures in my mind, ma'am. There were just pictures in my mind.

Q: You never told Detective Weintz that you were thinking about the abortion when this happened, did you?

A: No, ma'am. He asked me so many things and I just tried to explain everything, but I couldn't.

Q: And you were very upset because it was right after it happened, right?

A: Yes, ma'am; yes.

Q: After time passed you calmed down some, didn't you; over the months that have passed since then?

A: Ma'am, it's really hard to, even now, go through the situation. I really wish that I could forget about it.

Q: I'll bet you do.

A: I—yes. Yes, ma'am. I wish I could just forget about it now.

(Whereupon, the witness is in tears.)

THE WITNESS: Just right now.

BY MS. O'BRIEN:

Q: Mrs. Bobbitt—

A: Yes? I'm sorry. I'm sorry.

Q: You talked to some psychologists about this?

A: Yes, yes, I talked to a lot of people, ma'am.

Q: And one of them was Dr. Gwaltney, wasn't it?

A: Yes, yes.

Q: You talked to him with your lawyer, Mr. Lowe, in December, didn't you?

A: Yes.

Q: You spent two days with him?

A: I don't know how long I spent, but I spent a long time even talking to you, ma'am.

Q: And you never told me that you were thinking about the abortion, did you?

A: Ma'am, I thought so many things, so many things.

Q: But my question is, you never told me that you were thinking about the abortion, did you?

A: I don't remember what I told you, ma'am. I don't. I'm sorry.

Q: Do you remember talking to Dr. Gwaltney about everything that happened, about your life, and about everything that you were thinking and feeling that night?

A: Yes.

Q: You never told him that you were thinking about the abortion, did you?

A: Maybe no, maybe—there is so many things that I couldn't really place in the right day. There is so many things that I just could have forget about it, ma'am. There is so many. I'm sorry I couldn't remember detail.

Q: You talked to two other doctors about—

A: Yes, yes.

Q: And you never told either of them that you were thinking about the abortion, did you?

A: Like I said, I don't remember, really.

Q: Do you remember when the first time you told somebody you were thinking about the abortion was?

A: No, but I—that's what I was thinking. There were so many things. There was just pictures in my mind.

Q: But certainly, when you talked to those doctors, you told them everything you could remember, everything that was the truth, didn't you?

A: Yes, ma'am. I tried my best. I try really hard. I'm sorry if I can't remember.

Q: You don't remember leaving your apartment that night?

A: No.

Q: You don't remember picking up your purse, and Robbie's Game Boy?

A: That's what I assume so. I have to answer to myself. I—I have to answer to myself what I did.

Q: You don't remember it?

A: No, ma'am. I—no, I don't remember that. No.

Q: And the next thing you remember is when you were driving to your friend Janna's house?

A: Yes, yes.

Q: And you were getting close to a stop sign?

A: Yes.

Q: And you realized that there was something in your left hand?

A: Yes.

(Whereupon, the witness remains in tears.)

BY MS. O'BRIEN:

Q: And you realized it was your husband's penis?

A: Yes.

Q: And you were just horrified, isn't that right?

A: Yes.

Q: And you just wanted to get rid of it? Isn't that right?

A: Yes, yes.

Q: And you went and got rid of it? Just like that (indicating).

A: Yes, I throw it out.

(Whereupon, the witness remains in tears.)

(Pause)

THE WITNESS: I'm sorry.

BY MS. O'BRIEN:

Q: Mrs. Bobbitt you testified that Janna has been a very good friend to you?

A: Yes.

Q: And she had offered you a place to stay?

A: Yes.

Q: And you had lived with Mrs. Castro before?

A: Yes.

Q: And she had offered you a place to stay?

A: Yes.

Q: You had lived with Mrs. Beltran before?

A: Yes.

Q: And you knew you could turn to Mrs. Beltran if you needed help?

A: Yes.

Q: Diane Hall had offered you a place to stay?

A: Yes.

Q: She lived right downstairs?

A: Yes.

Q: And you had put some of your boxes in her apartment?

A: Yes.

Q: Tuesday night, Ella Jones said that you could stay with her?

A: Yes.

Q: Monday morning Stephen Rourke, from Juvenile Court explained that if you got a Protective Order, that your husband could be barred from your house?

A: Yes.

Q: Dr. Inman put you in touch with the Social Service people, who told you about getting a Protective Order?

A: Yes.

Q: Your friends, Lynn Acquaviva, and Roma Anastasi, had come and gotten you before?

A: Yes.

Q: You knew about calling 911 to get the Police?

A: Yes.

Q: You didn't want to get a divorce. Isn't that true, ma'am?

A: No, ma'am. I—but I—I wanted him not to rape me, and I wanted him to—not to follow me. I was very scared. I was really scared.

Q: You are saying, under oath, that you don't remember cutting him?

A: No, no. That's what I assume it happened. I want an answer to myself.

Q: Do you remember telling Dr. Gwaltney that you walked in the bedroom, you pulled the sheet back, you looked at this whole body, and then you did it, then you cut him?

A: (No response.)

Q: Do you remember saying that?

A: I'm not sure if I said that, but maybe I did say that. Every time I tried to say something, I—I tried to give it the right answer, and I tried my best. I really tried my best.

Q: You tried to tell the truth, didn't you?

A: Yes, I—I want an answer for myself, too.

Q: Mrs. Bobbitt, isn't that the truth? You looked at his whole body, and then you did it?

A: I didn't look at his whole body. I don't remember looking at his whole body.

Q: Mrs. Bobbitt, you testified that you were packing, to get ready to move?

A: Yes.

Q: Where were you going to move?

A: I was waiting for my pay check, in order to get a hotel room.

Q: Had you looked at any apartment complexes?

A: Yes, I did, in the newspaper.

Q: Where did you look?

A: I look around Centreville, and Manassas.

Q: Did you ever go to any of the apartment complexes to see about moving?

A: No, I call some.

Q: When did you call them?

A: I called some in May, and I called—I don't remember. I'm so sorry. I called some in May or—

Q: And that was when you knew Robbie was coming down, and you thought he was going to live with you?

A: Yeah, I think so. I'm not sure, ma'am. I'm so sorry. I'm not sure.

Q: You didn't like to have anyone living in the apartment, did you?

A: We didn't have enough space, ma'am. I'm sorry.

Q: And, in fact, you didn't like anybody staying there with you, did you?

A: It's okay to stay for two or three weeks, for a visit, but not to live in a small, tiny place, like we did have.

Q: Do you remember when Brett came to visit?

A: Yes, yes.

Q: Do you remember when you told Brett he had to leave?

A: I don't remember that. I just said if you come to work, and if you're not going to do anything, then how are we going to help you?

Q: You don't remember telling him he had to leave?

A: No, I do not. No, he was here in our house in Pine Street.

Q: You don't remember buying him a steak dinner the next night, because you felt bad about that?

A: I'm sorry?

Q: You don't remember buying him a steak dinner that next night, because you felt bad about that?

A: No; no, ma'am. No, I don't remember buying him a steak dinner, no.

Q: When you were leaving the kitchen—let me ask you this. You say you remember picking up the knife?

A: Yes.

Q: What were you thinking when you picked up the knife?

A: The pictures came up. The pictures came up in my mind.

Q: Did you think about cutting John?

A: No. No, I didn't. I just think of the pictures.

Q: And you had—you presume that you had the knife in your hand when you walked through the living room?

A: I presume so; yes, ma'am.

Q: Did you ever think about cutting Robbie?

A: The pictures were in my mind. I'm sorry. The pictures—they just—

Q: You never thought about cutting Robbie, did you?

A: I just saw pictures ma'am. I just saw pictures. Sorry. (Whereupon, the witness is in tears.)

BY MS. O'BRIEN:

Q: You would have had to have gone near Robbie to get through that living room, wouldn't you?

A: I don't know.

Q: You know where he was staying, don't you?

A: No, I didn't know where he was staying.

Q: Wasn't he staying on the fold-out couch while he was there?

A: I don't know. I don't know where he was staying.

Q: Well, where were his clothes when you picked them up, and you took the hundred dollars from him?

A: On Tuesday the clothes were all over the apartment. The clothes were even in the kitchen.

Q: And you just had one fold-out couch, didn't you?

A: Only one; yes, ma'am.

Q: So you presume he was staying on that couch, don't you?

A: I presume, but I didn't know.

Q: You said when you were driving down the road, and you had the penis in your hand, that was when your memory came back?

A: That was—

Q: That's what you remember now?

A: That's—that's where I realized, and I tried to explain myself what happened, ma'am.

Q: Do you remember that, now? Do you remember having the penis in your hand, while you were driving down the road?

A: Yes, that's when I found out about that, and I tried to answer myself, and I assume it happened, ma'am.

Q: How did you get rid of the penis?

A: I throw it.

Q: Do you recall in what manner you threw it out the window?

A: No, I—I just get rid of it, ma'am.

Q: You just wanted to get rid of it as fast as you could?

A: Yeah.

Q: There were a couple of times during your marriage to Mr. Bobbitt when you thought your husband was having an affair. Isn't that right?

A: Yes, he have.

Q: And that made you upset and angry, didn't it?

A: He had an affair, and I didn't know how to handle that. I just told him that if he wanted to have affair he had to be divorced first.

Q: Hadn't you told a friend, earlier, that if you ever found out he had an affair you would cut his penis off?

A: No. I did not say that, ma'am.

Q: You never said that?

A: No, ma'am; no.

Q: You never told Connie James that that is what you would do if you found out your husband was unfaithful?

A: I remember a Connie, but I don't remember saying anything to anybody, ma'am. I don't think I said that. No; no, ma'am.

Q: You don't think or you didn't say?

A: No, I—no, I did not say anything to anybody, ma'am.

MS. O'BRIEN: That's all I have. Thank you.

REDIRECT EXAMINATION

BY MR. LOWE:

Q: Now, Lorena, at some point you said to Detective Weintz, in your statement, "And then he say he doesn't care about my feelings. He did say that, and I asked him if he has orgasmed inside me 'cause it hurt when—me, when he made me do that before."

Is it the orgasm that hurt you?

A: No, sir; it was—

Q: Were you trying to lie to Detective Weintz about orgasm hurting you?

A: No, sir. No, no.

Q: What did you mean when you said that?

A: I mean that he hurt me when he grab me, and he hurt me when he force himself into me, sir. That's what I mean.

Q: So it's the forced sex that you meant there, it wasn't orgasm. Is that right?

A: Yes, sir; yes, sir.

Q: Now, the next thing you said to him is, "You cut him"—Detective Weintz says, "You cut him," and you say, "I—I—yes." Is that correct?

A: Yes; yes, sir

Q: Were you telling him that you remembered cutting him, or were you telling him something else?

A: No, sir; I—I—

Q: Did you believe that you had cut him?

A: Yeah, I—I found myself with my—

Q: Did you believe you were telling him the truth, even though you didn't remember it?

A: Yes; yes, sir. That's all I wanted to say.

Q: Now, let's go on to some of the other things in this matter.

A: Okay.

Q: There came a time in which John left the Marine Corps, did there not?

A: Yes, he did, sir; yes, he did.

Q: You had already bought—had you already bought the house when he left the Marine Corps?

A: Yes, sir; we did.

Q: And what happened to your finances when he left the Marine Corps?

A: I was struggling. I was—a desperate situation, sir.

Q: Did you go to Janna to work seven days a week?

A: Yes, sir; but she wouldn't let me work because she

said that she doesn't open on Sundays, but I wanted to work Monday through Sunday, because I had to—because I have a responsibility to pay, and I didn't have food in my house, so I—I needed to work.

Q: When did you steal the supplies?

A: When we buy the house, because I wanted to work in my house doing nails.

Q: And when did John find them?

A: When I show it to him. I show him when it was in the closet.

Q: When did you show them to him?

A: When he hit me, when he beat me up, and I said, "I don't understand why you doing this to me, but look what I'm doing. I just wanted to—I have a responsibility and I even stole this from my own friend, and boss, and because I wanted to work seven days a week," and I say that to him.

Q: When did you return them to Janna?

A: The same day. The same night that I show it to him.

Q: When was that, in relation to the time that she found out about the embezzlement?

A: Like a week later, or something like that.

Q: So the end of the summer?

A: Yes, the end of the summer.

Q: Now, what changes in your relationship with Janna occurred at work, as a result of finding out that you had been stealing from her?

A: She—she found that out, and I was try to put some money back, but I couldn't—I couldn't afford to put the money back, and eventually, it built up like more money that I owed to the cash register, and she understood what was going on, so she—she keep me working, and I pay her off, sir.

Q: How did you pay her back?

A: I pay her off by working—still working for her. She let me work there.

Q: Did she change something in the way you were paid?

A: Yes; yes, sir. She change it.

Q: How did she—what did she change?

A: I'm normally, regular earn fifty percent commission. She change it for forty percent commission.

Q: Do you still owe her any money?

A: No, sir; I finished pay.

Q: When did you see the divorce lawyer?

A: I really don't remember, but I went to see him.

Q: Let me ask it a different way. It sounded, in your direct testimony, that you saw him just a little bit before this incident happened. Was that true, or was it some other time?

A: Yeah, I think so, yes. I think it was before that that I saw him.

Q: Were you living together or separated when you saw the divorce lawyer?

A: We were separate.

Q: Were you separated the one week time, the two week, or two month time, or the year time, when you saw a divorce lawyer?

A: The two month time.

Q: Was that before or after the year time?

A: That was before the year time, sir

MR. LOWE: That's all I have, sir.

MARGARET MCGARY
DIRECT EXAMINATION

BY MR. HOWARD:

Q: Yes, ma'am; would you give us your full name, please, and where you were employed?

A: My name is Margaret McGary, and I'm employed at the Nail and Body Sculptor, in Centreville, and I'm a ballet teacher at the Russell School of Ballet, in Chantilly.

Q: Ms. McGary, did there come a time that you began to work with, and come to know Lorena Bobbitt?

A: Yes, sir. April 1990.

Q: When you first knew her was she married at that time, or single?

A: I believe she was married.

Q: Did you have occasion, at some point in time, after you initially met her, to see and meet her husband, John Bobbitt?

A: Yes.

Q: Did he ever come to the Nail Sculptor, where she worked, with any degree of regularity, if you know?

A: Oh, yes; quite often.

Q: What times of day would he come in there, ma'am?

A: When I was first working there, he was still in the Marines, so he wasn't there as often. Later, especially after he got out of the Marines, he was there, almost every day, and sometimes almost all day.

Q: Did you ever observe him in the area where she kept her purse?

A: Oh, yes. The first time I ever noticed anything that seemed odd to me was, he came into the shop, he said that he wanted to talk to Lorena, and she explained, "I'm with a customer right now, you need to wait."

And he grabbed her by the arm, forcibly, yanked her up out of the chair spun her around, took her in the back, again still holding her by the arm very tightly. I was also with a customer. I couldn't get up and leave, and go see what was going on, but a couple minutes later, John came out and picked up her purse and took money out of it and left.

A couple of minutes later Lorena came out. She had obviously been crying, and she apologized to her customer. She was very sullen and subdued, very down and heavy, and she just worked, and sniffed, and cried a little bit.

Q: Now, with reference to her purse, did you ever see any other situation while you worked with her, concerning Mr. Bobbitt and that purse?

A: Yes. I would see him, often, take money from her purse.

Q: On the occasions that you would see him do that, would that be close to where you were working?

A: Oh, yes; our tables are such that mine is here (indicating) and hers is here (indicating), so I sit facing profile, and she is maybe six, seven feet away from me, probably six feet away from me, and I face her table and her purse, all the time.

Q: When that would occur would there be any change in her demeanor, appearance, attitude?

A: Any time that John came around, she would become very tense, and the shoulders would go up, she'd be rigid, the face would set in in a rigid fashion, and after he would take the money and leave, she was always upset.

Q: Ma'am, will you tell us if you ever heard him make any remarks about her physical appearance?

A: Yes, I did. Not long after I came to work there, one of my first real impressions of him.. I would have to place it around, probably July, of 1990.

It was hot and the three of us were in the back of the shop, a little kitchen area, and John was looking through a bathing suit catalog, swimsuit catalog, and he said, "Oh, this one's got nice boobs. You need to have some like these, Lorena."

And I went over there, and I said, "What is this?" and he showed me the picture, and it was a very buxom, you know, model in a skimpy bathing suit. I said, "What's the matter with you?"

Q: What reaction, if any, did you observe in [Lorena], to that remark, made when you were present?

A: Oh, she was very embarrassed, shy, embarrassed, put her head down.

Q: Did you hear any other comments that he made about her, her heritage, background, anything like that?

A: I heard him call her, "stupid," and say—kind of relate that to being Spanish, and once he said, "You're lucky that I took you," or something; "Most men wouldn't want a foreigner like you."

Q: When any of those comments were made, did you see any reaction out of Mrs. Bobbitt?

A: Her face would just fall, you know, again, she would just drop down and physically, you'd see her shoulders and her head go down, and sometimes she would say, "Oh, stop it," but it was always so soft and meek.

Q: Did you ever have an occasion to notice any marks or bruises about Mrs. Bobbitt's person?

A: Yes. I did. The first time was in 1991. I had been there maybe a little over a year. I would guess we're talking about early June of 1991.

I was working late, everyone else had left for the day. Lorena finished with her customer, and she hung around, which she didn't always do, until I finished. She was— there was something about the way she was hanging around, and looking at me. I had the feeling she wanted to talk about something, and I said to her after I finished and she was still there, I said, "Do you want to go down to Jake's?"

And she said, "Yes," and we got there. After a while I said, "Lorena, it seems like you want to talk to me about something."

She began to speak to me, and her voice got shaky, halting, stumbling, nervous looking, and then she showed me some bruises.

I saw them on her neck and on her arm. It was summer and she was wearing a sweater, and she took the sweater off to show me the bruises on her arm, and she showed me on her neck.

That was the first time that I saw bruises.

Q: Did you notice any change in her attitude—and I'm speaking about her at work, interacting with the people there, at work—any change in her functioning behavior?

A: Over a period of time, yes, and there were different downs and ups.

She began to withdraw more, and seemed more pre-occupied when she wasn't working. When she wasn't with a customer she would seem preoccupied, dealing with a lot of paperwork on her desk, she would be on the phone, and facing the wall, speaking very low, so that no one could hear what she was saying.

She didn't interact with the people in the shop, and the customers, as much as she used to. She was just becoming more and more of a sad, withdrawn person, depressed.

Q: Did you ever offer her any assistance?

A: Yes, I did. The night that I first saw bruises I offered her to come to my home, and she did. She was afraid. She was afraid to go home, and I had her stay at my house.

Within a couple weeks, I had a phone call from Lorena at 2:30 in the morning. She conveyed to me that she was hurt. I won't tell you what she said.

She was crying. Again, her breathing was very erratic, her voice was shaky, she was pretty hysterical. I asked her if I could come and get her, pick her up, and she declined. She was afraid it would make it worse.

It happened again, a very similar phone call, within another two, three weeks; a little later, three something in the morning.

Both times, after the phone calls, I would observe her at work the next day, and I saw bruises on her wrists, behind her ear.

Q: Was she a lady that would wear a lot of makeup when she came to work?

A: I only saw her with a lot of makeup one time. There were not only some bruises, but her face was quite swollen in the jaw area here (indicating), and some up on her forehead.

It was summertime, I think, probably September of 1991, and she was wearing long sleeves, long pants, hair loose instead of—usually, when she works, her hair is held back away from her face, because it gets in the way.

I began to notice every time she had her hair loose and hanging in her face, and long clothes, I would be a little more observant and I would be concerned for her.

CROSS EXAMINATION

BY MR. EBERT:

Q: Now, are you aware of an embezzlement that occurred just prior to the separation, before Mr. Bobbitt left to go to New York?

A: Yes, sir.

Q: And would it be fair to say that the embezzlement, itself, had an effect upon her?

A: I don't know that.

Q: You saw no evidence of that, did you?

A: She was extremely remorseful, and embarrassed.

Q: Did she cry?

A: She asked us all to forgive her, and she cried when she did that.

SANDRA BELTRAN
DIRECT EXAMINATION

BY MR. HOWARD (through an interpreter):

Q: Mrs. Beltran, could you tell us whether you know Lorena Bobbitt, and her husband, John Bobbitt?

A: I met them on my mother-in-law, in a Christmas party.

Q: Ask her, if you would, if there came a time in 1992, that Lorena and her husband, John, moved into her home?

A: They move in September of 1992.

Q: Prior to moving in, was she aware, generally, of any problems between the Bobbitts?

A: Yes, I know—I knew.

Q: Prior to the couple moving into her house, did she speak directly to John Bobbitt?

A: Yes, I spoke with them before they moved to my home.

Q: What did she say to John Bobbitt, and what did John Bobbitt say to her?

A: When I talk with him—when I talk with both of them, I told him that I was—I knew everything what happened before, between both, and I was wishing that he in my house will have a good behavior.

He promised me that he was going to change, that he was not going to beat her anymore, that he was not going to have violence in her house, and he was going to try the best, because he love her.

And he was going to help her to pay the bills, and he was going to do the best.

Q: Now, after they moved in, I would like to direct her attention to New Year's Eve of that same year, New Year's Eve 1992.

A: That was for New Year's. They just was going to go out to celebrate the New Year.

Q: And who does she mean by, "they?" Would she identify who she is talking about?

A: She talking about Lorena, John, and his cousin, his brother, and a friend. They were supposed to go together, with Lorena that night. When comes the night, she came back alone.

Q: What time did Lorena come back alone?

A: Around ten or nine o'clock. When she came, she was crying. She went to her room, and she was crying all the time.

Q: After Mrs. Beltran and her family went to bed, did there come a time that something unusual occurred in her house?

A: Exactly, correct. I wake up and I was hearing her crying. When I came out, out of my room, I was hearing in the basement, there was crying. She was crying.

I came down the stairs and I saw John and Lorena, and he was screaming to her, and she was telling him, "John, this day is for being together," and he told her, "I went out with my friends to have a good time."

"John," again, and he put in front of him, and I got between them, and I put my hands in his chest, and I told him, "John, stop it. That's can't be. What happened?"

And he only stare at me with his big eyes, his face all red. I took her to my living room, and I tried her to calm down. When I came close to John, he was smell that he was drunk.

Q: On any occasion while the Bobbitts lived in her home, did she ever hear John Bobbitt say anything about his wife's physical appearance?

A: Yes, because he used to look at magazines of women that was with bathing suits, that Lorena didn't have the breasts that these women used to have.

That [her] hair was ugly, and that [her] legs was chicken legs.

Q: When these remarks were made in her presence, what reaction, if any, did she have? What reaction did she have, if any?

A: She put down her head, "Oh, John, don't say that. That's not good, that's not nice."

Q: Did Lorena ever talk about an abortion?

A: Yes. She was very sad when she was talking to me about. Her eyes was with tears because it was very hard for her talk about that.

CROSS EXAMINATION

BY MR. EBERT:
Q: Mrs. Beltran, you are related to the Castros, are you?
A: Yes, it's my sister-in-law.
Q: And you are very friendly with Lorena?

A: Yes, I met her through Mrs. Castro and we began to be good friends.

Q: Getting to the New Year's Eve, did she and Lorena stay up and watch the New Year come in?

A: We just ate and everybody go to bed that night.

Q: John and his cousin, brother, and amigo, had gone out and left Lorena, is that right?

A: When they—she said that, when they left that night, Lorena was working and she supposed to go with them that night, out.

Q: Does she know approximately what time it was that she was awakened by the arguing?

A: That was around three or four o'clock in the morning.

Q: Did she hear John scream at Lorena?

A: When I came downstairs, I saw him screaming to Lorena.

Q: Did she see Lorena scream at John?

A: I saw Lorena crying, telling him, once again, "It's New Year's, and we should be together."

Q: Did John tell her that he had hit, or Lorena had hit him?

A: She told me he hit me, he beat me, but then later he told her, "No, Lorena beat me." And that's why I came and go between them, and then I took her upstairs.

IRMA CASTRO
DIRECT EXAMINATION

BY MR. HOWARD:

Q: Would you tell the members of the jury when, and

under what circumstances you first had occasion to meet [Lorena Bobbitt]?

A: I met Lorena back in '87. She came to live with us. Actually, I met her from Eddie Coronid, who introduced us to Lorena, and she had—Lorena came to live with us because it was more convenient for Lorena to go to school.

Q: Ma'am, did there come a time that she met a young Marine at Quantico Marine Base while she was living with you?

A: Yes.

Q: Was that John Bobbitt?

A: Yes, it was.

Q: When they started dating, and seeing one another, did you play any part or role in that dating?

A: My sister and I, Mercedes, we were chaperons for Lorena's dating procedure.

Q: To the best of your knowledge, was there ever an occasion before they got married that you, personally, are aware of, where they were not chaperoned?

A: No, not to my knowledge.

Q: After their marriage, did you see much of this young couple?

A: I did not. I saw Lorena every once in a while when I went to get my nails done, but otherwise, I did not.

Q: Did there ever come a time that she came to your home, and you saw something unusual about her physical appearance, or her behavior, that was different than what you had seen in the past?

A: The night that she came over, she had called and said that John had left, and she was upset, she was crying. We told her to calm down, and to drive out to the house, and she did.

Q: When she got there, did you see anything about her physical appearance?

A: Yes, I did. She had bruises on her hip, she was really, really upset, but besides there were bruises on her back, but we took pictures of that.

Q: Did she ever confide in you about an abortion?

A: Yes, she did. It was very, very traumatic for her.

BARRY WHITE
DIRECT EXAMINATION

BY MR. LOWE:

Q: What kind of work do you do, Mr. White?

A: I'm an associate pastor at Bethlehem Baptist Church.

Q: What duties do you have there?

A: I work with young, married couples.

Q: Now, in the fall of 1991, did you have occasion to meet the Bobbitts?

A: Yes, I did.

Q: How many times did you see them?

A: In reference to coming to our church, sir?

Q: Yes, sir.

A: I believe approximately six times.

Q: How did the question of domestic violence arise?

A: I was approached by Lorena, after our [Sunday] class, and she came to me and told me that John had hit her.

Q: Was John present when that was said?

A: Yes, he was.

Q: Did you confront him with that?

A: I simply told John that, "That is not correct behavior. You shouldn't be hitting your wife." That's what I told him.

Q: Did he respond to that?

A: There was really no response at all.

Q: Was there any denial that he had recently hit his wife?

A: No, there wasn't.

CROSS EXAMINATION

BY MS. O'BRIEN:

Q: You said that you saw the Bobbitts about six times when they came to your church?

A: Yes, ma'am.

Q: Were you involved in any type of counseling with them?

A: I never served as a counselor, but as a Pastor, I like to let them know that any time they are in need, I am always willing to help.

Q: Did you get a sense that a time came when they were in that type of need?

A: Yes, I did.

Q: And would that have been in the late summer, early fall of 1991?

A: In the fall of '91, when they came to my home.

Q: Did Mrs. Bobbitt relate to you that her husband had discovered her theft from her employer, and was going to leave her?

A: Yes.

Q: And was she very upset about that?

A: Yes.

Q: Was there a point she said to you that she thought that was why he was leaving?

A: I believe so, yes.

a witness, was called for examination by counsel on

behalf of the Defendant, and, after having been duly sworn, was examined and testified, as follows:

SUSAN FEISTER
DIRECT EXAMINATION

BY MS. KEMLER:

Q: Good afternoon, Dr. Feister. Would you state your full name, for the record?

A: Susan J. Feister, M.D.

Q: How are you employed, Dr. Feister?

A: I'm the Medical Director of the Psychiatric Institute of Washington, D.C.

Q: Have you had occasion, during the course of your career, Dr. Feister, to ever work with, evaluate, or treat, battered women?

A: Yes. During the 1970s I was—during my residency training—I was a psychiatric consultant for the battered women's shelter in New Haven.

In that role I had the experience of working with, and evaluating, and assisting many women who had been battered, who had left their relationships, and were seeking a haven in the battered women's shelter.

I also worked with and evaluated their children.

Q: And in addition, during the course that you were working at the battered women's shelter in New Haven, and subsequently, have you had occasion to clinically treat battered women?

A: Yes, I have. I have treated hundreds of patients who have had a history of battering, or a history of being raped.

Q: Now, Dr. Feister, we're going to talk about your opinion and diagnoses, with respect to Lorena Bobbitt, but before we get to that I would like to ask you if you have an opinion, based on your experience and your evaluations in this case, as to whether or not Lorena Bobbitt is a battered woman?

A: My opinion is that Ms. Bobbitt, Lorena Bobbitt, is a battered woman.

Q: Dr. Feister, in preparing yourself to evaluate Lorena Bobbitt, and what happened in this case, were there some things that you did?

A: Yes. I met with Lorena for about thirteen hours, on four different occasions, and talked with her.

Q: And what was the purpose of those fourteen (sic) hours of interviews?

A: I interviewed her in order to do a comprehensive history of her past, perform a mental status examination, and examined her to determine if there were any symptoms of either previous or current psychiatric disorders that were present, that might be related or ones that might be unrelated to her current legal charges.

Q: And was there anything else that you did?

A: Yes, I looked at a number of records, including her Potomac Hospital Emergency Room record; records from her physician, Dr. Inman; Police records of statements that were made to the police by Lorena.

Also depositions and transcripts from the trial of John Bobbitt, and statements by close, personal friends, coworkers and acquaintances, and a variety of other important materials.

Q: And why was it important to you to talk to all of these individuals?

A: Because it's important not to simply take the word of the individual when one is doing an evaluation, but to gather as much information as is possible, from medical records, other kinds of records, and from other individuals who have observed the person, both for understanding more about their behavior, and understanding something about symptoms they might have had.

Q: Dr. Feister, I want to take you back to the time when you were interviewing Lorena Bobbitt, and ask, if you would, please, describe how she appeared during the course of those interviews.

A: Well, she—when I first saw her, it struck me that she was a very petite woman, very small. I believe she weighs only about ninety-three pounds, and she was a somewhat, almost retiring young woman.

She was neatly dressed, and she was very cooperative and courteous throughout the interview process, but it struck me as impressive that she broke down crying and sobbing, at times, and there were numerous times I had to stop the interview with her and take a break, so that she could compose herself, before we could go on talking.

Q: Dr. Feister, can you recall around what issues she would break down, and start sobbing?

A: Yes, there were several points at which she became extremely upset and distraught; one, when she talked about the violence which characterized her relationship with John Bobbitt.

The second occasion on which she broke down was when she talked about the unwanted abortion that she had had, during the time she was married to him.

Another time that was very impressive, when she became quite distraught and distressed, was when she was talking about the night that she was brutally attacked and raped by her husband, over a forty-five minute period, and subsequently cut off his penis.

Q: Did you think at all that when she broke down and

cried during those times, that it was inappropriate for her to do that?

A: No. It seemed quite appropriate a response at the time, and it seemed a quite genuine reaction.

Q: Now, Dr. Feister, during the course of your interviews with Lorena Bobbitt did you learn anything that was significant, for your purposes, about Lorena Bobbitt's upbringing?

A: Yes. I did. I learned that she had a very close knit family that spent time together, and had outings, picnics, and visited other family members.

I also learned that she was extremely religious, as was her family, that they were all strict Catholics who were faithful.

They attended church every Sunday, and both Lorena and her mother described this as being sort of an obligation, to attend church each week, and that they also had strong moral values that were consistent with their Catholicism; that is, believing that premarital sex is not proper, not believing in abortion, and not believing in divorce.

Q: What did Mrs. Bobbitt tell you, specifically about what she had been taught about marriage, and family, and children?

A: She told me that the woman is really the backbone of the marriage, that she believes the reason for marriage is to have children; that one should never divorce; that a woman would do really anything to try to keep a family together, and that if there is a problem in a family, in her culture, it's considered to be the woman's fault.

And also, she mentioned that if someone is to get divorced that there would be a good deal of gossip, and that the first question that would be asked is, what did the woman do?

Q: What, if anything, did you learn about any violence in her family, as she was growing up?

A: I learned, from her report, that there really was no violence in her family. Her father never acted violently. In fact, the father and mother, according to her comments, seemed to have a very loving relationship. They didn't even argue, that if they had disagreements, they would talk about their disagreements, sometimes behind closed doors.

Q: Was there anything significant that you learned about Lorena's relationship with her mother as she was growing up?

A: Yes, she was very close to her mother, and her mother was quite protective of her, as is typical in the culture that she grew up in, and that her mother had described to me, needing to know her every move, where she was if she went out, when she would be coming back, who she would be with.

Q: What, if anything, did you learn about Lorena's dating life as a teenager, her social life?

A: She told me that she really didn't date as a teenager, that she really enjoyed spending time with some friends and going out some as a group, but not spending time, individually, with boys.

Q: Now, all of these influences that you just described on Lorena, her upbringing and how she was raised, are those things significant to you, with respect to your conclusions in this case?

A: Yes, they are.

Q: Now, did there come a time when Lorena came to the United States?

A: Yes.

Q: And what did you learn about how that occurred?

A: Well, her first trip to the United States occurred when she was sixteen; it was a gift from her parents, and she visited for several weeks and stayed with relatives, and was quite enamored with the United States.

She really enjoyed her visit, but the second time she returned after she graduated from High School, with her mother, and sister, and brother.

Q: And how did it—how did it happen that Lorena decided to stay in the United States?

A: Well, the family had wanted to immigrate to the United States, so the plan was for Lorena's mother and the children to come to the United States, while the husband tried to—while Lorena's mother's husband tried to obtain a visa; however, after several weeks in this country, he could not obtain a visa.

He missed his family very much, according to her report; called frequently, and finally, the mother, Lorena's mother, decided to return to Venezuela.

At that time Lorena wanted to stay in the United States, so she begged and pleaded with her mother, could she stay in the United States, so her mother called her father, consulted with him, and they agreed to allow her to stay only under the condition that she would attend school, and with the idea that she would probably become homesick within a few weeks, and return to South America.

Q: Did Lorena know much English at the time she decided to stay in the United States?

A: No, she didn't.

Q: In fact, with respect to your interview of Lorena,

did you notice any difficulties because of any language barrier?

A: Yes, I did. There were times in which she had difficulty understanding some of the questions I asked her, so it required me to define words for her in simpler terms, and rephrase questions so that I could ensure that she understood what I was asking, and what kind of information I was trying to obtain from her.

There were also times in which she seemed to have some difficulty expressing her feelings, and expressing herself in general, but particularly related to her feelings.

Q: After her mother, sister, and brother returned to Venezuela, who did you learn that Lorena stayed with?

A: She stayed with Mrs. Irma Castro and her daughters.

Q: And were there any things about that living situation that were significant to you?

A: Yes. The Castro family are also immigrants from South America, and these people really embrace similar values as her own family, and they became really like another family to her, like her home away from home, and were really like her mother and sisters.

Q: And did Lorena tell you what she was doing at that time that her mother went home to Venezuela, and she stayed here with the Castro family?

A: Yes, she first took English—courses in English as a second language, and when her English language improved, she became—she obtained a job as a nanny for Janna Bisutti, and worked at that job for a period of time, and then later, became a manicurist at the Nail Salon which Janna Bisutti owns and runs.

Q: Now, I want to direct your attention, Dr. Feister, to the time when Lorena met John Wayne Bobbitt, her future husband.

Was there anything significant in your mind, during the course of your interviews with Lorena, about her description of about how she felt when she met John Wayne?

A: Yes, she was—she found him to be charming, handsome. She was extremely impressed by him, and also impressed by the fact that he was in the military.

She was so infatuated with him that she fell in love with him immediately, and she describes being swept off her feet, that it was love at first sight.

And, as she continued to date him over time she grew to love him more, and she felt that he was her everything, the man she had dreamt about, the man she wanted to marry and start a family with.

Q: Was there anything significant about—to you, for your purposes—about the manner in which they dated?

A: Yes, it's very interesting, because I should point out that they were almost never alone when they went out and were dating. They were almost always accompanied by one of Mrs. Castro's—one or both of Mrs. Castro's daughters, or other friends or family members.

Q: Was there any physical abuse, or any sort of verbal battering that occurred during the course of their dating relationship?

A: No, Lorena does not describe any abuse, whatsoever, during that time.

Q: How long had they dated before they got married?

A: They dated for ten months.

Q: Was there any change that occurred in terms of John and Lorena's relationship, early on, in the first month or so of the marriage?

A: Yes, within one month he struck her for the first time, and that happened in July of 1989.

Lorena and John, and John's brother, had gone to a club in the District of Columbia, and Lorena told me that John had been drinking, and on the way back, driving in the car, he was swerving the car and zig-zagging on the road.

She became very alarmed, thinking that they might have an automobile accident, so she reached over to grab the wheel from him, and he pushed her to the other side of the car. And then she again became alarmed as he continued to swerve and zig-zag on the road, and she reached over to grab the wheel again, and he punched her in the arm. Then, when the couple returned home, he grabbed her by the hair, threw her into the wall, and kicked her in the stomach.

Q: Was there anything significant to you about how Lorena reacted to this violence by her husband?

A: Yes. She described being extremely shocked and confused about the situation. She had not been previously exposed to any violence, and she did not expect that her husband would be treating her this way.

She was very attached to him, she loved him very much, and to her he was everything. They had just been married, newlyweds, and she was away from her family. She really felt very confused and had no idea how to deal with the situation.

She felt very embarrassed and humiliated that this had happened to her, and therefore, felt that she needed to keep it secret.

Q: Dr. Feister, when, if you recall, was the next time that John Wayne Bobbitt hurt Lorena?

A: It was about one month later. She and John, and Terri McCumber, and John's brother, decided to take a trip to Ocean City for the weekend.

They were on the beach, after arriving there, and Lorena and Terri McCumber went to a vendor to buy a key chain with John's name on it. Some men whistled at the two women, and as she described it, John came and grabbed her, yanked her back to where they were on the beach, pushed her around.

He called both Lorena and Terri, "whores," and he was in a rage of inappropriate fury over this incident. He then insisted that they return, immediately, to their hotel room, pack up their things, and get in the car and go back home.

And as Terri McCumber described, they were still in their bathing suits because there wasn't even time for them to change clothes.

When they arrived in the car this behavior didn't stop. John continued to be abusive toward Lorena, pushing her, hitting her, to the point where she was trying to crouch under the dashboard of the car to prevent him from hitting her, and Terri McCumber was trying to prevent him from striking her.

Later that night Terri McCumber received a call from Lorena, and she had been beaten after the couple arrived home in their apartment, and Terri McCumber went to pick her up.

I believe Lorena stayed with her for a period of time.

Q: After the second attack against her, did Lorena tell you about other ways in which John, her husband, began to batter her?

A: Yes. She described that, from that time on, every time she tried to talk to him about anything serious, that he would push her around and slap her, and tell her to shut up.

Q: And what about the kinds of things that Lorena told you about, in terms of what John would say to her?

A: She described that he began an intermittent barrage of verbal abuse. He would taunt her with repeated degrading and demeaning comments. He told her she was ugly, that she had a bad figure, that she was small, dark, Spanish. A number of them were comments that had racial overtones.

That she had small breasts, that she was too skinny, that she couldn't speak English, and he would also threaten to demean her and taunt her by telling her that he was going to get her deported back to South America.

Q: And you testified previously, Dr. Feister, that in your opinion, Lorena Bobbitt is a battered woman, and I would like to know if what you just described, in terms of the demoralizing, demeaning, and degrading comments, is that significant to you for that opinion?

A: Yes. Lorena started to believe a lot of the things that John was telling her, and it really started to have a very negative impact on how she felt about herself.

She began to have a very poor self-esteem, have a very bad image of herself, and in fact, feeling rejected, worthless, that she was unattractive, that no one would want her.

Q: Now, although you've described the first two incidents of violence between Lorena and John, with respect to the physical beatings and violence that her husband committed on her, can you describe the kinds of things that Lorena described to you, for the jury?

A: Yes. She described all the following kinds of beating and abuse that occurred to her: she described that John would slap her face; strike her on the head; grab her and yank on her arms; push and shove her; squeeze her face very hard; shove her into the wall; yank on her hair.

She described that he would practice martial arts moves on her, such as karate kicks and various kinds of holds.

He would butt her with his head into her head. He would drag her on the floor, either by her arms, or he would grab her by the hair and drag her across the floor by her hair, and causing her to have abrasions on her elbows and knees.

And he would also attempt to choke her, using a particular hold that he had learned, that she told me about, that he had learned in the Marine Corps, where he put his hands around her neck, and took his thumbs and pressed on the area right above the breastbone, which causes the windpipe to be compressed so that you can't breathe.

And, he would also punch her, and also kick her.

Q: And can you determine, at all, based on what Lorena told you, and the things that you were able to confirm, how often these beatings and attacks, head butts, the shoving, the pushing, and whatnot, that you described, occurred?

A: Yes. During the early part of the marriage it happened about once a month, but over time it gradually increased so that he was physically beating her and attacking her about once a week, and then, toward the very end of the time during the several months prior to when she cut off his penis, he was attacking her several times a week.

Q: And what, if anything, did you do, Dr. Feister, to determine whether Lorena was telling you the truth about the frequency and the nature of the beatings?

A: I reviewed records, including her medical records of a visit to Potomac Hospital Emergency Room.

Q: Tell me what those records from Potomac Hospital—what event did that confirm for you?

A: That she—Lorena had said that she went there to seek medical attention after being beaten once by John, and described to me that John had insisted on accompanying her to the emergency room, and being present when she received medical attention.

So, it was difficult to confirm exactly what had happened, because of his presence during that emergency room visit, but that was also interesting to me because it's very common in a classic battering situation, when a woman does try to get medical help, that the husband may try to accompany the woman to the physician, or to the emergency room, to make sure that the woman doesn't have an opportunity to let the doctor know about what has really happened.

Often, in these situations, they will tell a false story about what had happened to them.

Q: And in this particular incident, with respect to Lorena, what reason did she give to the emergency room doctors about her injuries, about the cause of her injuries?

A: I believe she said she had fallen, or twisted her ankle.

Q: Did there come a time in the spring of 1990, when Lorena became pregnant?

A: Yes.

Q: Dr. Feister, would you describe for the members of the jury, how she described her feelings about the pregnancy?

A: She was very—she was thrilled about the pregnancy. She was very excited and happy about it, and wanted to surprise John, because that's what her mother had done with her father. About six months after they were married, her mother became pregnant and surprised her father, who was overjoyed at the fact that the couple would be having a baby.

Tuesday, January 18

SUSAN FEISTER
DIRECT EXAMINATION

BY MS. KEMLER:

Q: And with respect to what you described earlier about upbringing and values that were instilled in her with respect to marriage and family and children, was that significant with respect to how she described her feelings about the pregnancy?

A: Yes, her values about marriage and family—the idea that people got married mainly in order to have children and that children were the very important focus of the family and also it fit in with her strong religious values—her Catholic religious values—in that she would be completely against the idea or concept of having an abortion.

Q: And would you please describe for the jury what happened when she told her husband of the news of her pregnancy.

A: He became extremely enraged and angry over the pregnancy and told her that she had to get an abortion.

He immediately pulled out the yellow pages of the phone book and started looking up numbers of abortion clinics. He told her that she would make a terrible mother and that if she did have a child that he would refuse to help out or support the child and, essentially, he told her she had to make a choice either between him or the baby.

Q: All right. And what, if any, effect did that have with respect to Lorena's dependency or emotional connection to John, her husband?

A: That was extremely difficult for her because she was being asked to choose between really the two most important things in her whole life—that is, her husband and a baby. So it put her into an extreme emotional conflict.

Q: And would you describe what thereafter Lorena did?

A: Yes, she really debated for a period of time and was really just absolutely distraught and finally made a very painful decision that she would get an abortion in order to try to keep the marriage together and in order to please her husband. But she did, nevertheless, feel extremely guilty and conflicted over it. She felt, in her words, that it was like killing the baby.

Q: Okay. And what exactly did John, based on what Lorena told you, tell her about what it would be like to have an abortion?

A: Well he accompanied her to the clinic for the abortion procedure and he told her it would be extremely painful; he told her that they would be inserting a very large needle into her and that it would really hurt her and she wouldn't receive any anesthesia. And it really frightened her even more and put her into a kind of state of terror.

Q: Did Lorena describe for you her feelings after having the abortion and her emotional well-being after the abortion?

A: Yes, she felt extremely guilty about having the abortion and she became quite depressed for several months after the time she had the abortion.

Q: Did she discuss with anybody the fact that she had had the abortion?

A: I don't believe she told anyone. She didn't certainly tell her parents or any people she was close to because she felt very ashamed of it.

Q: Now following the time frame when Lorena Bobbitt had her abortion, was that in June—around June 15 of 1990?

A: Yes, it was approximately that time.

Q: Did there come a time when Lorena and John moved to—or purchased a house?

A: Yes.

Q: Did Lorena describe to you what input she had in terms of the decision to purchase that particular house?

A: She really had very little input. It was John's decision.

Q: Now—and the house that we're talking about, that is the house on Pine Street?

A: Yes.

Q: Okay. Now did the—did you learn from Lorena and—during the course of your interviews whether the physical violence that John had been perpetrating upon her continued after they had moved to the Pine Street residence.

A: Yes, it not only continued but in the spring of that

year, it really—the violence took a very ominous turn for the worst.

Her husband had previously forced her to have sex, but now he began to rape her and for the first time forcibly sodomized her.

After this first episode of anal intercourse, he continued to threaten her with sodomy in the future and that was a way that he repeatedly forced her to agree to have vaginal sex with him in order for her to avoid him having anal sex with her.

Q: Following incidents of physical beatings or chokings or physical violence, what if anything would John do sexually?

A: It was not uncommon for him after he had beat her to try to comfort her, promise that he would be better in the future, and then attempt to have sex with her and often forcibly have sex with her after he had beaten her.

Q: What, if anything, would Lorena do as she described to you, Dr. Feister, to try to get away from him or avoid having him force himself upon her sexually?

A: Well since she was so much smaller, it was very difficult, but she would do things like struggle and push against him—she would try to hold her legs together. But she described to me that she never really struck back at him because she was extremely fearful that if she did so he would physically beat her and injure her even more than she had been beaten and injured by him under circumstances where she didn't try to fight back.

Q: Dr. Feister, did Lorena and her husband ever have consensual sex?

A: It's difficult to determine if it was really consensual because John used the threat of anal intercourse with her and often she would agree to have sex with him in order to avoid the worse punishment of having him forcing anal intercourse on her. So at times she agreed to have sex, but it's not clear that that's something she would have voluntarily done under other circumstances.

Q: Now, Dr. Feister, did you become aware during the course of your interviews with Lorena as to whether or not the parties had separations at all?

A: Yes, I believe they had two separate periods of separation, one for about six weeks in the spring of 1991 and then another that began in the fall of 1991 and lasted until September of 1992.

She stated that just prior to the [second] separation, John—she had learned about the second extramarital affair that John had been having. He originally had had his first extramarital affair that she was aware of in the spring and that's what led to their initial separation, and this time she had learned of his second affair. In fact, she learned about the name of the woman that he was seeing and did take the initiative to contact this woman and talk with her because she was so upset about it.

Q: And based on your discussions with Lorena, did you learn whether or not John found out that she had spoken with the woman with whom he was having this extramarital affair with?

A: Yes, I think he did find out about that and on the day that he discovered that she had talked to this woman, he flew into a rage and beat her very brutally. That was in—on September 18, 1991. And she received quite extensive injuries from that. He pushed her and shoved her in cabinets and caused an extensive amount of bruising on her left side, her hip, her side, and her shoulder. There's further confirmation of this not only from Lorena but at that time she left the house and went to her—a friend's house, Mrs. Castro's house—and not only Mrs. Castro but her daughters witnessed the injuries that she received at that time. And they took pictures of these extensive injuries because they felt it might be helpful if Lorena ever decided to get a divorce. In fact, these pictures were ultimately used when Lorena went to obtain a green card from the Immigration and Naturalization Service and these pictures were submitted to the Immigration Service and were used as a basis for her receiving her green card and the basis on which she received that card was spousal abuse.

Q: Now you mentioned the second affair that John Bobbitt had. Um, what if anything did Lorena describe to you about what John told her about his reasons for having an affair?

A: He, at one point, told her that he was performing an experiment. He told her that he would come in very, very late at night, in the early morning hours sometimes, and he told her he would—he had been with the other women, would have sex with the other women, and then would return home and want to have sex with Lorena and after that he would then state that he was making a comparison between the two women to see which he liked better.

Q: With respect to the first affair that you briefly touched on, what if anything—how did it come to Lorena's attention that he was having the first affair? If you recall.

A: I believe that he actually told her about it and taunted her with this information. He volunteered the information to her at the time it was occurring.

Q: During the course of your interviews with Lorena—

learn whether she and John remained in contact with one another during the separation?

A: Yes, they did remain in contact. Early on, they were in fairly frequent contact, but as time went on, the contact decreased in its frequency.

Q: Dr. Feister, why would Lorena who had just, you know, preceding the separation, having been violently beaten and attacked by her husband and having been raped on numerous occasions and verbally battered over the course of approximately two years, why would she continue to stay in contact with him?

A: In my opinion, Lorena Bobbitt was acting in a fashion that would be very typical, in fact, even classic of a woman who was a battered woman. And that is she continued to state that she loved her husband, she continued to hope that despite the abuse she'd endured and the violence that she endured that they would be able to possibly get back together and that the marriage would work out. In addition, according to her reports, John would also talk with her and promise that he would work more on his behavior, not be violent to her, act more responsibly, return and get a job. So he was at times pleading with her to get back together.

Q: Did there come a time when Lorena agreed to a reconciliation with John?

A: Yes. He returned in the fall—in September of 1992. Yes, they rented a room or a small apartment.

Q: Would you describe her and John's relationship was like after they resumed living together.

A: Yes. Despite his pleadings and promises that there'd be no abuse as is typical and classic with this kind of relationship, the abuse and violence started up again immediately, really at the level it was at before and continued to escalate and become even more furious . . .

Q: Was there anything significant to you about what Lorena described in terms of, you know, discussing these matters with like people she considered friends?

A: Yes. Even with people she considered friends, she was very reluctant to discuss it at length. Sometimes she would reveal a little information and then really not tell them much more. She would say she had been struck or hit but she wouldn't tell people the details of it. She felt very strongly, as she described to me, that she didn't want to hurt anyone else or hurt their feelings or upset them or make them worry about her.

Q: By the beginning of 1993, were you able to determine from your discussions with Lorena how frequent the physical beatings and sexual attacks were occurring?

A: Yes. She described them happening about twice a week.

Q: Did Lorena describe to you any discussions or conversations at all that she had had with John about a possible separation or even a divorce?

A: Yes. She said that she had brought up the possibility of a divorce. She had actually thought of the idea about a year before when she had, I believe, gone to see a lawyer, but had put that out of her mind. But she was beginning to feel that there that might be something that she would have to pursue. So she began to discuss this with him. In fact, she had purchased a small tape recorder and was attempting to tape the abusive conversations that he had with her so that she would have some information that might be helpful to her were she to pursue a divorce.

Q: What, if anything, did Lorena describe to you about the discussions about getting divorced from John?

A: During the week—just the week prior to the cutting episode when she brought up the divorce, he said to her for the first time that it really didn't matter if he divorced her or separated from her, because he would pursue her and he would find her no matter where she was. That he would come to her, find her, and have sex with her anytime that he wanted, anywhere he wanted, and any way he wanted.

Q: Based on your discussions with Lorena during the course of your many hours of interview, do you have an opinion as to whether Lorena believed that threat?

A: Yes. My opinion is that she really did believe that threat. That it was a very powerful threat for her and one that made her feel that there was no escape for her.

Q: Now during the week and a half or so prior to June 23, 1993, what if anything was Lorena doing to—to try to extricate herself from this situation?

A: Well for one thing she had started to talk with other people more about it—I described her going to the apartment managers and she was also beginning to talk to her friends. She was trying to really muster up every last drop of strength that she had to pull herself together to the extent that she could to try to escape from the situation. So she began to pack her things and actually started to move some of her things out from the apartment to a friend's house with the idea that she would soon be able to leave the apartment. She had a plan at that time that when she received her next paycheck which would be a couple weeks from that time that she would be able to use that paycheck to pay a number of outstanding bills and still have enough money left to make a down payment on a place to stay.

Q: On the Sunday before June 23, did Lorena describe for you anything that was significant to you for your purposes?

A: Yes, she said that she and John had sex, but that she agreed to the sex only because she felt that if she didn't he would beat her and be violent toward her.

Q: And did anybody come to stay at the apartment?

A: Yes, John brought a friend of his, Robbie, to stay at the apartment for a period of time.

Q: Is that Robert Johnston?

A: Yes.

Q: Did, was there anything significant to you with respect to Lorena staying at the apartment on Monday night and Tuesday night?

A: Yes, she—she described that she felt that because there was another person in the apartment at the time that she felt it was not—very unlikely that she would be abused or raped by John or that he would be very violent toward her because in the past, he had tried to be very careful and not be violent toward her when other people were present or nearby who might overhear the violence or overhear Lorena crying or screaming.

Q: And did Lorena describe for you whether she met and talked with Ella Jones?

A: Yes. On the night of the incident after she talked with Miss Jones, she spent a period of time before she returned home to her own apartment.

Miss Jones is the neighbor who lived right under the Bobbitts' apartment at Maplewood.

Q: And what, if anything, did Miss Jones discuss with Lorena?

A: Miss Jones had also been very concerned and alarmed because during the week prior to the cutting episode, she had overheard the—the physical violence that had occurred when John discovered that Lorena had been taping conversations on her little tape recorder. She was concerned about her safety and wanted to offer her a safe place to stay.

Q: Did Lorena take Ella Jones up on her offer?

A: No, she didn't.

Q: Did she also describe to you some concerns she had about Miss Jones and her age and condition?

A: Yes, and not only with Miss Jones but with other people who would, at times, offer her a safe place to stay, she declined because she was concerned that if she stayed with these people, John might come and pursue her and cause trouble or that there might be some violent incident which would involve the other person.

Q: Dr. Feister, [on] Tuesday, June 22, would you describe for the jury what Lorena described to you she did when she got home.

A: Yes, she turned on the television to see what was on television but there was nothing interesting on so she turned that off. She spent a few minutes looking at the brochures but put those down and went to bed.

She fell asleep and later on awoke briefly because she heard the door slamming when John and his friend returned home, went back to sleep and then, at some time during the middle of the night, awoke to find John on top of her raping her. And she attempted to struggle, to keep her legs together, but he was pulling—he had partially pulled her underwear down and continued to take it off with his foot while he held her hands very tightly at her side so she really couldn't struggle against him.

He pressed his body down very hard on her and as she described it had his shoulder pressed so hard on her face that it was almost impossible for her to cry out or scream. She also described him kissing her so violently that—and him putting his tongue so far down her throat that she felt she was choking and felt that it was hard to breathe and that she couldn't really cry out or scream. He then raped her for a period of time, Lorena isn't really sure how long this lasted. During this time he had vaginal intercourse with her; she wasn't prepared and it was extremely painful for her.

Q: Following this brutal rape by John, what were you able to discern about her state of mind immediately following the rape?

A: She was extremely distraught. After he finished raping her, he rolled over and sort of pushed her to the other side of the bed and she told me that she was lying there thinking, oh no, not again. Not this again. No, this is never going to end.

Q: How—if you have an opinion Dr.—Dr. Feister, did the fact that he had recently threatened her if she divorced him and left with following her, chasing her, finding her, and having sex with her any way he wanted it affect her at that time now that he had just raped her again?

A: It affected her because she, despite previously attempting to make plans to try to get out of the marriage and leave which was a very painful decision for her and an effort for her to make—at this point, she felt trapped. She was at an impasse. She felt there were no alternatives. She felt as if she was in a box.

Q: Dr. Feister, explain what, as Lorena described to you, she did following this rape by John.

A: Yes, she got up from the bed, she put on her clothes, and she went to the kitchen. At this point she was crying and extremely upset, and she went to the kitchen to get away from him and to try to calm herself down. She went to the refrigerator to get a glass of water and during this period of time, she described having a complete flood of memories and recollections that came into her mind. She had memories of the verbal abuse, the barrage of verbal abuse, she had recollections and memories of the abortion experience and her fear and terror at that time, she described recollections of the beatings, of many of the beatings that she received by John and the pain of her injuries and she described recollections of the times he had raped her, forced sex on her, and also the times that—the time that he sodomized her and how painful it was for her and how disgusting and awful the experience was for her. And she was flooded by this wave of emotion that had been set off by her—by her rape that night which had come out of the blue at a time she was asleep. And she described these memories and recollections as being extremely vivid, almost like pictures as if she were reliving these experiences right there while she was standing in the kitchen.

Q: And do you have any idea, based on your discussions with Lorena, how long this lasted?

A: Yes, it was only a few minutes.

Q: Is that significant to you, Dr. Feister?

A: Yes, it's significant to me in that in my view of these events—the events including the rape, the period of time in the kitchen and when she returned to the bedroom, I believe that this was all one continuous psychological event for Lorena. She experienced this as one continuous event that was happening.

Q: And during the course of having this flood of memories and recollections and thoughts and emotions, what did she describe to you that she did?

A: At the time she was feeling completely overwhelmed with this emotion, she was really having a difficult time even knowing what she was feeling. She described to me feeling abused, frightened, terrified, just being overwhelmed by fear, anger, actually—and described mostly having a lot of anger at herself and guilt. And when I interviewed her, she said, "At this time I'm still not able to describe how I really felt at that time. I felt that the whole world was in my body." Feeling this way, as she had the refrigerator door open, she noticed the knife on the counter in the kitchen and she described to me—recalls remembering picking up the knife and then going toward the bedroom with the knife.

Q: Let me stop you there. You talk about that she said she felt guilt and anger at herself. What does that mean?

A: Uh, well, again this is typical with women who have—many many women who have been battered. It's very difficult for them often to feel anger toward the person who's beating them and physically and sexually abusing them and often that anger is turned back on themselves and they blame themselves.

Q: What, if anything, did Lorena describe to you about what she did with the knife?

A: After she picked the knife up and went toward the bedroom, she describes to me that she does not really remember what happened from that period of time until the time that she found herself in her car at a stop sign.

Q: Now, Dr. Feister, you're aware that she gave a statement to Detective Weintz?

A: Yes, I am.

Q: All right. And in that statement she describes—in response to him asking what happened, she describes to him what she thinks happened.

A: Yes. Actually she describes other events occurring during the time after she picked up the knife into and during the time she entered the bedroom and after she left the bedroom. I asked her very closely probing questions and I asked her very closely about her memories and recollections during that period of time and when I asked her about—I asked her specifically about the statement she had made to the detective and I asked her if these were experiences that she actually remembered and she said no they weren't. And it turned out that she understood these as really reconstructions of what she must have done. . . .

Q: All right. Describe first, Dr. Feister, what Lorena told you about her memory of the cutting.

A: She described not having any memory of the cutting, but the things that—but described the things that she had said about what had happened were really reconstructions, not memories. She definitely said to me that she did not recall or have a specific memory of the cutting or a variety of other actions that took place during that period of time.

Q: And based on your training and experience as a psychiatrist, Dr. Feister, is that unusual for you?

A: No, it's not unusual because this woman, Lorena Bobbitt, is a trauma victim. She's been repeatedly victimized and she, that night, experienced a serious trauma, that is, a rape. Not only that, there was a second trauma that occurred that night when she cut off John's penis which was a very traumatic event to her also. So under the influence of both of those severe traumas, it's very common for people who have been in situations where they experienced something out of the ordinary and something that would be enormously distressing and upsetting to any normal individual for them to not have a complete recollection of the event.

Q: Do you recall Lorena's testimony that she looked down and her hands were busy is that significant to you—her description of what was happening as she was driving the car?

A: Yes, she then really describes the first time she has another memory from the time she picked up the knife is when she found herself at a stop sign in her car and realized that she was having difficulty trying to turn the wheel of the car. At that moment she looked at her hand and realized that she had John Bobbitt's severed penis in her hand. She became hysterically upset, shrieking, and since it was summer the windows of the car were open, tossed the penis from the car just to get rid of it as quickly as she could because she was so shocked and mortified that—that his penis was in her hand.

Q: And how about her other hand? Was it also busy?

A: Yeah, it was busy. She continued—but she did not realize at the time that she had the knife in her right hand. She then continued to drive her car until she arrived at the nail salon and at that point she described having difficulty using the key to open the lock on the door and at that time she realized she had a knife in her right hand and she also became hysterically upset and threw the knife in the garbage can right—right at the nail salon and then went into the salon where she was so upset that she's described falling down, she saw blood—saw blood on her hand, she became so upset she fell down on the floor then gathered herself up, went to the bathroom and washed herself off, and then immediately went to the phone where she tried to call her employer and friend, Janna.

Q: Dr. Feister, I want to shift focus here for a moment and talk to you about your diagnosis in this case if I might. Focusing in on Lorena Bobbitt's state of mind in the few days or few weeks even preceding June 23 and even that night of June 23, what is it about her feelings in terms of having made some efforts to extricate herself from the situation and in terms of how that is consistent with battered women in general.

A: Well, there have been a number of studies done that have shown that when the woman makes an attempt—actual attempt to leave her husband or spouse that—and makes actual visible efforts—says that she's going to leave and makes visible efforts to carry out that intention, that that is often in time in a battering relationship where the woman is at most risk of being injured. That is often precisely at that point in time when the violence escalates and the husband realizes that the wife finally is attempting to try to leave and escape from the situation and makes the violence more severe in order to insure that the wife remains a captive in the home.

Q: Dr. Feister, is what you've just described the constellation of symptoms that you've just described that Lorena Bobbitt suffered from—is that known as battered woman's syndrome?

A: Yes.

Q: All right. And is battered woman syndrome a mental illness?

A: No, it isn't.

Q: How is battered woman syndrome and the constellation of symptoms that underlie that terminology, how is that psychiatrically significant?

A: What is significant is that women who are enduring this kind of situation over a long period of time can develop serious psychiatric disorders as a result of being in this environment of constant violence—physical and sexual violence.

Q: All right, Dr. Feister. Without going into the details of each diagnosis, would you state for the members of the jury what your diagnosis—or diagnoses are.

A: Yes. She suffered from major depressive disorder, she suffered from post traumatic stress disorder, and she suffered from an anxiety disorder, that is panic disorder.

Q: Dr. Feister, I want to ask you, are you familiar with this book?

A: It's the Diagnostic and Statistical Manual of Mental Disorders, the 3rd Edition, Revised. This book contains the list of all the official recognized psychiatric disorders and all the official diagnostic criteria and—that are used to determine whether a mental disorder is present or not.

Q: All right. And are there different categories of mental disorders in this book?

A: Yes.

Q: All right. Would that be Axis I or Axis II?

A: Yes.

Q: Would you describe what an Axis I disorder is?

A: Yes, Axis I disorders are really the more serious psychiatric disorders. They're called the syndromal disorders that can, once they occur, can reoccur, often time during—as is common with a number of the disorders—can reoccur during a person's lifetime. The Axis II disorders in contrast are somewhat less serious disorders in the sense that they represent more longstanding personality characteristics and traits that the person demonstrates over a long period of time once they're adults.

Q: And with respect to the psychiatric diagnoses that you've just described—that is, major depressive disorder, post traumatic stress disorder, and panic disorder—are those Axis I or Axis II disorders?

A: Those are Axis I disorders.

Q: Dr. Feister, would you please describe for the ladies and gentlemen of the jury what major depressive disorder is?

A: Yes, it's a serious mental disorder and I'll describe the criteria to the jury. In order to have this disorder, the person must have five of the symptoms that must be present at least for a two week period of time, so it can't be just feeling down in the dumps or depressed for a day or two as is common with normal people.

Q: And these symptoms that you're describing she had at the time that she cut off her husband's penis?

A: Yes, these are symptoms that she had at that time.

Q: Okay, and prior to that time?

A: Actually, these are symptoms that I determined that she had for several—a several month period of time prior to cutting off his penis.

Q: Okay.

A: She did have a very depressed mood which occurred almost every day most of the day according to her. She did describe having a very limited interest in the kinds of activities that she would have previously taken pleasure in and enjoyed. She had a weight loss and was not dieting. She had insomnia. She described having fatigue or loss of energy nearly every day. She also described feeling worthless and also having excessive guilt. She also described having difficult with her ability to think and her concentration and attention. She also described having difficulty making decisions. She also had thoughts of death—reoccurring thoughts of death, thinking about the possibility of suicide, but did not have any specific plan and did not wish to really harm herself or kill herself. So she met actually more than five of the symptoms for the major depressive disorder.

Q: Okay. Now, doctor, we all get depressed from time to time. Is what you're describing here the criteria that Lorena met for major depressive disorder—is that a severe mental illness?

A: Yes it is and, in addition—in addition to determining if the disorder's present, there's a rating system for rating the severity of the depression. The depression would be considered mild if the person just met the number of criteria necessary, moderate if the impairment was a little—if the interference with their functioning was a little worse, and severe if they had several symptoms in addition to the minimum number and that those symptoms were markedly interfering with their ability to function either in the social arena or, for example, at work. And based on my interview with Lorena and other people's observations, I felt that she really suffered from a severe level of depression because she had symptoms in addition to the minimum that were necessary to make this diagnosis and, in addition, she had quite significant interference with her daily functioning.

Q: Now I'd like to direct your attention, Dr. Feister, to your second diagnosis and that is panic disorder. What, if any, symptoms did Lorena meet based on your observations and interviews with her and as confirmed by documents and other witnesses for panic disorder.

A: In order to be diagnosed with this disorder, the person has to have had one or more panic attacks and that's a certain period of time, a discrete period of time when the person experiences intense fear or discomfort, and I'll describe that a little bit more in a minute. And that these episodes have to come—they have to be unexpected; that is, they come out of the blue, and they're not triggered by situations in which the person's the focus of somebody else's attention; for example, if you're the center of attention at a party or you're giving a talk or something like that. And Lorena did have these episodes which were unexpected and weren't triggered by situations in which she was the focus of other people's attention.

Q: Now you also described for the jury that she was suffering from post traumatic stress disorder at the time that she cut off her husband's penis. And I'd like you to take your time describing this psychiatric disorder for the jury.

A: Yes, this is a rather complicated disorder, so let me just take you through it. The first necessary criteria is that the person has to experience an event that is outside the range of usual human experience. And one that would be very distressing to almost any person—that is, for example, a serious threat to one's life or one's physical integrity, serious threat or harm to other people that you are close to, destruction of your home or community such as a natural disaster, for example. Lorena, I feel, experienced that kind of event which is outside the range of the normal person's experience in that she had been repeatedly raped.

Q: Okay. What is the next criteria?

A: There are three sets of criteria. After the person's experienced this traumatic event, then there are three groups of symptoms that the person can experience as a result of that trauma. The first grouping of symptoms have to do with reexperiencing the event and the person needs to have at least one of the following symptoms; that is, after the traumatic event they have difficulty getting the thoughts out of their mind, and it's very upsetting. Lorena did describe to me that she had repeated upsetting memories and recollections of the abuse and other people's observations appear to confirm this.

The second symptom under that category is experiencing repeated distressing dreams about the event. Lorena describes to me how the frequent dreams, on almost a nightly basis, and what she would dream about—her husband John raping her and locking her up so that she couldn't escape. The third symptom under that category is suddenly acting or feeling as if that traumatic event, for example, the rape, were recurring. Something like a flashback. Lorena describes at least one episode in which she was driving down the highway and she was driving so radically that a car was honking its horn behind her and she was, at that time, reliving one of her rape experiences and came to her senses and had to pull the car to the side of the road and spent some time crying and composing herself before she could continue on.

And the fourth symptom under that group of the persistent reexperiencing of the event is for the person to experience intense psychological distress if they're exposed to events that resemble some aspect of the trauma. In Lorena's case, if she were watching television or a video and there was any kind of violence that it started to appear on the television, it would be intensely distressing and upsetting to her.

Q: All right, Dr. Feister, what is the next set of symptoms?

A: Let me just mention that then of that first grouping of symptoms, the person needs to have at least one of the symptoms and Lorena had all four of those symptoms which is also significant. The next grouping of symptoms involves avoidance. The first one is that the person makes efforts to avoid thinking about the traumatic event, and having feelings that are associated with traumatic events. Lorena would describe having these destructive recollections and then making great efforts to try to put it out of her mind, busy herself, do other things.

The second symptom is efforts to avoid activities or situations that would cause her to recollect trauma. And in this case she would avoid, for example, watching certain television programs, . . . particularly any kind of violence toward women on the television.

She had markedly diminished interest in significant activities. Although her work was important to her, she was really much less interested in her work and found that she had no interest in socializing with others which were things that she previously enjoyed.

Feelings of detachment or estrangement from others. Lorena described that as she continued to experience the rapes and abuse that she felt more and more detached from other people, that it was difficult for her to make an emotional connection with others. The sixth is a restricted range of affect. She describes having a good deal of difficulty being able to have loving feelings or emotions toward other people.

And finally the seventh symptom is a sense of a shortened future. Lorena described very vividly that she would never have any children and felt that there really was no future for her at all.

Q: All right. And how about the third category of symptoms.

A: The third category of symptoms has to do with increased arousal. The person needs to have at least two of the symptoms that I'll be telling you about. Difficulty falling or staying asleep and, as I've already mentioned when I described depression, Lorena had a great deal of difficulty falling asleep and staying asleep. The second criteria is irritability or outburst of anger. Now, although Lorena describes not having any outburst of anger, she did describe feeling very irritable and described that simple little annoyances that would occur when she was at work would really bother her a great deal and she just felt very sensitized. The third symptom is difficulty concentrating and, as I've also described with the depression. The fourth symptom is hyper vigilance and that really means that the person has a sort of increased level of fear and watchfulness and she described really feeling that she had to be constantly vigilant and watchful because so many bad things were happening to her. She also had the sixth symptom which is physiological reactivity. When she's exposed to events that symbolize an aspect of the trauma—what this means in simple terms is that if she were watching TV and some episode of violence came on the video or the television, for example, seeing a woman being raped or violence toward a woman, she would feel nauseous, she would become sweaty and breathe heavily in reaction to watching. So she met all those criteria and then these symptoms all have to be present for at least a one month period of time and in my interview with Lorena, it was clear that these symptoms were present for at least several months—two to three months at least, prior to the cutting episode.

Q: Okay. Now how, doctor, were you able to determine that all of these three disorders that you just outlined for the jury—that is, major depressive disorder, panic disorder, and post traumatic stress disorder—if those were all present in Lorena at the time that she committed the cutting on June 23, 1993.

A: Well I interviewed her extensively and asked many questions about the symptoms which she reported on.

Because this was such an unusual situation—cutting off a penis—I felt that in addition to the extensive clinical interview I felt it was important to obtain some psychological testing to really see if there were other psychological factors that might be present that would confirm my view or disconfirm my views. And the kinds of things that might not be possible to learn about simply through asking the personal questions in an interview situation.

Q: Okay. And what, if anything, did the psychological testing reveal for your purposes?

A: It revealed a number of things that I felt were significant. The psychological testing showed that Lorena had a borderline normal intelligence level—on the low end of normal. And that was even after the score was recalculated to take into consideration the fact that because of her Spanish background, she might have difficulty with some of the language parts of the intelligence test. Those items were taken out and the test score was recalculated, according to my discussion with the psychologist, she still ended up with an IQ of 83 which as I mentioned is a borderline normal level. In addition, the Rorschach test better known to most lay people as an ink blot test showed that Lorena was a person who used very rigid kinds of defenses and rigid ways of coping and that under situations of extreme emotion or extreme stress that her normal reasoning process would break down and the kind of rational thinking changed. At those times, she actually had what would be considered psychotic-like aspects to her thinking or aspects to her thinking that would almost suggest a break with reality.

Q: Dr. Feister, based on what you've just explained to the jury about these three major mental disorders that she—that Lorena Bobbitt was suffering from at the time that she took the action in cutting off her husband's penis, what if anything in your opinion, based on a reasonable degree of medical certainty, did those disorders have to do with her ability to control her impulses on that night?

A: I believe that these disorders that I described—the depression, the anxiety, and the post traumatic stress disorder, which were present, were already signifying that she had had a significant deterioration in her functioning and in her mental state. She was already experiencing severe distress as is evidenced by a number of symptoms of a number of disorders such that this vulnerable person already experiencing several severe psychiatric disorders and symptoms—when subjected to the additional trauma of feeling that she was most likely going to be safe in her home that night and was raped and then had this flood of—flood of emotions and feelings—that she had an acute deterioration of her mental state at that time and became psychotic.

As I understand it, this was a woman who was young, almost childlike in terms of her lack of life experiences, very naive, a kind of starry-eyed person with high hopes, she had met her dream man and married him, also with high hopes to have a wonderful marriage and children and family situation. Her dream though, ended up turning into a nightmare. She began to be subjected to episode after episode of violence, of verbal abuse, physical violence, and ultimately sexual violence and sodomy. After years of increasingly horrible beatings, attacks, rape, and sodomy by her husband, she really had—was experiencing a horrible ordeal over a long period of time. She made many efforts to try to cope with this, and actually was able to cope reasonably well although she did experience a number of psychiatric disorders which I believe were at least in part a result of the horrible abuse that she experienced in her marital relationship. So she attempted to pull her strength together and cope as best she could, but she really is a very fragile individual and, as her psychological testing showed, someone who's very vulnerable. She is limited intelligence and really didn't have a lot of emotional resources or life experience. She had already done some things like reporting the abuse to the police and reporting it to the Marines, but these hadn't been terribly effective in terms of protecting her from any future abuse.

Despite all the abuse, [Lorena] showed a remarkable strength of character to try to pull herself together to finally get herself out of this relationship. Despite several separations, she had gone back to her husband partly because of her cultural values of the importance of marriage, the idea that it was really improper to become divorced and that it would be humiliating for that to happen. However, she was trapped in the relationship by John's repeated threats, that no matter where she went, he would control her life by seeking her out and demanding—and forcing sex on her whenever he felt like it. So it was partially the intimidation and violence of her husband that kept her in the relationship at the same time that she was making efforts to finally leave. This created for her an impasse. She had a breakdown. She felt desperate because there was really no place for her to go. If she stayed in the relationship, she would continue to be violated and abused and if she left the relationship, her husband would pursue her relentlessly. At this point, she—because of this extreme stress and this impasse which is a common occurrence in a person who undergoes a deterioration into psychosis, she became psychotic and at that point in time, I believe, was overwhelmed by the kind of flooding of emotions that she experienced and under the experience of these overwhelming emotions, she attacked the weapon which was the instrument of her torture, that is, her husband's penis.

Q: Dr. Feister, how much control did she have at that moment?

A: I don't believe that she had control over her actions at that point in time.

Q: Dr. Feister, as Lorena Bobbitt sits here today, is she suffering from any mental disorders?

A: Yes.

Q: Would you briefly describe that for the jury?

A: Yes, she continues to suffer from the symptoms of major depressive disorder that I described previously and she also continues to suffer from symptoms of post traumatic stress disorder which I previously described as well.

Q: And in that context of post traumatic stress disorder, is there anything in the criteria that you previously outlined about post traumatic stress disorder that have to do with memory?

A: Yes, one of the criteria is that the person may have a partial amnesia for the event.

Q: Do you have an opinion as to what if any impact

the actions that she took that night, that is cutting off her husband's penis, had on Lorena?

A: Yes, I think that was an extremely traumatic event, equally traumatic as the rape that occurred.

Q: As she sits here today, Dr. Feister, is Lorena Bobbitt a danger to herself or others?

A: No, I don't believe that she's a danger to herself or others at this point in time.

Q: Are you familiar with the law in Virginia as it relates to the defense of irresistible impulse?

A: Yes. For irresistible impulse, it's necessary that the defendant knows the nature, the character, and the consequences of his or her actions and that they know that the act is wrong but that the person's mind is impaired by mental disease such that they're unable to resist the impulse to commit a particular action.

Q: All right. And Dr. Feister, do you have an opinion based on a reasonable degree of medical certainty as to whether or not the actions that Lorena took on June 23, 1993—whether that was consistent or inconsistent with irresistible impulse as defined in Virginia law?

A: I believe her behavior was consistent with the irresistible impulse.

Q: Thank you very much.

CROSS EXAMINATION

BY MR. EBERT:

Q: Now you felt as a result of that that she suffered an irresistible impulse. Is that correct?

A: Yes.

Q: And did the other maladies that she suffered have any bearing on your opinion in that regard?

A: Yes, I believe I've already testified about how I understand those disorders related to the brief reactive psychosis that she experienced at that time. That is, they preceded it, they were an example of the symptoms—she was already under distress, she was already experienc— experiencing which led her to be already in a vulnerable state so that when an additional major stress came upon her, she further deteriorated into the psychotic state.

Q: All right, ma'am, let me ask you something. You're basing much of your opinion on what Mrs. Bobbitt told you, isn't that right?

A: No, not really. I'm basing my opinion on what Mrs. Bobbitt told me, in addition to my review of medical records, in addition to my review of transcripts and depositions and in addition to my review of police reports, in addition my review of her medical records, the Marine records of Mr. Bobbitt seeing a social worker.

Q: So what she tells you is not important to you?

A: Yes, what she tells me is important to me. I simply said that that was not the only basis for my opinion.

Q: I ask you if much of your opinion was based on that.

A: Certainly the interview with the client and my personal interview with her is important information, yes.

Q: And the history is very important in your profession, is it not?

A: The history is important, yes.

Q: And if what she told you was not the truth, would that change your opinion?

A: It would depend on which aspect of what she told me was not the truth and how central that was to my professional opinion. There might be pieces of information that were really irrelevant or not very important. That—that were they altered, would not have a significant impact on my professional opinion.

Q: All right, let met just—just let me ask you a few questions about the history that she gave you. I think you testified that her background and her upbringing had a great bearing on how she reacted to what she was experiencing, is that right?

A: Yes.

Q: And would it be fair to say that she had a strict Catholic upbringing?

A: Yes, my understanding is that it was a relatively traditional Catholic household.

Q: Yet she was married in a civil proceeding, isn't that right?

A: Yes.

Q: You are aware that the only church proceeding was an Episcopal proceeding which was arranged by Mr. Bobbitt's parents sometime after the civil proceeding, isn't that right?

A: I really don't have any knowledge of who arranged the proceeding.

Q: But you are aware that they did have a church proceeding in Niagara Falls.

A: Yes.

Q: And you are aware, are you not, that Mrs. Bobbitt at the time of their marriage was concerned about have to go back to Venezuela?

A: I'm not sure what you mean, concerned about going back to Venezuela.

Q: Well you realize that her visa was about to expire.

A: I wasn't aware of that.

Q: Well in your conversations, in your evaluations, did [Ms. Bobbitt] indicate to you that she was frightened that she may have to go back if something happened to her marriage?

A: Well she described that John had made numerous threats that he would report her to immigration or try to have her deported, yes.

Q: Matter of fact, when they separated and he went back to New York, prior to that time she had certain pictures made and sent to the Department of Immigration in an attempt to show that she was shall we say a battered wife.

A: Actually, I don't believe she had those pictures made. I believe that when she was severely beaten at—on the evening when her husband left, she went to Mrs. Castro's house and at their suggestion and initiation, Mrs. Castro's daughters took pictures of her injuries. I don't believe she had anything to do with initiating that.

Q: Well in any event, whether she did it or somebody on her behalf did it, they did in fact send those pictures to the Department of Immigration, did they not?

A: Yes and that seems quite appropriate.

Q: And that was an attempt to make sure that she would not have to go back to her native country, isn't that right?

A: Yes, I assume that that material was used as part of the processing for her receiving her green card.

Q: Did you have occasion when you reviewed the records you had the police reports, did you not?

A: Yes.

Q: And did you also have occasion to see the hospital reports when Mrs. Bobbitt was admitted to the hospital for an examination on the date this occurred?

A: Yes.

Q: And did she indicate, if you know, was she able to give a history to the emergency room people when she came in?

A: I'm not sure. I don't recollect exactly the details of what she said on that report.

Q: I'll read you the quote. "I was really angry. I opened the sheets and I cut him. I was driving and I threw it in the bushes." Did you ever look at that—see that statement?

A: Yes I did.

Q: You know, do you not, that she mentioned being really mad and really angry?

A: Yes.

Q: Do you feel that she felt any anger during any of these episodes?

Q: Let's say—just take the episode of when she cut her husband.

A: I feel that anger is certainly one of the strong emotions that she was experiencing at that time, yes, but only one of many.

Q: When you went down the list on the post traumatic stress syndrome, you said she met all the symptoms except no outburst of anger. Do you remember saying that on your direct examination?

A: Yes. I don't believe I said no outburst of anger, but for that criteria it is either irritability or outburst of anger and I said that I felt she met the criteria for irritability.

Q: But not outburst of anger.

A: But, no, I did not get a history of outburst of anger.

Q: But all other characteristics set forth in that anxiety disorder she met in your opinion.

A: All the ones that I testified to, yes.

Q: If at some time during the course of this she had said if her husband had been unfaithful to her she would cut off his penis, would that have an effect on your opinion?

A: It would depend. I really have to have further information about who said that, who reported that, under what circumstances that was said, when it was said, when that information came to light. It might or it might not have any impact on my opinion.

Q: Well if she said it to a co-worker, would that have any bearing on your opinion?

Q: All right. Now were you aware that Mrs. Bobbitt was—had stolen some $7,000 from her employer?

A: Yes, I was.

Q: And were you aware that Mr. Bobbitt was very upset about that?

A: Yes.

Q: And were you aware that he accompanied Mrs. Bobbitt to talk with Janna, her employer?

A: Yes.

Q: And were you aware that Janna assaulted Mrs. Bobbitt?

A: No, I wasn't aware of that.

Q: Aware she pulled her hair?

A: No.

Q: Slapped her?

A: No.

Q: Would that have any bearing on your opinion?

A: On my—on which opinion?

Q: The opinion that you've rendered here today as to whether or not she suffered an irresistible impulse.

A: No, not necessarily.

Q: While I'm thinking about it, doctor, did you look at the medical records at the hospital to determine whether or not there was any physical damage or ripping done in the rape on the night in question?

A: No, I don't believe they found any serious physical damage to the vaginal area.

Q: So I take it her characterization of being ripped was not physically borne out.

A: Well I believe she said she felt as if—it was painful and she felt as if her vagina were being ripped apart and I don't believe she characterized it as her vagina was being ripped apart. She said that was her feeling or it was her way of describing her experience of that rape.

Q: And with regard to the anal intercourse, did she tell you that happened on one occasion?

A: She said it happened on two occasions.

Q: Two different occasions—in four years?

A: It happened first in the spring of 1991 and one other time.

Q: Did she tell you that as soon as she experienced pain that Mr. Bobbitt stopped?

Q: Doctor, if Mrs. Bobbitt had a memory of the event including the cutting of her husband—would that make a difference in your opinion?

A: It might or it might not. That is not the main issue on which I base my opinion.

Q: So if she had a memory and had planned in some degree what she did, that would not change your opinion.

A: Well you just added another factor in there. We were initially talking about memory and now you said if she planned. Sir, are you talking about having a memory or are you talking about if she planned it?

Q: You've already told us if she had a memory of it, it wouldn't change your opinion.

A: Not necessarily, no.

Q: But it might.

A: It wouldn't necessarily change my opinion.

Q: But it might.

A: I don't think it actually would because the irresistible impulse is the issue is not necessarily based on whether there's an actual memory of the event or not.

Q: Well, certainly the lack of memory has a basis on your opinion about psychosis, doesn't it?

A: Yes, it helps contribute to my impression.

Q: Thought so. If she had the ability to plan and reflect in any respect, that would have a basis on your opinion, would it not?

A: There's a difference in my mind between having an ability to plan versus actually engaging in planning thoughts and behavior.

Q: Put it this way. If she did plan or have the ability to reflect and act upon those reflections, would that change your opinion in any way?

A: It would have some impact on my opinion. For example, if she had planned to carry out an act and then carried out the act that would raise some questions as to whether it was simply acting under an irresistible impulse.

Q: And you will agree, I take it, from your interviews with Mrs. Bobbitt and other people that she had offers—many offers of places where she could go to live during the course of these traumatic events which she experienced.

A: She had offers of places to stay as I described to the court the reason she gave for not accepting those offers at different points in time—

Q: And she had even gone to the extent of looking for apartments prior to the event, hadn't she?

A: Yes, I believe she was looking in the newspaper to try to see what might be available.

Q: And would it be fair to say then that, in your opinion, she knew a separation was imminent?

A: No, I think it would be fair to say that she was mustering up her resources to try to make an attempt to break away from Mr. Bobbitt again.

Q: Now you say in your opinion she suffered a brief psychosis?

A: A brief reactive psychosis.

Q: And in order to fit the criteria set forth in the manual, it would have to last for several hours up to a month?

A: Yes.

Q: And when is it, in your opinion, she began to experience the psychosis?

A: I believe that she began to experience the psychosis during the period of time that she was having the flood of memories. When she was in the kitchen. But it may be possible that she experienced some of that even prior to it—it's really hard to know exactly when the onset of it was. It's a little more fluid than—than one can pin down to a particular minute or moment.

Q: I think you testified that after the rape she lay in the bed and thought for a while before she got up.

A: I don't believe I testified to that, no. I believe I said that after the rape he rolled off her, pushed her to the bed, she got up and put her clothes on.

Q: Excuse me, I must have misunderstood you. Did she stay in the bedroom for any length of time?

A: I don't think so. I think it was moments—just the time it took her to put her clothes on.

Q: And did she tell you that she said she sat on the side of the bed and said "Why do you do this to me?"

A: No, she didn't tell me that.

Q: Did she tell you that "It hurts me inside. It hurts my heart. Why do you do this to me?"

A: She did not use those words when I interviewed her.

Q: Did she tell you she talked to him in any respect before she left?

A: No, she didn't.

Q: Did she tell you that she talked to him in any respect after she came back?

A: No she didn't because she told me she couldn't remember.

Q: Doctor, she had, I take it, in your opinion, a real fear of her husband. Isn't that right?

A: Yes.

Q: In that respect, she was in touch with reality, was she not?

A: Yes, that could be taken, I guess, to be one aspect of reality, yes.

Q: And psychosis, by its very definition, is one who's out of touch with reality, isn't it?

A: Well, but that's not inconsistent with the statement I just gave a moment ago.

Q: And do you have an opinion as to when she stopped suffering this brief—brief reactive episode?

A: At some period—at some time after the event, it may have been, some time after she was at Janna's house, sometime between then and when she went to the police station, possibly sometime when she was at the police station. It's very hard to know exactly when she started to reconstitute herself. Obviously she was described as being hysterically upset, crouched in a fetal position, when she was at Janna's so it's clear that she was in a deteriorated mental state at that time still. And she had a difficult time offering any coherent account of what had happened.

A: Um, I believe that between—the event is thought to have happened sometime between 3 a.m. and 4 a.m. and by the time—it was about between 5 and 5:30 by the time she arrived at the police station for questioning.

Q: And at that point in time there can be question that she was able to—to relay to Janna and the authorities the location of the penis. Is that right?

A: She did, I believe, tell them where she was when she threw it out the window. I'm not sure she was sure exactly where it was, but she gave a description of where the car had been at the stop sign.

Q: You're—you are aware of the fact that the penis was found some 45 feet to the rear of the stop sign, so she would have had to stop the car before getting to the stop sign. Are you aware of that?

A: No, I wasn't aware of the exact location of the penis.

Q: Well if that were the case, there would have been no necessity for her to have to turn 45 feet before reaching the stop sign.

A: Actually I don't know the facts of whether it would be possible to turn the wheel of a car with a penis in your hand.

Q: But understand—she told you—she got ready to turn, that's—and she was prevented from doing that by the fact that's what she had in her hand.

A: That's what she reported to me.

Q: And I guess you took that to be the truth.

A: I took that to be her report as best she could give

me of what she was experiencing at that time. It's difficult for me to determine what the truth is often.

Q: Thank you.

JOHN WAYNE BOBBITT
DIRECT EXAMINATION

BY MR. EBERT (Rebuttal):

Q: Directing your attention to the Sunday preceding this event, what did you do, sir, after you had consensual sex with her?

A: After my friend Robby knocked on the door, she wanted to continue having sex, because she didn't have an orgasm. You know, I did have. I thought she had one, and so she wanted to continue after that. But, I said, give me like a few minutes until, you know, because I wasn't ready.

She was kind of like frustrated and then Robby knocked on the door, and just came in from New York. So he kind of like interrupted us. Lorena answered the door and said Robby's here. I got dressed. Then that's when we had the big discussion on getting divorced, who was leaving, who was doing what, you know.

Q: Did there come a time when you left and went to the pool?

A: Yes.

Q: How were you dressed, sir?

A: I was wearing black shorts, like nylon shorts.

Q: When you got up to the pool, what did you do?

A: I stayed down there and talked to a friend. Then he introduced me to one of his friends and I stayed down there for like about a half an hour.

Q: Did you go swimming while you were there?

A: Yes.

Q: Did you have her keys at any time?

A: No.

Q: What happened then?

A: Lorena came down to the pool and the guy I was swimming with, he says, "Your wife's over there." And I looked and I went over to her and she said, "What's taking you so long? You know, I thought you were coming right back."

I said, "Well, okay, I'm sorry." We went back to the apartment.

Q: What happened after you got back in the apartment?

A: Well, we continued making love again, because she wasn't fully satisfied the first time, and so we tried it, you know, we did it again.

Q: Did you see Robby after that?

A: After that he came back because he had to make a phone call, was trying to contact his parents, and I guess he went to McDonalds to get something to eat.

Q: Approximately how long was it after you went up to the apartment with your wife before Robby arrived back at the door?

A: About fifteen minutes to a half hour he arrived back.

Q: All right, now, sir, there's been testimony that your wife had an abortion. Is that correct?

A: Yes.

Q: When was that? Do you recall?

A: That was like in June of 1990. I remember we were at Lakewood Apartments then.

Q: Tell the ladies and gentlemen of the jury what occurred and how that came about?

A: Well, I didn't know nothing about the pregnancy at all until she came home from work one day and she put a bib around me and said, you know, that she was pregnant, and I said—I was kind of shocked because I wasn't ready for something like that, and I told her we weren't ready for children.

I mean, we were just getting settled and we didn't have money, we didn't have financial security. We weren't prepared for it. I wasn't ready; she wasn't ready, so we both agreed of getting an abortion. She talked to Janna at the time and Janna told her she had a couple abortions and it wasn't that bad.

Q: Did there come a point in time when you did accompany her to the place to have an abortion?

A: Yes.

Q: Where was that?

A: It was in Alexandria.

Q: Do you know how that was selected, the clinic was selected?

A: She made all the arrangements. I just took her. I just drove her and drove her back home.

Q: When you got there, what occurred?

A: She went in there and she just did some paperwork and I think she talked to a lady, and then we both went into a room and watched a videotape and then—then I waited. I waited out—wait until the procedure was done.

Q: Did you ever chide your wife or say anything to her about it was going to hurt or anything like that?

A: No, I didn't. I didn't say that.

Q: After the abortion, what was her attitude?

A: Yeah, she was pretty upset because, you know, I guess she felt real bad about doing it, and I took her home after that, and it took her about a day, the rest of the day, to settle down, you know, because she was really upset about having the abortion.

Q: Did Lorena give you another reason why it would be in everybody's best interest to have this abortion?

A: Alls I know is she couldn't—she couldn't have it anyways, because one of Janna's [employees] was already pregnant and she didn't want, you know, two people getting pregnant and being, you know, taking all this time off from work.

Q: Someone else at the shop was pregnant at that time, to your knowledge?

A: Yeah.

Q: How long did your wife remain upset over the fact that she had this abortion?

A: On the way home and I think almost the rest of the day, and then the next day. By the time we went to bed, she was all right.

Q: Did you try to comfort her in any way?

A: Yeah. When we got home, I hugged her and I told her, you know, just forget about it. It's over, you know.

Q: Did she ever talk to you any more about it after that day?

A: No, not at all. I mean, it didn't come up.

Q: All right. Now, sir, have you ever had anal sex with your wife?

A: Well, we experimented with anal sex.

Q: How many times did you experiment?

A: Once.

Q: All right, would you tell the ladies and gentlemen of the jury what happened and whether or not you actually completed the act?

A: No, we didn't.

Q: Tell us what happened. Why didn't you?

A: Because, well, it was consensual. We both started to, but, you know, then she said that she didn't like it. You know, it hurt and she didn't want to do it, so she just got up and she said something, you know, "That's not where God intended you put it," you know.

And, she went in the bathroom and came back out, and then she said she didn't want to do that any more. So, I said okay.

Q: Did you ever do it again after that?

A: No. We both agreed we didn't want to do it after that.

Q: Did she bleed?

A: I think she said she did. She told me she did.

Q: You didn't see her bleed but she said she did?

A: Yeah, a little bit. She went in the bathroom and she said she bled a little bit.

Q: Did you ever—did you ever threaten her with the prospect of that again?

A: No, not ever, because I didn't want to do it anyway after that.

Q: When was it that you went to work at Legends, sir?

A: It was, I think, June 14th, 1993.

Q: Did you—did your wife's attitude change towards you when that happened?

A: Yes.

Q: In what respect?

A: Basically, I already had the job a month in advance, and I told her I'd be working at this really nice bar, and she said she didn't want me working there. You know, I explained to her it was better, you know, better pay. And it was convenient.

It was like right across the street, and she didn't like that at all, me working there, for a number of reasons. She said that girls would try to pick me up and vice versa. She said she'd be spying on me, you know, checking me all the time, making sure I'm not doing anything wrong at work.

You know, I think I started working there June 14th, but a month prior, our relationship just went bad, just basically we went our separate ways. I mean, we didn't speak to each other, we didn't communicate, we didn't get along. Just the only time we got along was in bed.

Q: Back to the abortion question, did you ever tell her she wouldn't be a good mother?

A: Never, no, I didn't. I never told her that.

Q: In your opinion, would she have been a good mother?

A: She'd make a great mother.

Q: Did you ever threaten to leave her?

A: Did I ever threaten? No, I left her twice, but I never threatened her. I just got up and just left twice and moved to New York.

Q: Sir, when you separated the last time from her, why is it that you came back?

A: Because, I still have feelings for her and I felt bad about leaving, and I had a lot of responsibilities that I left behind that I felt obligated to and I wanted to come back and take care of them and try to work it out with Lorena.

Q: How did you get the money to return?

A: Well, first time that I left, I was gone for like two months. I wrecked my car. It was in the shop, and I had no way of getting back, so I told Lorena I need money to get back, and so she sent money for a bus ticket.

She sent like a hundred dollars for a bus ticket to go back. And, you know, when I got back in Washington, she picked me up at the bus station, and I remember we went and had dinner and she was happy that I was back and all that. That's the first time I left.

Q: The second time you left, why did you come back, sir?

A: The second time I left—that was the second time, to work it out, to just take care of my responsibilities.

Q: Both instances you and she agreed to try to work it out? Is that right?

A: Yes.

Q: Let me ask you, sir, after this happened, even after your wife had done what she had done to you, do you still have some affection for her?

A: Yeah.

CROSS EXAMINATION

BY MR. HOWARD:

Q: Mr. Bobbitt, on June 24th of this year, do you recall having conversations with the police here in Prince William County while you were at the hospital?

A: I guess I remember. I'm not sure.

Q: You were in the hospital on June 24th, weren't you?

A: 24th, yes, I was.

Q: You talked to Dr. Sehn that day, didn't you?

A: Dr. Sehn? Yeah, in the morning.

Q: Yes, and, when you talked to Dr. Sehn, you were fully coherent? You had no problem understanding the conversation you had with Dr. Sehn, did you?

A: No.

Q: Later that day you talked to Investigator Weintz and you also talked to an Investigator Morgan, did you not?

A: Weintz and Morgan? Later on that day or after the surgery?

Q: At any time that day, June 24th, Mr. Bobbitt?

A: No. No, not until after the surgery.

Q: Okay, after the surgery, then, did you talk to Investigator Weintz?

A: Yeah, I remember them being there but I don't remember what was said.

Q: You've told this jury today that on the Sunday before this incident, before Robby arrived, you had sex with your wife?

A: Yes.

Q: You're trying to tell this jury the truth today, aren't you?

A: Yeah. That's the truth.

Q: It's your recollection today that, after Robby arrived, there was some discussion between you and your wife about separating.

A: Uh-huh.

Q: And she also made sure that you understood that she hadn't gotten enough sex that morning, that she wanted more sex?

A: Right.

Q: That's what you're telling this jury today?

A: I'm telling you that—that's what exactly happened.

Q: So, it went from sex to a discussion of separation and moving out to her coming to the pool and getting you and bringing you back and having more sex with you?

A: Correct.

Q: And then, after that, as soon as that sexual act was over, she finished packing her bags and took them downstairs?

A: Yes, that's exactly what happened.

Q: That's the sequence that you want them to believe that occurred on Sunday?

A: Well, that's the truth.

Q: Do you think your recollection of what occurred that Sunday is better today, as you've testified, than it was back on June 24th, 1993, within two or three days after the Sunday events?

A: Yes.

Q: You think it's better today?

A: My recollection of that Sunday is a lot better than my recollection on June 24th.

Q: Do you deny, Mr. Bobbitt, telling those two investigators on June 24th that the last time you had any sex with your wife at all was Sunday morning before your friend, Robby, arrived?

A: I don't remember saying that to them. No. I told you that I don't remember the conversation.

Q: If you told that to the detectives back on June 24th, would you say that you were mistaken when you told them that?

A: Well, maybe I didn't give them all the facts because I just got out of surgery and I was, you know, I was like kind of out of it.

Q: You just told us that you had a conversation with Dr. Sehn that morning and you understood everything he said and that you felt fine.

A: Yeah, but that was before the surgery. I was in a nine-and-a-half-hour surgery and, when I got out, I talked to Detective Weintz and Detective Morgan.

Q: All right, let me ask you this, sir: with respect to the abortion, there's no question in your mind that your wife was upset about that abortion? Is that true?

A: She was pretty upset about it.

Q: All right, and are you telling the members of the jury that, when she went to the clinic that day, that she was not frightened about what was going to happen to her?

A: I know she was uncomfortable about going through the procedure, you know, of having an abortion, you know. Then after she was really upset about doing it.

Q: All right, let me ask you this: did she ask you any questions about what was going to happen to her when she went there that day?

A: What was going to happen to her?

Q: What was going to happen to her when she went into that clinic?

A: I don't remember.

Q: Do you remember telling her that they would probably have to stick some needles in her during the course of that procedure?

A: I don't know nothing about an abortion.

Q: Okay, so, you don't remember saying those things?

A: No. I remember reading a magazine in the lounge.

Q: Might you have said those things?

A: No, I wouldn't have said that to her. I would not say that to her.

Q: You still maintain that you don't get any pleasure, excitement, out of anal sex or forced sex?

A: No. No way.

SHERRY BIRO
DIRECT EXAMINATION

BY MS. O'BRIEN:
Q: Do you know the Defendant in this case, Lorena Bobbitt?

A: Yes, I do.

Q: Have you seen her prior—have you seen her socially prior to this date?

A: Yes, I have.

Q: In 1991, Sherry, where were you and your husband living?

A: In Dover, Delaware, which we still do.

Q: You still live there now?

A: Yes.

Q: Would you occasionally socialize with John and Lorena Bobbitt?

A: Yes.

Q: How was the relationship between the four of you?

A: Friendly. John and Bud were brothers, so they got along really well.

Q: How did you get along with Lorena?

A: We didn't disagree or anything. It was friendly.

Q: Let me direct your attention to the summer of 1991 on your birthday. Did you and Bud socialize with John and Lorena?

A: Yes, we did.

Q: Where did you go? What happened?

A: We made plans to go to Kings Dominion.

Q: What were your plans for that evening? Where were you planning to stay?

A: At John and Lorena's, just for the night.

Q: Did there come a time when you got to Kings Dominion when something unusual happened with John and Lorena?

A: Yes, we were standing in line waiting for the bumper cars. I was standing ahead of Bud and John, which were facing each other, and behind them were Lorena. And John and Bud were talking, and, all of a sudden, Lorena, for some reason, got upset and she scratched John and then stormed out of the park.

Q: What did the three of you do?

A: We went after her.

Q: Did you catch up with her at some point?

A: Yes, John got the car and we all jumped in, and we went after Lorena, which, when we found her, she was sitting on a little island, just sitting there waiting, I guess.

Q: What did she do when you all pulled up?

A: She started yelling at John and then she started trying to like scratch his face and she was punching him, and John just—he just stood there, because he really didn't know what was going on.

Q: Did she calm down after a few moments?

A: Yeah, me and Bud had gotten out of the car and so did John, and John and Lorena talked, and then we went back into the park and we spent the rest of the evening there.

Q: Where did you go after you left the park?

A: We went to a diner, Mike's Diner.

Q: Did something—was something said by the Defendant while you were in Mike's Diner?

A: We were talking. Me, her and my husband were having a friendly conversation.

Q: Where was John?

A: He went to the bathroom.

Q: What did Lorena say?

A: She told us we were not welcome to stay at her house that night.

Q: What happened after you left Mike's Diner?

A: We all went back to their house. Me and my husband grabbed our clothes and we left.

Q: Did you drive back home that evening?

A: Yes.

Q: How long was that?

A: It's a two-and-a-half-hour drive.

Q: At about what time did you get in?

A: It was about two-thirty, maybe a little bit later in the morning.

Q: Did someone arrived at your residence shortly after you got there at two-thirty?

A: Yes, John did.

Q: How long did he stay?

A: He stayed a few days.

Q: Did you have occasion after that incident to socialize with them again?

A: Yes.

Q: About how regularly would you see them then?

A: About once every couple of months.

Q: During that period of time, did the Defendant ever make any complaints to you that John was abusing her?

A: No.

Q: Did you ever notice any bruises or marks on her?

A: No.

CROSS EXAMINATION

BY MR. HOWARD:

Q: Was there any discussion in your presence over that period of time of Kings Dominion incident concerning a girl by the name of Rhonda?

A: No.

BRETT BIRO
DIRECT EXAMINATION

BY MR. EBERT:

Q: Are you related to John Bobbitt?

A: I'm his cousin.

Q: Did you grow up with John?

A: Yes, I did.

Q: All right, now, did there come a point in time, specifically in January of '91, when you came to this area to visit John and Lorena?

A: Yes, I did.

Q: What was your occasion for coming here?

A: I came down kind of to visit John, maybe look for a job and get a job down here. See, I had just gotten out of the Navy.

Q: Where did you stay when you came?

A: I stayed at Lorena's house.

Q: How long were you there?

A: I was there approximately four days.

Q: How long had you planned to stay?

A: I didn't really plan to stay, you know, either—if I found a job, I was going to move out and get my own apartment or, if I didn't find a job, I was going to go back home. I didn't plan to stay around and live with them.

Q: Why is it that you left when you did?

A: Well, because Lorena asked me to leave.

Q: Was John on the telephone just prior to your leaving?

A: Yes, he was talking to my mother.

Q: Did something occur that was unusual while he was talking to your mother?

A: Yes, Lorena was mad at him and wanted him to get off the phone.

Q: What did she say?

A: She told John, "You've been talking to your mother long enough. Get off the phone."

Q: What did she do?

A: At that point, after John hung up the phone, she pulled the phone out of the wall.

Q: What happened then?

A: At that point, nothing really happened after that. Before that, I had cooked dinner for John and Lorena that day, and John complimented me on the dinner and Lorena got mad because John was complimenting me on how good the dinner went.

I went in and took a shower and I hear John and Lorena arguing. I looked out of the shower and Lorena was smacking John.

Q: What happened then?

A: I went back in the shower. I came out of the shower, put my clothes on, and they both acted like nothing happened. Then Lorena asked me to leave.

Q: Did you leave?

A: I left that night; I went and stayed at a hotel. I stayed there one night, then I went to a base billeting at Quantico.

TODD BIRO
DIRECT EXAMINATION

BY MR. EBERT:

Q: Are you related to John Bobbitt?

A: Yes, sir

Q: What is your relationship?

A: He's my cousin, but we consider each other brothers.

Q: Incidentally, were you raised with John?

A: Yes, sir, I was.

Q: Your mother actually was his foster mother to him? Is that correct?

A: Yes, sir.

Q: How many people lived grew up in your home?

A: Six boys and my parents.

Q: Now, Mr. Biro, you—in the past you have been a drug abuser, have you not?

A: Yes, sir.

Q: How long has it been since you abused drugs?

A: About four years.

Q: What kind of drugs did you abuse?

A: Cocaine.

Q: Did there come a time when you came to live with the Bobbitts?

A: Yes. Not too long after they were married.

Q: At that time, were you abusing drugs?

A: Yes, sir.

Q: Sir, are you a convicted felon?

A: Yes, sir, I am.

Q: What have you been convicted of and where and when was it?

A: It was in Niagara Falls, about three years ago. It was for second degree attempted burglary.

Q: After that, after your arrest and conviction, did you cease using drugs?

A: Yes, sir.

Q: Now, when you were living with the Bobbitts, did you use drugs at that time?

A: Yes, sir, I did.

Q: How long was it that you lived with John and Lorena, and when was it?

A: About three months, and then I lived with another family that were acquaintances of theirs for another three months.

Q: What was the name of that family?

A: The Beltrans.

Q: Where were you living when you lived with John and Lorena?

A: In Asten Park Apartments in Manassas, Austin Park Apartments. I'm not sure of the name.

Q: What time, what year was that?

A: I think it was 1989.

Q: Did there come a point in time, sir, that you had occasion to go with them to a nightclub known as Chelsea's in Washington, D.C.?

A: Yes, sir, there was.

Q: Were you able to enter the establishment?

A: No, we weren't able to enter because John had wore running shoes instead of dress shoes.

Q: In any event, he was not able to enter. How was Lorena dressed?

A: Lorena was dressed in a dress.

Q: How were you dressed?

A: I was dressed in dress pants and dress shirt and boots.

Q: Approximately what time was it that you arrived there?

A: It was early evening; it wasn't late. That was the first place that we had went to.

Q: Do you recall what happened then?

A: Yes, we went to the door and the bouncer at the door wouldn't let John in because he was wearing running shoes, and Lorena went into a frenzy and started screaming at him in front of the bouncer and all the customers that were waiting in line saying, "It's all your fault that I can't get in."

At that time, John walked out to the car and the argument continued, and we got in the car and left. On the way home, she started punching him in the face, curling up her fists and punching him, and kept punching him and punching him.

Q: Let me stop you, sir. Did you go anywhere else after you left Chelsea's? Did you go to any other bar?

A: No, sir, we went home.

Q: What happened then?

A: Lorena jumped on John's back and scratched his face and, at that time, I walked out of the apartment, down the stairs and into the parking lot and stayed there.

Q: Why did you do that, sir?

A: Because this is the first time that I'd ever seen anything like that happen between them, John and Lorena.

Q: Up to that point, you'd never seen anything, any violence or any hostility between the two?

A: Not any—not any physical.

Q: Did you return back to the apartment?

A: Yes. Then I went to bed.

Q: When you went to bed, where were they?

A: I think they were in their room.

Q: At that point in time, did you hear anything unusual between the parties when you went to bed, or was it over with?

A: No, I didn't hear anything unusual.

Q: Now, did there come a point in time when you had occasion to go to Ocean City with John and Lorena?

A: Yes, sir, there was.

Q: Do you recall approximately when that was?

A: It was Memorial Day weekend, I believe.

Q: Something unusual occur on that trip? Incidentally, who went along on that trip?

A: Myself, John, Lorena and a girl named Terri.

Q: When you went to Ocean City, what was the seating arrangement going up?

A: Seating arrangement was John driving, Lorena in the passenger seat and myself and Terri in the back seat.

Q: Did you spend the night there?

A: Yes, sir.

Q: How many rooms did you get?

A: One.

Q: Who did you sleep with?

A: I slept in the same bed as Terri.

Q: Did you have sex that night?

A: No, sir.

Q: Why not?

A: She had her period.

Q: Did there come a point in time when you left?

A: Yes, sir, we did.

Q: What was the seating arrangement when you left?

A: I drove home. John sat next to me and Lorena and Terri sat in the back seat.

Q: What happened then?

A: There was a car driving next to us with some guys in it, and Lorena and Terri were in the back seat and I don't know if they were waving to each other. I didn't see what was happening behind us, but something was happening.

John rolled down the window and got upset and asked the guys, do they have a problem. And then he turned around to Terri and said, "You're a bad influence on my wife. I don't want you hanging around her anymore. You're making her do things that I don't want her to do."

Then we took Terri to her father's house and dropped her off.

Q: Did you see any argument between John and Lorena other than what you've accounted at this time?

A: I seen them argue lots of times.

Q: Well, on this occasion?

A: No, not on this occasion.

Q: How is that you left the apartment and went to live with the Beltrans?

A: Their apartment that they lived in was a studio apartment and there was really—there really wasn't much privacy for them with me there.

Q: Lorena express some concern about that or dissatisfaction with that arrangement?

A: Yes.

Q: John ask you to leave, as well as Lorena?

A: It was a mutual agreement.

CROSS EXAMINATION

BY MR. LOWE:

Q: Mr. Biro, you indicated that you had a drug problem when you were staying with your cousin and Lorena?

A: Yes, sir. Cocaine.

Q: What instruments were you utilizing to use that cocaine?

A: A needle.

Q: So, you were shooting cocaine? Is that correct?

A: Yes, sir.

Q: Were you keeping drugs in their home?

A: Yes, sir, at one time, I did.

Q: You knew John was in the Marine Corps, didn't you?

A: Yes, sir, I did.

Q: So it would ruin his career if he had got caught with drugs, wouldn't it?

A: It could have.

Q: You knew Lorena was an immigrant, didn't you?

A: Yes, sir.

Q: You knew it would ruin her ability to remain in America if she got caught with drugs in her house, wouldn't it?

A: Oh, I didn't know that.

Q: You didn't worry about those sorts of things?

A: Well, at the time, I guess I didn't worry about it. I had a pretty severe drug problem.

Q: Did you use any when you went up to Ocean City?

A: No, sir.

Q: As far as you know, Terri doesn't ever use any drugs, does she?

A: Not as far as I know.

Q: All right. You grew up with John, didn't you?

A: Yes, sir, I did.

Q: And you'd do anything you could to help him, wouldn't you?

A: Yes, sir, I would.

Q: You all ever known as the Bruise Brothers?

A: Yes, sir, it was a nickname given to us by our vice principal of our high school.

Q: Now, Mr. Biro, in the process of doing whatever you could for John, have you threatened to and gone out to look to harm Lorena after this incident on the 23rd?

A: I mentioned that one time, sir. On Jenny Jones' show, but that was my feelings at the time, but I would never take the law into my own hands.

Q: Didn't you in fact say on the Jenny Jones Show you and your brother—cousin—who just got off the stand, that you all went out looking for Lorena to kill her?

A: That was my feelings at the time, sir.

Q: Did you say that on national television, sir?

A: I said that if I'd seen her, that I would have killed her. That was my feelings.

Q: And you actually said "went out looking," didn't you?

A: I don't know if I actually said I went out looking because, when we got to the emergency room, we were greeted by two police officers which strictly forbidded (sic) us from going out to look for her. But, my intentions on the way down to Virginia were go to look for Lorena; yes, they were.

But, again, that was just my feelings at the time. Once I got to the emergency room and talked with the police officers and seen John was okay, and I asked John, "What do you want us to do, John?"

He said, "Nothing, Todd. Don't do anything."

REDIRECT EXAMINATION

BY MR. EBERT:

Q: Mr. Biro, would it be fair to say, when you heard about this, you were pretty upset? Isn't that right?

A: Yes, sir, extremely.

Q: The entire family was upset?

A: Yes, sir, my mother was screaming at home and as far as I knew, that John was very critical and close to death, and me and my brother left as soon as we got ready. We left first, but we were quite upset and angry. That was our first reaction, sir.

When Jenny Jones asked me that, what my reaction was, that was—that was my reaction.

Q: Your reaction was you wanted to kill her for what she had done to the person you consider as your brother?

A: Yes, sir, but I would never have took the law into my own hands, sir.

Q: Now, sir, you say you would do anything for your brother?

A: Yes, sir

Q: Would you lie for him?

A: No, sir, I wouldn't lie.

Q: What you told us here today is the truth?

A: Yes, sir.

MARYLYN BIRO
DIRECT EXAMINATION

BY MR. EBERT:

Q: How long have you been married?

A: Twenty-eight years.

Q: How many children do you have?

A: Six.

Q: You say you have six children born to you; is that correct?

A: No, four—we have four of our own and two that we've raised since they were small.

Q: One of the children that you say you supported is adopted?

A: Yes.

Q: Which one of the children is that?

A: Bud.

Q: Now, you know John Bobbitt, do you not?

A: Yes.

Q: Did you raise him?

A: Since he was five years old.

Q: How did he come to live with you, he and his brothers?

A: Well, we took them out of a bad home life. His mother wasn't mentally capable of taking care of them.

Q: She's related to your husband?

A: Yes. She's his sister.

Q: You say she was mentally unable to take care of them?

A: Yes.

Q: When was it that they came to live with you and how did that occur?

A: They came in September when they were five and six years old. I don't remember the exact year.

Q: How about the baby? When did he come to live with you?

A: When he was eight days old. He had been home from the hospital for a day.

Q: When was that, with relation to when John and his brother, other brother, came to live with you?

A: We took the boys three years later—no, it wasn't three years later. I'm trying to think of the difference in their ages. Four years later.

Q: All right, ma'am. Did there come a point in time when John left your home?

A: Yes.

Q: When was that?

A: When he went into the Marines.

Q: While he lived with you, did you learn that John had some attention span deficit?

A: Yes, he did.

Q: Ma'am, after John went in the Marine Corps, did there come a point in time when you became aware that he was to marry?

A: Yes.

Q: Did you talk with Lorena concerning that?

A: Yes, I did.

Q: Did you have any conversation with her concerning the proposed marriage?

A: Well, at first we had a conversation with John, and we were real concerned because he said he was going to get married because Lorena's green card was running out. When we talked to Lorena, she said that that wasn't the reason why she was going to get married. She said that she loved John and she wanted to marry him.

Q: What was the reason that you related to her that made her respond in that respect?

A: Because, you know, we had said that we were concerned. We talked to John and Lorena about the green card. They said her green card was going to expire in a few days.

Q: Did you talk to her about that?

A: Yes, I did.

Q: What did you tell her in that regard?

A: I just told them both that, you know, that's the reason why we're concerned. You know, if that's the only reason why they were getting married; and we suggested to both of them why didn't she go back and get another card and wait a year, and, if they really loved each other, then they could wait a year.

Q: What was her response to that advice?

A: Oh, I don't remember her true response, but they did want to get married and their mind was made up.

Q: Did there come a point in time when you were aware that they did marry?

A: Yes.

Q: As a result of that, did you make any arrangements for another ceremony?

A: Yes, I did. John and Lorena had both talked to us

on the phone, and John had said that they wanted to have their marriage blessed because they had only gotten married by a justice of the peace, so we said we could arrange that for them.

He said they were going to come home, so I said, "Just let us know when you're coming home and we'll have a reception for you," because they had, you know, nothing. They just got married by the justice of the peace.

Q: Did you make arrangements for a church ceremony?

A: Not really a church ceremony, just to have their marriage blessed by the priest.

Q: Now, did you talk to Lorena concerning the plans that you made?

A: Before they came up?

Q: Right.

A: Yes, I did, and she said she would bring her wedding dress and John brought his navy blues.

Q: Now, when they failed to appear, did you make any other arrangements to reschedule the ceremony?

A: Yes, we rescheduled the ceremony for the next day and the reception had already been scheduled for three o'clock on Saturday afternoon.

Q: When you had this reception, did you see anything unusual occur at that reception?

A: Yes, I did.

Q: Would you tell the ladies and gentlemen of the jury what that was?

A: Okay. My niece came up to John and wanted him to come to the truck to look at some pictures. Lorena was standing talking to someone else, so he proceeded to go over and look at the pictures.

When he came back, she pulled him aside where we

could see but didn't hear what she was saying and she was letting in to him.

Q: Did you talk to Lorena about it?

A: Yes.

Q: Was she angry at that time?

A: Yes.

Q: Tell us what you said and what her reply was.

A: I said, "Don't be jealous. That's his cousin. She lived with us at one time. They're very close." And she just said, "He could have taken me with her"—or "with him."

Q: Did you make arrangements for them to stay there that night?

A: Yes, I did.

Q: What were those arrangements?

A: We have two trailers, a small trailer and a bigger trailer. The small trailer is like right behind, and that's what my husband and I use for our personal bedroom. Well, when they came for that weekend, we gave it to them for the weekend.

Q: Did they stay there?

A: Yes, they did.

Q: When is the next time you visited them?

A: Thanksgiving time.

Q: Did you bring anything with you at that time?

A: Everything. We brought all kinds of food. We brought a turkey. We even brought the cookware to cook in. We bought a portable, like a folding table.

Q: Did you tell Lorena that you were going to do that?

A: Yes, I did.

Q: Had you talked with her about your plans?

A: Yes, I had.

Q: She respond to you when you told her?

A: Right.

Q: What did she say?

A: At first, you know, she was kind of, just a little bit hesitant; but then, after we talked, she was fine. We made all these plans and, when we got down there, when we got there, Todd and Lorena and John took us out for dinner, and I can't remember the name of the place.

And, when we came back, she said, "I cut up"—she had two little containers of celery and carrots. She says, "I cut these up in case you need them for dressing or for dinner."

Q: I take it you returned, you went home; is that right?

A: Yes.

Q: Did you notice anything unusual between John and Lorena during that day?

A: She got mad at him and left for two days.

Q: Do you where she went?

A: No, I don't know where she went.

Q: You and your husband stayed at their residence at that time?

A: Yes, we did.

Q: Where did you sleep during that period of time?

A: On the floor, except when Lorena wasn't there. Then we slept in the bed.

Q: Where did John sleep?

A: When Lorena was there, he slept with Lorena.

Q: Well, I mean after she left.

A: He slept on the floor.

Q: Did there come a point in time when you had occasion to return and attend a Christmas party on Christmas Eve at the Beltrans' with your husband?

A: Yes, we did.

Q: What happened then?

A: Well, we were invited to this Christmas party because

we had met them when we went down at Thanksgiving time and they wanted us to come back to this party.

Q: How did you get along with them?

A: We got along well with them and, in fact, we had to talk Lorena into going, because she didn't want to go to this party.

Q: Did she in fact go to this party?

A: Yes, she went to the party.

Q: Did you see any exchange of gifts on that occasion?

A: No gifts.

Q: Did you see any fights or anything like that?

A: No.

Q: I direct your attention specifically to the summer of 1991. How long did John stay with you that summer?

A: I think it was about six weeks, and then he went back and then he came back again.

Q: While he was living with you, did you have any calls from Lorena?

A: Many, many, many calls, over and over and over again.

Q: Where would she call you?

A: She called me at home. She called me at work. She called my sister's house. She called at camp, where we camped.

Q: To your knowledge, did she talk to your husband?

A: She talked to all of us—my husband, Todd, Brett, myself. I mean the phone would ring and it rang so many times that we would say, "I'm not going to answer it; I'm not answering that phone." Everybody said they weren't going to answer the phone.

Q: When you talked—when you talked with Lorena, what did she say to you?

A: She said, "Send him home. You're his mother. You can make him come home. Make him come back home."

Q: What did you tell her with regard to that request?

A: Well, I told her that we couldn't make him come home and then, you know, she proceeded to say other things, too.

Q: What else did she say?

A: She said, you know, "I know why"—she'd say, "I know why he left me. He left me because I'm stealing." And I said, "That's not the only reason why he left you. He left you because you're mean."

So then she would call and say, "I'm reading the Bible. I'm going to church. I'm sorry I was so mean. I'll tell all the boys I'm sorry I was so mean."

Q: Then, to your knowledge, did she tell everybody she was sorry?

A: Yes, she did.

Q: Oh, just incidentally, did she ever talk on any of these phone calls about needing money?

A: No, never.

CROSS EXAMINATION

BY MR. HOWARD:

Q: Ms. Biro, as John's mother, I understand why this entire matter has been very upsetting to you; is that correct?

A: Yes, it has.

Q: Now, you come back for another visit to the Beltran—you came back for a visit around Christmas time and you went to a party at the Beltran house?

A: Yes.

Q: Would you tell the members of the jury roughly how long you stayed there that evening?

A: I'd say three or four hours.

Q: Okay. During the three-to-four-hour period, were there occasions where you would be engaged in conversation with people there at the party that you didn't see John or Lorena?

A: There may have been but the house was kind of small and set out where you couldn't more or less see what was going on on that floor.

Q: Okay. So, there were times because of the arrangement of the house and your being engaged in conversation that you couldn't see what everybody in that house was doing, correct?

A: Right.

Q: You didn't see any gifts being exchanged between John and Lorena that night, did you?

A: We didn't see any gifts between anybody.

Q: And, if that occurred, it happened out of your presence?

A: Right.

DAVID CORCORAN
DIRECT EXAMINATION

BY MR. EBERT:

Q: State your full name, sir, and give your place of employment.

A: David Michael Corcoran, Prince William Hospital Emergency Room.

Q: What is your position there, sir.

A: I'm one of the staff physicians.

Q: Would you tell the ladies and gentlemen of the jury what your duties are in that capacity?

A: I take care of people who come in through the emergency room.

Q: And part of your duties, is that to examine alleged rape victims?

A: That's correct.

Q: Did there come a point in time in the course of your employment that you had occasion to see Lorena Bobbitt?

A: That's correct.

Q: When was that?

A: The 23rd of June, '93.

Q: What was your occasion for seeing her?

A: She came into the emergency room saying she'd been raped.

Q: And what time was it?

A: 7:39 in the morning.

Q: At that time, would you describe her condition and her demeanor at the time of your examination?

A: Her demeanor was very calm.

Q: Did you have any conversation with her?

A: Yes, I did.

Q: Did you explain the procedure that she was to undergo?

A: I explained to her that, for the evidence to stand up in court, the procedure had to be done very exactly and asked her to cooperate. She said she would.

Q: Did she appear to understand and comprehend what you said?

A: She did.

Q: Did you take a history from her at that time?

A: Yes, I asked her what happened.

Q: What did she tell you?

A: Well, I have it in quotes here. Shall I read it to you?

Q: Yes, sir. Read it loudly, so the jury can hear you, please.

A: "Claims husband "raped her" here at about 4:30 in the morning. Patient claims she resisted, regular vaginal intercourse. Doesn't know if ejaculated. Put back on clothes. Went to kitchen to drink water. "I saw a knife. I was really angry. I opened the sheet and I cut him. I was driving. I threw it into the bushes."

Now, this is what she also said. "Husband did not pull on hair; did not hit."

Q: Did you do an examination of her?

A: Yes, I did.

A: Well, it's a screening physical examination and then a vaginal examination.

Q: Well, you say a screening physical examination. What do you mean by that?

A: You listen to her heart and her lungs and check her stomach.

Q: And the vaginal examination, what does that consist of?

A: You look at the labia, the lips, to see if there's any bruises or tears, and then you put a speculum inside and see if there's any discharges, and then you see how big or tender the uterus is.

Q: Did you find any discharge?

A: There was a slight clear cervical discharge, yes.

Q: Did you make any preparation for a microscopic examination?

A: No, I took the samples for the rape exam kit that goes to the forensic lab.

Q: You say you took samples. What were the samples that you took?

A: Samples of the discharge I found sitting next to the cervix, samples of the cervix, and then on the outside.

Q: Did you see any evidence whatsoever of trauma to Mrs. Bobbitt?

A: No.

Q: With regard to her—you noted a tenderness of the uterus; is that correct?

A: That's correct.

Q: Is that customarily traumatized in forcible intercourse?

A: Usually not, but you'd have to ask an obstetrician for this.

Q: Did you ever see it in your practice, sir?

A: No, I haven't, but it's possible, I suppose.

Q: Certainly, no ripping or tearing of the vagina from your observation?

A: I did not see any.

CROSS EXAMINATION

BY MR. HOWARD:

Q: Now, the exhibit in your hand has just been admitted into evidence and I'd like to draw your attention, please, to the quotes that you have given us.

Right above those quotes, there's a priority block on that report.

A: Uh-huh.

Q: There's three categories there: one, two and three. Can you give us or interpret what the meaning of those priorities are?

A: Well, one, a priority one is a heart attack, which comes before everybody else—somebody who is close to dying. And then it goes down to two and then to three. Three would be the lowest priority.

Q: All right. Would you be good enough to read to the members of the jury what appears in that block?

A: Under priority three?

Q: Yes, sir.

A: "Arrived by rescue. Patient states—'My husband forced me into having sex with him.' Patient crying and appears upset."

Q: Okay. Does that refresh your recollection, sir, as to her condition when you saw her that morning?

A: That's what the nurse saw when she—it's called triage. When the nurse sees her first, she writes down what she sees. Then I write down what I see. The nurse was Carolyn Hansborough.

Q: Do you have any reason to disagree with what Ms. Hansborough put down there?

A: I wasn't there, so I don't know.

Q: All right, sir. And the time that she put down that she made these observations of Ms. Bobbitt was 6:30 a.m.?

A: 6:30 a.m.

Q: What time did you see her?

A: 7:39.

Q: Oh, you saw her an hour later?

A: That's correct.

Q: After she had been seen by the nurse?

A: That's correct.

Q: Do you know how many people had talked to her and what had been done in the intervening hour or so before you saw her?

A: No, I don't.

DIANE HALL
DIRECT EXAMINATION

BY MS. O'BRIEN:

Q: Ms. Hall, directing your attention to June the 23rd of 1993, did you know John and Lorena Bobbitt on that day?

A: Yes, I did.

Q: Where were you living on that day, ma'am?

A: Maplewood Apartments, Apartment Two.

Q: Do you know what apartment they were living in?

A: Apartment Five.

Q: Directing your attention to the early summer months of 1993, did you ever have occasion to socialize with John and Lorena Bobbitt?

A: A few times, yes.

Q: What would those social occasions consist of?

A: Dinner.

Q: During this period of time, the early summer months of 1993, did you ever observe any bruises on Lorena Bobbitt?

A: No.

Q: Did you ever see the couple having any physical fights during that period of time?

A: No.

Q: Let me direct your attention to the weekend of June of the 20th and ask you if you saw Lorena Bobbitt during that weekend?

A: I saw her Sunday.

Q: How did you come to see her Sunday.

A: Well, she came down to the apartment. She had already stored some stuff in my apartment, and she came down to tell me about it on Sunday night.

Q: Did you know why she had stored things in your apartment?

A: Not until she came down on Sunday night and told me.

Q: When she came down Sunday night and talked to you, did you offer her your apartment as a place to store items and a place to stay?

A: Yes.

Q: Did she appear to understand that offer?

A: Yes.

Q: Did she take you up on that offer?

A: No.

Q: Did you in fact have dinner with her that night?

A: Yes.

Q: Where did you have dinner?

A: At the apartment, mine.

Q: What did she tell you with regard to her future plans?

A: She was leaving John.

Q: Did you see her again after Sunday night?

A: I think I saw her Monday.

Q: Did you renew your offer to her to store things and stay in your apartment if she needed to?

A: Yeah, well, the stuff was still there. Everything was there.

Q: Did she indicate to you she wished to stay in your apartment on that day?

A: No.

Q: Ma'am, when you had dinner on Sunday night, did Lorena talk to you at that point about any problem she was having?

A: She said things were—you know, about John beating her and raping her.

Q: She told you that on Sunday night?

A: Yeah.

Q: After she told you that, did you offer your home to her?

A: Yes.

Q: Did she indicate any hesitancy about going back upstairs?

A: No, it was late when she went back up.

Q: You said you saw her again the next night?

A: I think so, yeah.

Q: Did you all have dinner that night, or do you know?

A: Well, I don't remember if we had dinner.

Q: Were you—did you support her idea of leaving?

A: Yeah, sure, yeah.

Q: What did you say to her?

A: I just agreed with her. If she wanted to leave John, that was fine.

CROSS EXAMINATION

BY MR. LOWE:

Q: Ms. Hall, as I understand it, during this last week or so before this incident, Lorena reported to you that she intended to leave John?

A: She told me that Sunday night.

Q: Okay. She told you that he'd been raping her?

A: Yeah, that he had raped her and beat her, but she didn't say when.

Q: She told you that he beat her? She also told you, did she not, that he could get any girl that he wanted?

A: Yes.

Q: Did she also tell you that she was tired of the abuse?

A: Yes.

Q: Did she also tell you that her husband would track her down or had threatened to track her down whatever she did?

A: She said he always came and found her when she left him.

Q: Did she actually say—the last time you testified that she reported to you that he would track her down?

A: Yes.

Q: She did not appear to you to be either vengeful or mad, did she?

A: No.

Q: You had an impression of her that she was a quiet, nice girl who just wanted to be happily married?

A: Yes.

CONNIE JAMES
DIRECT EXAMINATION

BY MR. EBERT:

Q: Ma'am, was there a time when you had occasion to reside in this area?

A: Yes.

Q: When was that?

A: That was in '89 and '90.

Q: How did you come to be here?

A: My husband got stationed in the Marine Corps in Quantico.

Q: In that capacity, did you come to know John and Lorena Bobbitt?

A: Yes, I did.

Q: What was your relationship with them?

A: Lorena worked with me, and my husband worked with John.

Q: Were you friendly?

A: Yes.

Q: Have you continued to be friendly up to this date?

A: Yes.

Q: Ms. James, what kind of work did you do?

A: I used to do nails and teach aerobics.

Q: You say Lorena worked with you. Where was that?

A: Fit and Pretty in Stafford, Virginia.

Q: Was she working at that point in time any place else?

A: Yes, she was.

Q: Where was that?

A: She never mentioned the name of the salon, but she said she was doing nails at another salon.

Q: So, to your knowledge, she was working two places?

A: Yes, she was.

Q: Did you and she become friends?

A: Yes, we did. We just became friends because both of our husbands were stationed together and they worked together, and she was from a Hispanic background and I'm Mexican, so we had a lot in common. And we were newlyweds, so, that's how we became friends.

Q: Did you socialize with her?

A: Yes, I did at work.

Q: From your observation, did you notice anything unusual about Lorena's actions towards John while she was at work?

A: She seemed very possessive of John. John would pick her up from work and, if he was even a minute late, she would be pacing back and forth and she would get on the phone to call John right away to see where John was.

Q: Did you and she have conversations about John's potential infidelity?

A: Yes, we did. We always discuss about our lives at home and our husbands, and we had a discussion what would we do if our husbands ever cheated on us, and we had a discussion about that.

Q: Tell the ladies and gentlemen of the jury what that conversation consisted of?

A: It consisted of I made a joke and I said, "You know, I would probably kill him," and I said, "I'm just kidding. I'm probably going to take everything and leave him." Then I asked Lorena what would she do, and Lorena stated, "I would"—can I say it exactly like—

Q: You can say exactly—

A: Lorena stated, "I would cut his dick off because that would hurt him more than just killing him."

Q: How did she appear to be when she made that statement?

A: She appeared to be serious. She wasn't joking. She didn't say anything after that.

Q: Now, there came a point in time when she ceased to work with you; is that right?

A: Yes, after three months, we stopped working together.

Q: Why was that?

A: She couldn't coordinate her hours between the other job and the job with me.

Q: Did you and she stay in touch despite that?

A: Oh, we stayed in touch. We probably communicated about once a week or so, and then, all of a sudden, she just stopped returning my phone calls.

Q: When did you become aware that something had occurred between John and Lorena?

A: I saw John and Lorena's picture on 20/20. My husband and I, we were sitting around, and then we looked at each other and we go, "Oh, my God, that's the couple, you know, about the penis and stuff and we know them." And I go, "I can't believe she went through with it." That's the comment I made to my husband.

Q: Did there come a point in time when you had occasion to contact a radio station concerning what you had heard while you were in this area?

A: Yes, I was driving on my way to work and I heard John Bobbitt on the radio station. I told myself, you know, I'm going call him and just say hello and see how he's doing.

So, I did. I got to work and I dialed the number and I finally went through and I proceeded to speak to John. And then I told him, you know, I just said, I, I thought it was funny that this actually happened to you when I knew about it in 1990, and then they stopped me from speaking to John. I couldn't proceed with my comments.

Q: You consider yourself to this day to be a friend of Lorena?

A: Yes.

Q: And a friend of John, likewise?

A: Yes.

CROSS EXAMINATION

BY MR. HOWARD:

Q: Let me ask you this. I listened closely to your direct examination and, as I understand it, when this conversation took place between you and Lorena, you were joking with her, is that correct?

A: We were having a normal conversation. We weren't joking through the whole thing. No, we weren't.

Q: But didn't you tell this jury just a few minutes ago that you jokingly said to her that you'd kill your husband if he ever ran around?

A: Yes, I did.

Q: And you conveyed it to her in that way, didn't you? As a joke?

A: I told her it was a joke.

Q: You made that very clear to her.

A: That's right.

Q: And her response to you was, between two ladies, "Well, I wouldn't kill him. I would cut his dick off." That's what your recollection is, is that correct?

A: Right.

Q: Now, that evening, did you go home and call John Bobbitt?

A: No, I did not.

Q: When was the first time you ever told John Bobbitt about what she had said?

A: On the radio station.

Q: Three years later?

A: Yes.

Q: Did you tell your husband about this that night when you got home from work?

A: I sure did.

Q: Is he here to testify today?

A: No, he's not.

Q: He couldn't make it to court?

A: We have a child and he takes care of the child.

Q: All right. You indicated that you first saw something about this case on 20/20?

A: Yes.

Q: Did you remark to your husband at that time about the fact that this case was getting a lot of publicity?

A: No.

Q: All right. Did it occur to you that when your friends were on television like that, if you came forward with this information, perhaps you could get a little publicity?

A: No, sir, I don't care about publicity.

Q: You were brought up here when?

A: I was brought up here last Tuesday.

Q: Where did they have you stay ma'am?

A: They had me stay at a hotel in Manassas.

Q: All right. Was that the Holiday Inn?

A: Yes, sir.

Q: All right, now, the entire John Bobbitt family was staying at the Holiday Inn, also, isn't that true?

A: Yes, sir.

Q: Did you get together with them during the period of time that you were at the Holiday Inn?

A: To eat breakfast.

Q: Okay. So, you socialized with them and you were with them at breakfast and you were in their company over there at the Holiday Inn?

A: Yes.

Q: Did you discuss with them your testimony and what you were going to testify to in this case?

A: No.

Q: How many times were you in their company while you all were staying over there at the Holiday Inn together?

A: Probably just for breakfast a couple of times and dinner two times.

Q: Ma'am, on any of these occasions—you had dinner with them, breakfast with them—did anyone pay for your food or drinks or anything that you had?

A: A couple of times.

Thursday, January 20

EVAN NELSON
DIRECT EXAMINATION

BY MS. O'BRIEN:

Q: Doctor, let me ask you if you have an opinion with a reasonable degree of medical certainty as to whether the defendant in this case was suffering from mental illness at the time that she committed the crime.

A: Yes, I do. It is my opinion that Mrs. Bobbitt was suffering from a mental illness known as major depression.

Q: And would someone who is suffering from major depression generally act impulsively?

A: No. Quite the opposite. Folks who are depressed or lethargic or lacking in energy really don't feel like doing much of anything. They don't usually act on impulses at all. Well, let me clarify that. As a rule they're not impulsive folks. In general; what they're doing is sitting around feeling sad and lost in their lives.

Q: And was that consistent with what you observed from your evaluation and the items that you reviewed concerning Mrs. Bobbitt?

A: Oh, very much so.

Q: Doctor, may I ask you if you've considered any other diagnosis of mental illness?

A: Yes, I considered, post traumatic stress disorder.

Q: And why is that?

A: Well, I went back through all the information that I had from Mrs. Bobbitt, the interviews, the statements that she made for police, the 700 plus page deposition that she made in August and September, and I looked at all the other types of information from other people who had observed her and talked with her and, of course, I spoke with a number of folks and what I saw is that her explanation of what was happening at the time of the crime changes over time. It starts out very clear and succinct. When she makes her statement to Detective Weintz let's look at the language of what she says. "I was hurt, I went to the kitchen to drink water. I opened the refrigerator and I got out a cup of water. Then I was angry already." She stated a feeling. Hadn't stated any other feelings or confusion about feelings at that point in time. There's nothing about pictures rushing through her mind or intrusive thoughts here.

"And I turned my back and the first thing I saw was the knife. Then I took it and I was just angry." Now at this point in time, my first hypothesis is she's saying that she was just angry. She's identifying that there's one clear emotion that's driving her behavior at this point in time. She's not describing any confusion here about how she's feeling, she's not describing problems with thoughts and feelings rushing through her mind.

She goes on. "Then I took it and I went to the bedroom and I told him he shouldn't do this to me, why he did it. And then I said, I asked him if he was satisfied" and it goes on and then she says, "I was just mad." Again, she's saying the exact same emotion, it's the third time that she said she's angry in the same 3 or 4 sentences, and two of the times she says I was just mad. There's no indication of any confusion about her feelings. There's no indication of any problems in her head of reexperiencing trauma or having intrusive thoughts of the past trauma.

When she gets to the emergency room, the quote that's written down by the emergency room doctor is "I was angry." Again, there's no report of any confusion whatsoever. It's a very succinct statement about her feelings

But what happens over time is that Mrs. Bobbitt's ability to recollect what's going on changes., By the time she gets to her statements in her deposition in August and September, she starts to say that she doesn't really remember picking up the knife and she said "I guess I cut him" indicating that she's not sure herself if she remembers it—"I guess I ran out," indicating that the memory for the traumatic event of cutting off the penis seems to be unclear at this point in time. She seems not to remember what her actions are vividly. But she doesn't mention at that point in time pictures flooding through her mind. She does indicate that she had many thoughts and feelings.

By the time she's interviewed in late November, early December, she has a slightly different version of things and as she told us she remembers looking down at her husband, looking him up and down and pulling down the sheet. So at that point in time she seems to have a little bit more memory and she describes having lots of thoughts and feelings going through her mind at that point. When we saw her on 12/20/93, she said that she was "in a dreamlike state" with images of current and past spouse abuse.

So clearly what's happening over time is initially she gives us a very succinct explanation of how she feels and what's going through her mind, but as we get further and further from the event, her own ability to recall and understand the events are changed.

My own personal opinion is that's because she now has Post Traumatic Stress Disorder and folks who've had Post Traumatic Stress Disorder often have spotty remembrances for the trauma. They may have some things that they remember some days correctly, some things that they remember incorrectly on other days, and other periods of time where they don't remember at all. So her change in the memory, I think, makes it confusing. What we seen now is PTSD.

There's additional information to this, too. I watched Mrs. Bobbitt testify here on the stand and I saw how when she was remembering these things the sort of the glazed look in her eyes—she's clearly not completely connected with the topic matter that she's discussing at this point in time. She is obviously an individual in great agony at this point in time. You don't see that described anywhere in her statement. On top of that, I looked at all the other things because clearly Mrs. Bobbitt's self report wasn't going to be real reliable because it's changing over time as the symptoms develop.

We looked at all the other things that people said here on the witness stand as well as the statements. She's consistently described as sad and tearful and in some cases he's described as anxious. Nowhere is there any description of Mrs. Bobbitt saying thoughts are flooding through my mind, I can't get these images of abuse out of the way.

So I'd started to ask myself well why was that? Is it possible that she didn't tell anyone. Well she's certainly telling us in the interviews that, no, she didn't like to talk about these things, but when I looked back to the depositions, that really didn't turn out to be true at all. She talked about the rapes and the abuse and her desire to have the marriage change and to leave with many people. So Mrs. Bobbitt spent a lot of time talking about the abuse that she experienced, but no one in the depositions or in their statements here has said that Mrs. Bobbitt was reporting problems with intrusive images that she couldn't get out of her mind. If she was experiencing symptoms as severe as we saw on the stand right now which would clearly meet the criteria for the diagnosis, it would seem likely that somebody at that time would have noticed it or that she would have complained to somebody in all the different discussions that she had.

Q: Doctor, are you aware that two of your colleagues have changed their opinion about whether she was suffering from Post Traumatic Stress Disorder at the time of the event?

A: Yes.

Q: And based on their opinion and their testimony, is it still your opinion that she was not?

A: We spent a lot of time talking about that and I still believe from the data that what Mrs. Bobbitt had was major depression and not PTSD.

Q: Now given the information you have reviewed and your diagnosis, can you explain your opinion of Mrs. Bobbitt's mental condition at the time of this offense, June 23?

A: It's my impression that Mrs. Bobbitt had a pretty

terrible marriage. I don't think that's very disputable. And that she had been depressed. But something changes for her after Mr. Bobbitt comes back and, specifically, after they moved into their own apartment in March or April of '93. What changes is even though she's been wanting to make the marriage work, she has a recognition that it's not going to work. And she starts to take efforts to leave the marriage. She's got a clear intent on going to get a divorce and, starting in May all the way through to the time when she leaves, she's beginning to make more and more changes in her life in an effort to get out of the marriage. That's very clear.

What's happening is she's starting to get stronger. She's starting to get more control over her life and to take actions to fix her problem. I think what happened on the day of the alleged crime in terms of her mental status is that Mrs. Bobbitt was beginning to feel better, as scared as she was that her husband was going to do something, she'd pursued six or seven things which indicated that she was going to leave the marriage. For example, she pursued contacting divorce attorneys, she had pursued getting the audiotape, she had pursued contacting the apartment managers to find out about breaking the lease, she had pursued trying to stay out of the house more often during those last few days, she had gone to a physician to complain about her symptoms, something that she hadn't done before for other types of symptoms such as the symptoms of major depression that she was having, she'd pursued a temporary protection order, she'd made a decision about whether or not she was safe if she did or did not get that order.

In general, she was starting to get more control. When Mr. Bobbitt did what she perceived as a rape, that was a challenge to her sense of control and, at that point in time, I believe that because she was starting to feel more in control. What was different for her was that she got intensely angry and rather than rationalizing it or putting up with it, this was a tremendous emotional insult. When she's standing in the kitchen, I think her description in June is the most reliable piece of information because, as I've described, I think her ability to report how she felt about the situation has changed over time. She very clearly says, I was just angry. I was just mad. And that anger comes for having been violated, and anger comes from having had her increasing sense of control challenged.

So when she picks up the knife at that point in time, it's my opinion that she was having an impulse of anger and that she was feeling very angry towards her husband. When she went back into the bedroom, she pauses. She pauses, according to her own report, to stop and talk to him. "Then I took it and I went to the bedroom and I told him he shouldn't do this to me. Why does he do it?" She's got the knife, she's gone back to confront him, and she challenges him or she says to him, "I asked him if he was satisfied with what he did and he was just half-asleep or something. I was just mad." So when she goes to him and says "Hey, you talk to me, do you like what you just did to me? Because I'm about to tell you how much I don't like it. And he says he doesn't care about feelings. He did say that and I asked him if he has an orgasm in me 'cause it hurt me—when he made me do that before he always has an orgasm and he doesn't wait for me to have an orgasm. He's selfish. I don't think it's fair. So I pulled back the sheets and I did it."

What we have is the anger starts to emerge in the

kitchen, she goes back to the bedroom to confront him, and he doesn't give her the satisfaction of sitting up. She's standing there with a knife over him and she's saying *Talk to me. I'm angry with you. I want to know how you feel about this because I need to tell you how I feel about this.* He doesn't even do that. It not only fuels her anger more, and it's my opinion that when she cut him, the key emotion, the clear emotion by her own description, is anger.

Q: Let me ask you this, doctor. What is the likelihood that her mental illness and her mental state at the time of the offense would have led to an irresistible impulse?

A: Well from what we know about major depression and from what we know about Mrs. Bobbitt, it seems very unlikely that this would have been an irresistible impulse. For example, she picks up the knife, she goes into the bedroom, but she pauses. She stops long enough to have a conversation with him. So that clearly suggests that the impulse of whatever she's going to do with the knife—and in truth we don't really know what she's going to do. Was it her intent just to scare him, to give herself a sense of power, is she going back to kill him? She tells us in a later interview, "I just wanted him to go away." But I think, again, that this effort for her to try and remember things is a little muddy. We know that she's depressed. Depressed people don't usually act on impulse. We know that during the days before that she's had lots of opportunities where she might have acted on impulse but, instead, what she's done is acted very rationally and a very controlled manner pursuing these six or seven very logical, sequential things that she needs to do to leave the marriage. So it doesn't seem to suggest that Mrs. Bobbitt is losing control of her impulses during those last few days, but the opposite. She's gaining more control over herself.

Q: Along those lines, doctor, there has been a great deal of testimony from Dr. Feister about the defendant suffering from what she describes is a battered woman syndrome. Would that be your conclusion as well, sir?

A: I think that Mrs. Bobbitt was a battered wife. I don't think that there's any doubt in my mind that there were incidents of violence and abuse, both verbal and physical and sexual, that Mr. Bobbitt may have engaged in a great deal of intimidation. It's my impression that during the period of 1991 before the long separation that she probably was exhibiting more features of that syndrome but, at the time of this event and those last few months, I don't think she fits that.

Q: The specific features that I recall Dr. Feister testifying about were being trapped, inability to tell people, denial, reluctance to seek help. What of those features do you see her fitting or not fitting?

A: Can you say those to me one at a time.

Q: Being trapped.

A: Okay. Being trapped. What do we know about Mrs. Bobbitt? Well, battered woman syndrome actually was brought about by the observation that women were being beaten to a pulp and staying in their marriages and it didn't make sense. To some degree, it's an outgrowth of mental health professionals' frustration that when you're sitting in a room with an individual who's bruised and depressed and frightened and it should seem obvious for them to leave but they don't, and that's really why that feeling emerges. And the trapped feeling that battered women describe who meet the syndrome is feeling trapped because they don't believe that they're capable of making it on their own and feeling trapped because they've had so many episodes where their husband has made it clear that if they leave there's going to be great violence to them and in ways it makes them feel like it's unsafe to go. In 1991, from things Mrs. Bobbitt reported, I think she really did believe that if she fleed, her husband would find her and get her. In 1993, she has a somewhat different approach. She goes and gets the temporary protection order, she's offered multiple opportunities to go someplace else and makes rational decisions about why she doesn't go. She doesn't say I can't go to all these different places because I'm at serious risk, can't go because there's cats and this person's on oxygen, I don't want to go impose on this person, I don't want to go because it's safe at home. Most specifically, very clearly again and again why is she getting back together with Mr. Bobbitt, why is she staying? Because of her religious and cultural values. That is not being trapped in a battered women syndrome. That is trying to adhere to what she sees as her personal ethic in life.

Q: How about the inability to tell or relate these views?

A: Well as I've said, I think she's done a wonderful job of telling lots of folks. She's alerted everybody from the military through to most of her friends, her neighbors in the apartment complex, Mrs. Castro and the Castro children—there are lots of folks that she's talked about the abuse with.

Q: What about the denial of the abuse?

A: The denial of the abuse? Well, again, she's not denying that it's existing, she's telling other folks. In fact, she's getting her bruises photographed and, in a number of ways, at this point in time she's very open about it because she's getting more angry during the last couple of weeks prior to the crime.

Q: And is reluctance to seek help another characteristic of the battered woman syndrome?

A: Often, yes. That's part of the feeling trapped.

Q: And was that exhibited in this case?

A: Well, again, it may have been in 1991.

Q: How about 1993?

A: But in terms of the current mental status, again, the same things apply. Mrs. Bobbitt is not at all reluctant to seek help, she is contacting folks for temporary protection order, she's asking a neighbor may I please start to bringing things over to your house because I'm starting to move out, she's asking folks for assistance in terms of how can I break my lease to leave—there's a whole host of those types of activities in which she's engaging.

Q: Doctor, you are familiar with Dr. Feister's report and you were present during her testimony?

A: Yes.

Q: Do you recall her characterizing the defendant's mental status being in the midst of a brief reactive psychosis at the time that she committed this offense? What, first of all, is your understanding of that term brief reactive psychosis?

A: Again, you need to put this in the context of where brief reactive psychosis fits in in the diagnostic scheme. It's in a broad category known as psychotic disorders not otherwise classified. And the general hallmark of psychosis are people who are having very bizarre thoughts and ideas, engaging in bizarre, disorganized behaviors—in general, people who don't have a sense of reality.

The four criteria that are really most important for psychosis are: incoherence or marked loosening of associations. What this means is an individual who starts talking and what they're saying makes zero sense.

Loosening of associations means that the topic that someone's discussing keeps changing so they may be talking about one thing one moment but the very next sentence they're talking about something else and it doesn't seem sequential, you can't figure out how they got off the idea.

Delusions are false belief. It's when somebody firmly believes that something's happening and there's no reality.

The third is hallucinations—seeing things and hearing things that aren't there. Most commonly people hear voices telling them to do things, sometimes they see things—they'll see the devil standing in the corner or they'll see dogs barking at them—other types of things.

And then the fourth one which is the one that Dr. Feister sees as the criteria for brief reactive psychosis says catatonic or disorganized behavior. The first part of that, catatonia, refers to a symptom of a specific type of schizophrenia—a psychomotor disturbance—where people's physical movements are bizarre. For example, you may have heard of catatonic rigidity. This is somebody who sits rigidly in a position. So rigidly that when you try and move them, their whole body moves as if the muscles are locked. Or catatonic excitability. Where somebody is flailing all around and there's no reason for any of those movements at all.

That clearly doesn't apply at all to Mrs. Bobbitt.

And the last part of that is disorganized behavior. That's a tough term. We need to remember that this is brief reactive psychosis. Disorganized behavior doesn't mean here that you pack your suitcase and you remember something you forgot and go back and put it in. It means, like with criteria number one, a marked loosening of associations. That the behaviors that someone's engaging in don't seem to be related to each other, in general, they don't seem to make sense.

Q: And did you see those behaviors exhibited at all by your evaluation of Ms. Bobbitt and the materials you evaluated?

A: No, not at all. Certainly, I don't think there's been any debate at all about the fact that she's not having psychosis during the days before all of this. The question is, starting with the rape forward, is there any evidence of brief reactive psychosis. Well she goes to the kitchen to get a glass of water. Even though we can't be in her mind although she does tell us because she's feeling when she gets to the kitchen, looking at the behavior, there's nothing disorganized about going to the kitchen getting a glass of water. She picks up a knife. Well, is that an organized behavior or not? Let's see what she does next. She takes it to go back to her husband. Oh, well there's a purpose here. She's going back to confront him and to tell him how angry she is. That's very organized. She pauses when she gets to him. She doesn't do anything illogical—she makes a beeline back to the bedroom and stands over him and says I want to talk to you. She cuts him.

Now all of those behaviors fall in a very organized way. It's certainly a goal directed behavior. Even after the event, her behavior is organized and this is important because brief reactive diagnosis doesn't mean that somebody was crazy for an instant. We're talking about a period of time, hours or days, in which somebody is showing these symptoms.

Afterwards, she's clearly shocked with herself and she's disoriented as to time. It's clear that she's not thinking about the fact that it's 5 in the morning. But her clear intent for everything she does in the next hour is *I'm gonna find Janna and the other folks who I feel are an emotional support*. And all the behaviors that she engages in are essentially towards that end. She flees the house and remembers to take her keys. Why did she take the Nintendo [sic]? Well, I think she's pretty disoriented as to time, I think she's in shock, she bundles it up and she runs out. She gets in the car. She doesn't get lost driving around. She's not confused. She ends up at the beauty salon. She gets there, she opens the door—that means using the key, understanding how to get in, finds no one there and she does the next logical organized thing. She picks up the phone and calls Ms. Bissuti at home. Gets no answer. She does the next logical organized things. She gets in the car and drives over to their house.

Now there were things in here that indicate that she was so focused on fleeing and I think after cutting the penis, her own shock and dismay at what she'd done— we don't know but I think it's reasonable to speculate as an expert that she would be afraid of what her husband might do if he jumped out of bed at that point, and she heads out of there with the penis in one hand and the knife in the other and she is so focused on finding Janna in her distress that she doesn't notice these things. And when she does notice them, she gets rid of them.

Q: The disorientation that you described after the event—could that have been caused by the commission of the crime?

A: Very much so. I've seen numerous cases of individuals who had this type of thing. Remember what we know about Mrs. Bobbitt. It's very important to her to perceive herself as a non-violent, nice, upright, Catholic individual. Now separate from whether or not one agrees or disagrees with that, that is part of her identity. And she has legitimate reasons to be afraid of her husband. He has hurt her terribly, he had just hurt her a few minutes before and he's demonstrated that he can do it again because of the number of times that he's assaulted her one way or another over the years.

So her disorientation probably stems from shock and dismay at having committed a violent act that was inconsistent with her sense of self. Having committed one that was so close to sexual issues when clearly those are very uncomfortable topics for Mrs. Bobbitt, and she's fleeing from her husband because she doesn't want to stay around to find out what he's going to do. That may have been a very wise thought. So her energies are focused on that—not on trying to keep track of what time of day it is.

Q: Doctor, going back to the concept of an irresistible impulse, what is your understanding of an irresistible impulse under Virginia law?

A: They're talking about an impulse that someone has but they cannot stop themselves from doing it because the disease of the mind impairs their ability to control themselves. In this case, the impulse is clear—it's anger and it's to cut off her husband's penis. But there's nothing here indicating that she can't control herself.

Q: In fact, are there any indications to the contrary?

A: Yeah. All the things that I've described in the days beforehand that demonstrate that she's controlling herself and then again, afterwards, she makes a conscious decision to go to the kitchen to have some space from all of this, to have a drink of water—when she picks up the knife and she goes back to the room, she pauses indicating she's controlled her impulse long enough to at least try and talk with the guy, but lo and behold he doesn't give her any reason to stop whatever it is that she's thinking of doing.

CROSS EXAMINATION

BY MR. HOWARD:

Q: Doctor Nelson, you are not a medical doctor, is that correct?

A: That's correct.

Q: And doctor, is it true that although you see many people that are referred to you for evaluation of mental illness for alleged psychotic behavior and so forth, you cannot prescribe any kind of medication for those people, can you?

A: That's correct. I cannot.

Q: And it is also true that you cannot commit those people, not withstanding whatever your opinion is for those individuals?

A: I would need to double check on that, Mr. Howard, because my practice in Virginia is limited specifically to working in a hospital. It's a different context.

Q: You've never ordered the commitment of anyone yourself, have you?

A: Not here in Virginia, no.

Q: Doctor, you were ordered by this court to do an evaluation of Mrs. Bobbitt and you were ordered in connection with Dr. Ryans who is a psychiatrist and a medical doctor and Dr. Gwaltney, is that correct? Are these gentlemen that you have been—are those gentlemen that you have worked with on a regular basis at Central State Hospital?

A: Yes.

Q: Would you tell the members of the jury, do you have respect for their opinions?

A: They're very experienced individuals.

Q: Do you think they're honest and objective in their conclusions and in this case, do you respect their opinions in this case?

A: I certainly do respect the differences in their opinions, yes.

Q: All right. Let me take you to that if I may, sir. Bear with me, let me make sure I get the right page. Bissuti, yes. Since you brought it up about the deposition where she talked to Mrs. Bissuti and her husband, let me ask you to turn to page 24 of your report.

Mrs. Bobbitt said in her deposition that she told Mrs. Bissuti and her husband, "I did something to him. I cut him." The conclusion of the three of you doctors when you reviewed her statement made to Mrs. Bissuti and her husband was this suggests that she either knew what she had done or was able to reconstruct it from the obvious evidence of a knife, the blood on her hands, and the severed penis. That was your conclusion.

A: Yes.

Q: And you're not changing that today, are you sir? I mean that still is your belief.

A: That either of those could be true, but the one is more likely.

Q: Now, doctor, you said, and I listened closely to your examination, you said that in your opinion this was—this act was impulsive. I know you disagree with irresistible impulse, but you did say it was impulsive. You also said that this was an act that had occurred after a very emotional, very traumatic event. There's no question about that.

A: No question about it.

Q: Can we agree that she was in an extremely high state of emotion?

A: She doesn't tell us what her emotions are until she starts talking about anger. However, what we know about people who have been raped, I think it's fair to predict that she was very emotional at that point.

Q: All the verbal abuse, with the threat that had been communicated to her that I'll find you, whether we get a divorce, whether we get a separation, I'm gonna find you, I'll have sex with you any way I want. With the deposition and the sworn testimony of Diane Hall that she told me he would track her down—knowing all of that, you have to know that this woman was not thinking with a healthy mind. Isn't that true, sir?

A: No, sir. As a forensic psychologist, what I have to do is look at the statements that people make but also look at all the other information that's available at this time about it. And we have a number of descriptions for Mrs. Bobbitt at the time and we have descriptions that have changed over time. At that point in time, I'm sure that there was a lot of distress. The emotion that's driving her is the anger.

Q: Are you telling this jury that at the time she had that experience of the rape that her mind was healthy?

A: We don't know how she's feeling until she picks up the knife and describes her anger. The gap between after the rape and the time when she's in front of the refrigerator, we really don't have any information on except to agree that people who have been raped usually have a number of different emotions afterwards that's going to vary depending on the individual and the situation.

Q: All right, let me just ask you this, sir. You have concluded in this case that she was suffering from a major depression disorder. You agree that that is a severe mental disorder, an anxiety disorder.

A: No, it's a mood disorder.

Q: Mood disorder, okay. Would you agree that she was suffering from that disorder late that night?

A: Yes.

Q: Okay. Are you saying that a severe mental disorder—a person with a severe mental disorder has a healthy mind?

A: A person with a severe mental disorder has a mental disorder.

Q: Exactly. They don't have a clear healthy mind like the members of this jury or yourself, do they?

A: She has a mood disorder.

Q: Exactly. So she didn't have a completely healthy mind that night when she underwent the rape, did she?

A: Not before or during or after.

Q: All right. And there's no question that it is your opinion, sir, that she was suffering from a lot of fear of her husband.

A: Yes.

Q: As a matter of fact, I believe it was your testimony that it was that fear that motivated her to flee—the fact that she had the knife and that she was standing over him with the knife and she could do anything with the knife—in her mind she was still in fear. She wanted to get away from there. Isn't that true?

A: Before or after cutting the penis?

Q: After cutting the penis. She's just cut the penis. She's still got the knife. This man is laying in the bed. She's standing over him.

A: After the offense, I think she was very scared.

Q: She was very scared and very frightened and she had been frightened of him before this event ever took place. Isn't that true?

A: That's correct.

Q: He threatened her, told her what he was going to do to her, told her that he would find her and rape her any way he wanted and he had just demonstrated he was capable of carrying out the threat, isn't that true?

A: Yes.

Q: Doctor, you realize that in his report you alluded to the fact and I think you testified to it today that she was disoriented. And disoriented is another way of saying that she was disorganized.

A: No, not at all. Disoriented refers to whether somebody's aware of who they are, where they are, or what they're doing. In this case, she's not oriented as to time. That's the only dimension in which she's confused.

Q: Do you believe then that at all times that she knew that what she had in her hand, she knew that she had the penis in her hand and the knife in her hand, she knew she was picking up the Gameboy, do you think she was completely oriented to all those facts?

A: No.

Q: Okay. So she was a little confused about things that were going on. When she went down to the shop that morning at 4 a.m. in the morning. 4 a.m. in the morning

expecting people to be there, that wasn't organized thinking, was it?

A: It was organized, but it was disoriented as to time.

Q: That was fear and disorientation.

A: Disorientation.

LORENA LEONOR BOBBITT
DIRECT EXAMINATION

BY MR. HOWARD (On Rebuttal):

Q: Ms. Bobbitt, you saw the witness Connie James testify here the other day.

A: Yes, I did.

Q: Tell the members of the jury that name Connie
James, when it was that you first placed that with a face.

A: It was right here when I just saw her the other day.

Q: Okay, now let me ask you this, Mrs. Bobbitt. What
is your recollection as to when you worked at Fit and
Pretty and tell the jury whether that was full time or part
time.

A: It was only one day a week during the month of . . .
I would say like middle of March to beginning of April.
Maybe three weeks.

Q: And what year do you recall working at that salon?

A: 1990.

Q: All right, tell the members of the jury when you
worked there on a part time basis, was that one day a
week?

A: Yes.

Q: Did you become friends with this lady?

A: I hardly see her. I do not did any kind of social
friendship with her, no.

Q: Did you ever go to lunch with her?

A: Never, no.

Q: Did you ever go to dinner with her?

A: Never, no.

Q: Did you ever go out with her husband and you and your husband on dates and—get together in group activities?

A: I had a full time job and I did not have time for social time. I was working 6 days a week—7 days a week.

Q: And the final question. You heard her testimony and you know what your testimony was the other day about denying ever making these comments. Has your position changed on that? Are you still denying that you made that statement?

A: Yes, sir.

Q: Thank you very much. That's all.

CROSS EXAMINATION

BY MR. EBERT:

Q: You saw you were working so much that you didn't have the opportunity to socialize with her? Is that what you're telling me?

A: Yes, sir.

Q: And I take it you didn't have the opportunity to socialize with anybody else during the year 1990, is that correct?

A: That's right, sir.

Q: You and your husband never went out anyplace?

A: Me and my husband most of the times when he finished work he would come home and I would be still 'working and then I go home. We never really socialized too much.

Q: Never went out. Period.

A: We did go out, but we—

Q: So you did have time to socialize, isn't that correct?

A: Yes, but not with Mrs. Connie James.

Q: You didn't call her on the phone?

A: Um, I never know her phone number, sir, no.

INSTRUCTIONS TO THE JURY

HERMAN A. WHISENANT, JR.: I'll ask you to please listen carefully as these instructions are read to you. These instructions will be given to you for you to take back to the jury deliberation room during your deliberations as will all of the exhibits that have been placed into evidence. After I have concluded reading these instructions, you will then be hearing the closing arguments by counsel after which you can start with your deliberations.

Ladies and gentlemen, the Defendant is charged with the crime of maliciously causing bodily injury. The Commonwealth must prove beyond a reasonable doubt each of the following elements of that crime:

One, that the defendant caused bodily injury by any means to John Wayne Bobbitt.

Two, that such bodily injury was with intent to maim, disfigure, disable, or kill John Wayne Bobbitt.

Three, that the act was done with malice.

If you find from the evidence that the Commonwealth has proved beyond a reasonable doubt each of the above elements of the offense as charged then you shall find the Defendant guilty of maliciously causing bodily injury and fix his punishment at a specific term of imprisonment but not less than 5 years nor more than 20 years. Or two, a specific term of imprisonment but not less than 5 years nor more than 20 years and a fine of a specific amount but not more than $100,000.

If you find from the evidence that the Commonwealth has proved beyond a reasonable doubt each of the first two elements of the offense as charged but that the act was done unlawfully and not maliciously, then you shall find the defendant guilty of unlawfully causing bodily injury and fix her punishment at:

One, a specific term of imprisonment but not less than 1 year nor more than 5 years.

Two, confinement in jail for a specific time but not more than 12 months.

Three, a fine of a specific amount but not more than $2500.

Four, confinement in jail for a specific time but not more than 12 months and a fine of a specific amount but not more than $2500.

Now ladies and gentlemen, the Defendant is presumed to be innocent. You should not assume the defendant is guilty because she has been indicted and is on trial. This presumption of innocence remains with the Defendant throughout the trial and is enough to require you to find the Defendant not guilty unless and until the Commonwealth proves each and every element of the offense beyond a reasonable doubt. This does not require proof beyond all possible doubt, nor is the Commonwealth required to disprove every conceivable circumstance of innocence. However, suspicion or probability of guilt is not enough for a conviction. There is no burden on the Defendant to produce any evidence. A reasonable doubt is a doubt based on your sound judgment after a full and impartial consideration of all of the evidence in the case.

Now ladies and gentlemen, you are the judges of the facts, the credibility of the witnesses, and the weight of the evidence. You may consider the appearance and manner of the witnesses on the stand, their intelligence, their opportunity for knowing the truth and for having observed the things about which they testify, their interest in the outcome of the case, their bias, and if any have been shown their prior inconsistent statements or whether they have knowingly testified untruthfully as to any material fact in the case. You may not arbitrarily disregard believable testimony of a witness. However, after you've considered all of the evidence in the case then you may accept or discard all or part of the testimony of the witness as you think proper. You are entitled to use your common sense in judging any testimony. From these things and all the other circumstances of the case, you may determine which witnesses are more believable and weigh their testimony accordingly.

You may have heard that every person intends the natural and probable consequences of her acts. The Defendant is presumed to be sane at the time of the crime. In order to be found not guilty on the ground of insanity, the Defendant must prove by the greater weight of the evidence that she was insane when the crime was committed.

Now ladies and gentlemen, it is your responsibility to decide whether the Defendant was insane at the time the crime was committed. You are not required to accept the opinion of any expert witness or whether the Defendant—as to whether the Defendant was sane or insane. You should give the testimony such consideration as you feel it is entitled along with the other evidence in the case.

If you believe from the evidence that the Defendant or any witness previously made a statement inconsistent with testimony at this trial, that previous statement may be considered by you as proof that what the Defendant previously said is true. If a person leaves the place where a crime was committed, this creates no presumption that the person is guilty of having committed the crime. However, it is a circumstance which you may consider along with the other evidence.

Now ladies and gentlemen, malice is that state of mind which results in the intentional doing of a wrongful act to another without legal excuse or justification at a time when the mind of the actor is under the control of reason. Malice may result from any unlawful or unjustifiable motive including anger, hatred, or revenge. Malice may be inferred from any deliberate, willful, and cruel act against another, however sudden.

Heat of passion excludes malice when the heat of passion arises from provocation that reasonably produces an emotional state of mind such as hot blood or rage, anger, resentment, terror, or fear as to cause one to act on impulse without conscious reflection. Heat of passion must be determined from circumstance as they appear to the Defendant, but those circumstances must be such as would have aroused heat of passion in a reasonable person. If a person acts upon reflection or deliberation or after his passion has cooled or there has been a reasonable time or opportunity for cooling, then the act is not attributable to heat of passion.

You may infer malice from the deliberate use of a deadly weapon unless, from all of the evidence, you have a reasonable doubt as to whether malice existed. A deadly weapon is any object or instrument that is likely to cause death or great bodily injury because of the manner and under the circumstances in which it is used.

Every person is presumed to be sane and to possess a sufficient degree of reason to be responsible for her crimes until the contrary is proven to the satisfaction of the jury. And even though you may believe from the evidence that the Defendant was laboring under some type of defective mental condition at the time of the offense charged against her, nevertheless, if she was able to understand the nature, character, and consequences of the act and to perceive that it was wrong and that she possessed with all a will sufficient to restrain any impulse to do the act that may arise from the diseased mind, then the Defendant cannot rely upon the doctrine of irresistible impulse as set forth in another instruction as a defense.

Planned means a specific intent to act adopted sometime before the act but which need not exist for any particular length of time. Now if you believe that the Defendant was without thought in provoking or bringing on the incident and if you, further, believe that the Defendant reasonably feared under the circumstances as they appeared to her that she was in danger of being killed or that she was in danger of great bodily harm, then the incident was in self defense and you shall find the Defendant not guilty. Now in order to find the Defendant acted in self defense, you must find that the Defendant reasonably feared, under the circumstances as they appeared to her, that she was in danger of being killed or that she was in danger of great bodily harm; however, in order for her fear to be reasonable under the circumstances as they appear to her, there must be some act by

John Bobbitt placing the Defendant in present peril of an impending attack or something in the attending circumstances indicative of a purpose on the part of John Bobbitt to make such an attack.

If you find from the evidence that the Defendant knew the nature, character, and consequences of her act and knew that her act was wrong, you may still find her not guilty by reason of insanity. If you find the greater weight of the evidence that her mind was so impaired by disease that she was unable to resist the impulse to commit the crime.

Now ladies and gentlemen, if you have a reasonable doubt as to the grade of the offense, then you must resolve that doubt in favor of the Defendant and find her guilty of the lesser offense. For example, if you have a reasonable doubt as to whether she is guilty of malicious wounding or unlawful wounding, you should find her guilty of unlawful wounding. If you have a reasonable doubt as to whether she is guilty at all, you should find her not guilty.

CLOSING ARGUMENTS

MARY GRACE O'BRIEN: Ladies and gentlemen, let me take a moment and thank you. Thank you for your time and attention to this testimony, thank you for your patience during the bench conferences and the arguments between the lawyers, and thank you for the very real sacrifices that you have each made to be here these past two weeks.

This is an important case and it's not an important case because of the media attention. It's not an important case because of the notoriety that it has received. It's an important case because it deals with the crime of violence. It deals with the crime of violence by one person against another person and in our system the courts are the recourse for justice and in this case you are the recourse for justice. This is a criminal case and in spite of what you've heard the last six and one half days it's not a divorce case. It's a serious case. It's a criminal case, it is the Commonwealth's contention that what it is is a calculated and malicious act of revenge. You have seen explicit photographs, you have heard graphic testimony of the injury visited upon John Bobbitt by the Defendant, and I suggest to you that the defense team does not want you to think about the crime. They do not want you to focus on the crime. Instead, they want to talk about the marriage. They want to talk about the four years that these people lived together before June 23. If they want to talk about the marriage, let's talk about the marriage for a minute. There is one thing I think that everyone involved in this case agrees upon and that is that these people should not have been married, that they certainly should not have stayed married. I think when one of the Castro girls was testifying about her mother having some hesitation about Lorena Bobbitt marrying John Bobbitt, Mr. Howard said well your mother's a perceptive person, isn't she? And she is. And Mrs. Biro said the exact same thing. She said when I heard they were getting married I said wait. Give it a year. See if you really care about each other. That, I think, is something everyone agrees on. That is probably the last thing about this marriage that everybody agrees on.

There are witnesses who say there was physical abuse,

there are witnesses who rebut that physical abuse. I am not going to rehash all of that with you, ladies and gentlemen. I will tell you this. I will tell you that I think the evidence shows you that there certainly was some physical violence in 1989 and 1990. I think all those witnesses you heard from from the defense, some of the customers and people who saw Lorena Bobbitt, I don't think they're lying to you. I think they are telling you the truth. I think there's evidence to support that.

However, if you remember what one of the defense lawyers said in the opening, she characterized this marriage as a reign of terror. And I don't think the evidence supports that. I think that if you think about the argument that these people would have, they were almost ridiculous.

When you would hear about an argument Thanksgiving day about whether they're going to watch the parade or the football game and she turns the channel so he goes outside and unplugs the cable or takes the antenna down, she locks him out, he breaks the door down—you hear testimony of an argument at the end of the marriage where she's taping him secretly, he goes into her purse, she yells give me my purse, grabs her purse back, he takes the tape out of her purse, flushes the tape down the toilet—at that point she says he raped her and he denies that.

As I said, I'm not going to rehash that. I think you people have heard more about this marriage than you ever needed to know to decide this case.

There are two points, however, which are significant when you consider the testimony you've heard over the past week. They go to the crime and they go to the people who have appeared to describe the people who have appeared before you today. The first is the testimony that you heard about the abortion. There's no question that the Defendant had an abortion in 1990 and the way she relates the facts of that abortion and the way her husband relates the facts of that abortion are very different. She tells you that because of that abortion three years prior— three years and a half month prior to committing this offense she was suffering from a mental disease or mental illness that caused her to commit the offense. And what she tells you was "He forced me to have the abortion. I didn't want to have an abortion. He forced me into it. He told me that they would use big needles, they would go through my bones and they would hurt me and he told me I wouldn't be a good mother, if I didn't have the abortion he would leave me."

I suggest to you that you should consider what John Bobbitt says about the abortion. He says yes, "We decided we weren't ready to have children and she should have an abortion." He acknowledges that she was upset about that. I believe he said "I comforted her afterwards and I thought she should have an abortion." Well, folks, if he thought she should have an abortion, he isn't going to sit there with her and tell her about how the needles are going to hurt her when the abortion is performed. And perhaps most significantly, when you think about this testimony on redirect and you think about the specific question that was asked when one of the lawyers said did you ever tell her she wouldn't be a good mother and he said no. "She'd be a great mother." That's what he told you, folks. He didn't answer the question, but I think if you consider the way that he testified, it's inconsistent with her testimony concerning that abortion.

The second point. There are two sides to every story and in this particular case, when you consider it to whatever degree you consider this marriage, I ask you to remember that and I ask you to remember as Mr. Ebert mentioned in his voir dire that sometimes people are not exactly what they appear. That if you saw the Defendant, you might not conceive of her as someone who would commit a violent and malicious act. And certainly she was suggested to you as someone who was described as a delicate, petite, naive woman who was raised in a strict Catholic household and came to this country, left without family and lived with friends. That's not exactly accurate. And it's not exactly accurate that if you would believe her she never got angry during the course of this marriage.

Look to the argument they had New Year's Eve of this year. They have reconciled, they're living together in the Beltran household and according to her her husband's friends are visiting, they go out New Year's Eve, leave her behind, she spends New Year's Eve alone. She tells you she's sad. She tells you she's upset. If you remember, when I would ask her questions, she wouldn't say angry. She'd say everything but angry. Her husband goes out with his buddies drinking New Year's Eve and leaves her alone and she's not angry. That doesn't make sense, folks. Sure she's angry. Probably rightly so. But she doesn't tell you that. She says no, I wasn't angry. She tells you that he came home and she tried to talk to him and he got upset and he raped her and to escape him raping her she ran downstairs where his friends were. And he tells you something different. He said I came home, she was angry. Of course she was angry. "I came home, she was angry, I ignored her, she went downstairs"—and his friend

Robert Johnston verifies this—"she came downstairs and she told us to leave."

They were renting one bedroom and the basement room. She told us to leave and she had done that to John's family before, she had told them to leave. They get into an argument, Mrs. Beltran comes downstairs—and Mrs. Beltran is telling you the truth, folks. Mrs. Beltran says "I heard an argument, I didn't see anyone hit anyone, they were yelling at each other, I separated them—this is like two children. I separated them, she said he hit me, he said she hit me, I went upstairs and comforted her."

The only reason that that particular argument was significant is because it supports the contention that things are not exactly the way they appear in this case. Things are not black and white.

There are, I expect, some other things that you did not hear about in all the extreme detail you've heard from the Defendants about this marriage. You heard probably close to a day of testimony from her on direct examination about where they lived, where she worked, where he worked, the abuse she suffered, her unhappy married life, and the separation. And it wasn't until I got up on cross examination that you ever heard of not the one, not the two, not the three, but the four instances of stealing that she's involved in.

And again, think about her explanation for that stealing. In 1990 I was stealing because I had moved into this house that I really didn't want to live in but he had forced me to buy and I was going to try to work at home and do some manicuring at home. So that's his fault. In 1991 I stole two dresses from Nordstrom's because I wanted to look nice for him because he was having an affair. That's his fault. In the end of 1991 I embark on a 9 month or 6—6 to 9 month embezzlement from my employer because he wouldn't work and I had to pay the bills. That's his fault. And perhaps most significantly, the stealing is the incident that occurred the day before she cut her husband's penis off—the incident in which she took the hundred dollar bill belonging to her husband's friend. And what does she tell you about that folks? She tells you not "I was angry at my husband because he was working and he was using all his money to go out and he wasn't giving me any money for rent." No. She tells you that hundred dollar bill was kind of hanging out of his wallet and so I took it. And that's not so. He says that's not so. He says that he tucked it up and put it in the corner of his wallet.

There is no question that the Defendant was upset about the abortion that she had in 1990. There is no question that at the time of this act their marriage was in shambles and there was no question that the night before that act in which she cut off her husband's penis she felt that he had forced her to have sex against her will. But having said that, John Bobbitt is not on trial here. John Bobbitt had not been charged with being a bad husband, he's not on trial for giving two separate statements to the police when they interviewed him after the surgery.

This is a criminal case, Lorena Bobbitt is on trial, and let's take a minute or two and talk about the crime. For you to find her guilty, you have to find that we have proved to your satisfaction that she caused bodily injury with intent to maim, disfigure, disable, or kill and that that act was done maliciously. And what the Defendant has told you is that I have two defenses. I either was acting in self defense when I committed this act or I was legally insane but I don't really remember anything that happened, so you choose.

Let's talk for a minute about the self defense aspect. You received some instructions from Judge Whisenant about self defense. I ask you to review those instructions. Because for you to find the Defendant acted in self defense, you have to find that she reasonably feared, under the circumstances as they appeared to her, that she was in danger of being killed or in danger of great bodily harm. However, important, significantly, in order for her fear to appear reasonable under the circumstances as they appeared to her, there must be some act by John Bobbitt placing the Defendant in present peril of an impending attack or something in the attending circumstances indicative of a purpose on the part of John Bobbitt to make such an attack.

Even if you believe her, even if you believe her testimony completely about what happened that night, she's in no danger. There is no self defense here. This is a man who is asleep in his own bed. He is defenseless.

Now I expect the defense lawyer may say well she was afraid that if she left he might come and follow her and force her to have sex whenever he wanted. That's not what this instruction talks about. Present peril of an impending attack. There's no present peril of an impending attack. Even if you believe her testimony concerning the events of the night of June 22, early morning of June 23, the incident is over. When she cuts his penis off, that's not self defense. That's revenge.

Let's turn for a second to the other defense which is

asserted by the Defendant and that's the defense of insanity, specifically an irresistible impulse. And I ask you to focus on those words and review the jury instructions concerning irresistible impulse because that's what it comes down to. You've heard a lot of talk about psychotic behavior, post traumatic stress disorder, battered women and other psychological jargon, but if there's no irresistible impulse, if she's not acting from the irresistible impulse, there's no insanity. And you start from the presumption that everyone is sane. You have an instruction on that. Everyone is presumed to be sane and the Defendant is no different. You heard in her defense from Dr. Feister, the psychiatrist she hired who said that she was insane and the jump that Dr. Feister makes is sort of interesting. She says she was a battered woman and because she was a battered woman, that led to post traumatic stress disorder, because she was suffering from post traumatic stress disorder, that led to a brief psychotic episode, because she has a brief psychotic episode, that led to an irresistible impulse.

Now folks, that's quite a jump. It's a very sweeping conclusion with what I suggest to you was some insufficient information. When Mr. Ebert asked Dr. Feister about her sources of information, she said she spoke to the Defendant, she spoke to people who knew the Defendant, she reviewed depositions—she said she never talked to John Bobbitt at the defense lawyer's recommendations and perhaps more importantly, she never talked to anybody from John Bobbitt's family. So this person who Dr. Feister characterized as someone committing all these awful acts upon Lorena Bobbitt was never investigated by her.

She does acknowledge that the issue here is the Defendant's state of mind at the time that she committed the offense. And what Dr. Feister says is that state of mind can be determined by two things—by somebody's actions and by what they relate about the offense. And it is common sense, I suggest to you, that what somebody relates most immediately after the offense concerning how they felt is the most accurate reflection of how they felt.

The first person besides Janna Bissuti who the Defendant spoke to was the nurse at the emergency room and then Dr. Corcoran at the emergency room. She told Dr. Corcoran her husband raped her, she put on her clothes, she went to the kitchen to drink water, quote "I saw a knife, I was really angry, I opened the sheets and I cut him. I was driving and then I threw it into the bushes." There is no suggestion that she was trying to reconstruct that, there was no suggestion of any hesitancy, there was no suggestion that that memory was being suggested to her.

She also talked to Detective Weintz and you will recall that when I asked her some questions, she said that the Detective was someone with whom she felt comfortable—that he was kind to her, that he was gentlemanly, and that she told him the truth. And you have the statement that she made to the Detective, and you've heard excerpts from that statement and I suggest when you go back to the jury room, review the entire statement. Read the entire statement. But the significant portion to determine her mental state is as follows.

Detective Weintz said after "He forced you to have sex this morning can you tell me what happened then?" "Yes," says the Defendant. "He pushed me away like when he's finished like he did it before, sometimes push me away like make me feel really bad because that's not fair, that's not nice. I don't feel good when he does it and I don't even have my shirt off and I put my underwear back, my other shirt, my spandex shirt on, and I was hurt. I went to the kitchen to drink water. I opened the refrigerator and I got a cup of water, then I was angry already and I turned my back and I—the first thing I saw was the knife. Then I took it and I was just angry. Then I took it and I went to the bedroom and I told him he shouldn't do this to me. Why he did it. So I asked him. I asked him if he was satisfied with what he did and he was just half asleep or something. I was just mad. And then he say he doesn't care about my feelings, he did say that, and I asked him if he has orgasm inside me 'cause it hurt me when he made me do that before. He always have orgasm and he doesn't wait for me to have orgasm, he's selfish, I don't think it's fair, I pulled back the shirt—the sheet, and then I did it." Detective Weintz says, "All right, you cut him?" And Mrs. Bobbitt says yes. There's no hesitation here. There's no reason for Detective Weintz to say are you really sure you cut him? Are you sure you're not just sort of reconstructing that? She tells him she cut him, she tells him why she cut him. She makes a similar statement to Dr. Gwaltney. She even goes into more detail. She tells him she saw the knife, picked it up, remembering many things that had happened to her and what he had said and done, specifically about the abortion, and all the sexual, physical, and psychological abuse—she said she walked into the bedroom with the knife in her hand, looking at him laying in bed, she reports she felt she just wanted him to disappear, to go away. She said she lifted the sheets, looked at his whole body and then I cut him really fast.

This week what she tells us is I don't really remember. I just don't remember. A number of independent doctors, all examined the Defendant as well. And you heard, again, probably more than you need to know about their evaluation and their determination. But again what's significant is whether she had post traumatic stress syndrome or not, they all agree there was no irresistible impulse. They said the behavior has to be random which means Robert Johnston could have been as likely a victim as the victim, they say there has to be no preplanning, it has to be sudden.

And those doctors also told you that to have an irresistible impulse you'd have to have what they call "the policeman at the shoulder." That you would still commit this act if there was a policeman at your shoulder. So if you think that Lorena Bobbitt still would have done this act if a policeman had walked in that apartment, she would have just gone ahead and cut her husband's penis off, then find her not guilty by reason of insanity. But that's not what the evidence shows you. And I suggest to you, you don't have to have a medical degree from Yale to realize this. It's common sense.

There is no insanity in this case. There also is no issue about whether there is serious bodily injury, whether it was caused by the Defendant, what she intended, and that it was done with malice.

I want to talk to you for just a minute about malice because there's a distinction here. If you find this act was done with malice, it's malicious wounding. If you find it was done unlawfully in a heat of passion, it's unlawful wounding.

Think about the act in this particular case. Think about the weapon that was used. Is this a deadly weapon? You bet. This is what she used. Her husband forced her to have sex, she wasn't happy, she got up, she tried to talk to him, he wouldn't talk to her. She pulled on her clothes, she finds her clothes at the end of the bed. She's crying. She gets out of bed. She walks through the apartment to the kitchen. In the kitchen, she decides she's going to have a glass of water. She walks to the cabinet. She takes a glass out of the cabinet. She makes the decision the water's going to be cold water in the refrigerator. She walks to the refrigerator, gets a glass of cold water, she turns, she sees the knife. She walks over, picks up the knife, walks from the kitchen through the bedroom, through the living room, into the bedroom. She's in the bedroom, she lifts up the sheet, she looks at her husband, she looks at his whole body, she take his penis in one hand, the knife in the other, and she cuts his penis off.

At that point, ladies and gentlemen, she becomes upset instead of angry. She leaves the apartment and her testimony is that she doesn't recall anything else that happened until she was driving along. She said she was driving along and she had the knife in one hand and the penis in the other hand and she was horrified or appalled to realize she had the penis in her hand and she disposed of it. And when I asked her, when I pushed her a little bit about how she disposed of it, she couldn't tell.

Remember the physical evidence in this particular case and, again, I ask you to use your common sense. This penis is found 45 feet back from the stop sign, 24 feet from the center of the road. Is that consistent with somebody who was driving along and sees something in their hand that they realize is just awful, they don't want to have it there, so they're just gonna throw it down, you're gonna get rid of it as quickly as possible.

I suggest to you what happened was partially what she told you—that she was driving along, she realized the penis was in her hand, she stopped the car, she got out of the car and threw it into the bushes. That's why she was able to describe to the police with such specificity where they could find the penis. She is disposing of evidence as she disposed of the knife.

So, folks, this is not a case of heat of passion. If he had forced her to have sex, she had rolled over, if there was a knife there, she had picked the knife up and cut him, that would be heat of passion. This is not a case of unlawful wounding, it is a case of malicious wounding. It is truly a fairly straightforward case. It is not about self defense, it is not about insanity, and it most certainly not about what was offered to you in opening statement, a choice between a life and a penis.

This is a case about anger, it's a case about revenge, and it's a case about retribution. Her husband came home, he was drunk—I think you have sufficient evidence from which you can find he was under the influence of alcohol—he was drunk, he wanted to have sex, she didn't, that's her right. He forced her to have sex, she was angry and she retaliated against him. But, you know, folks, we don't live in a society that is governed by revenge. We don't live in a society in which whoever has the biggest knife wins. We live in a society of law and that's why you're here today.

And I will tell you this. This is not someone who was lost and adrift, innocent and naive in a foreign country. She had options and she knew about those options. She had a support system that was emotional, that was mental, that was physical, that was legal, that was religious— you heard from that support system in the defense case. They all would have taken her in. Barry White gave her religious support. There were a number of people who were there for her in every capacity they could have been.

In addition, she knew about the legal resources available to her. She could have called 911 a number of times. She knew about juvenile court and juvenile court obtaining a protective order. It was explained to her that if she obtained the protective order she could have her husband barred from the house. She had resources, and she knew about them.

And I will tell you, if you say to her that despite those options what you did is somehow justified or somehow excused because you felt that harm had been visited upon you and it was appropriate to seek revenge, what you tell her is you don't have to be like those women who pick up two or three children in the middle of the night and swallow their pride and go to somebody's house. You don't have to inconvenience yourself to wait for a protective order, and you don't have to avail yourself of the remedies which we, as a civilized society, provide for you. You can take the law into your own hands.

Ladies and gentlemen, what she did cannot be excused, it cannot be condoned, and it cannot be justified. I ask you to find her guilty of malicious wounding and impose whatever penalty your collective wisdom feels is appropriate. Thank you.

BLAIR HOWARD: Thank you on behalf of Lisa Kemler, Jim Lowe, my client, Lorena Bobbitt. I, too, am aware of the inconvenience—the imposition—the source of interruption that this has been in all of your lives over this last two weeks. We started out this trial thinking it was going to be three days and it went a whole lot longer. We've been separated from our families, we've been separated from our homes and our loved ones. And all of us including the Commonwealth appreciate that and we thank you for that very much.

I will point out to you however that we have really experienced together over this last two weeks one of the most cherished rights that is guaranteed to any citizen (the right of a trial) when you're charged with a criminal offense by a jury of your peers.

I will tell you that in every criminal case that is tried across this country there is one principle that is consistent. It is woven into the fabric of our judicial system. And ladies and gentlemen, that principle is that every Defendant who comes into the courtroom is presumed to be innocent, and that is what this court has instructed you, that the burden is upon the prosecution to prove a defendant's guilt beyond a reasonable doubt.

Beyond a reasonable doubt.

Now all our lives, each and every one of us have heard that phrase beyond a reasonable doubt. What does it really mean? Does it mean that it is the Commonwealth's burden in a criminal case to prove the Defendant's guilt beyond all conceivable doubt? No, it doesn't mean that. That would be absurd. Does it mean that the Commonwealth can satisfy its burden if it proves that the Defendant's guilt is probable or even more probable than innocence? That's not enough. The burden is upon the Commonwealth to prove the Defendant's guilt to the exclusion of every reasonable hypothesis of innocence.

Now what does that mean. If you look at all of this evidence and that evidence in part sustains the hypothesis of guilt, but if you look at some more of this evidence and that sustains the hypothesis of innocence, and those two hypothesis are equal, then your verdict should be not guilty. Their burden is to exclude every reasonable hypothesis of innocence before you can convict. Suspicion, no matter how strong, is not enough to convict beyond a reasonable doubt. I think it's important before I talk about the evidence, with your permission, to look at some of the instructions that have been given to you in this case. I think it's very important now that we've talked about reasonable doubt that you look to what are the options of the charges that had been placed before you by the Commonwealth.

The Commonwealth suggests to you that this is malicious wounding. What, then, do they have to prove beyond a reasonable doubt? Well, first of all they've got to show that there was a wounding. I don't think anybody's going to take issue with that. We'll give them number one. Number two says that the wounding has to be with the intent to maim, disfigure, disable, or kill. And number three says that the act has to be done with malice. Now there's an important instruction in association with malice. Remember, for malicious wounding there has to be the intent to maim, disfigure, or kill and malice. If you eliminate the malice, it becomes unlawful.

How do you deal with malice? Well there's an instruction respectfully that I believe will assist you in that regard. It's instruction number 9. It tells you that malice is a state of mind which results in the intentionally doing of a wrongful act to another without legal excuse or justification at a time when the mind of the Defendant or the actor, as the instruction reads, is under the control of reason. You have to find that the person charged has the wherewithal, the capability, the mental ability to understand, that they are fully in control of reason.

But the instruction goes on to tell us this. Heat of passion excludes malice when the heat of passion arises from provocation that reasonably produces an emotional state of mind such as hot blood, rage, anger, resentment, terror, or fear as to cause one to act on impulse without conscious reflection.

Heat of passion excludes malice. It means that at the time she committed this act that she was acting under heat of passion; that is, that her emotions were high arising out of same provocation. I respectfully suggest to you I think of no greater provocation than the act of rape.

I heard a lady say one time that a woman's body is her home. That her body is the most intimate contact that she has with her soul. To rape a woman is not only a violation of her body—I would respectfully suggest to you, gentlemen—I know the ladies know what I'm talking about, but I would respectfully suggest to you, gentlemen, that it's also a ravishment of her soul. It was on a direct attack on the emotional structure that holds a woman together, that gives her dignity, that gives her pride, that gives her self confidence.

It's a given in this case, and the prosecuting attorney just told you that she was raped that night, they concede she was raped that night, that's not even an issue.

Of what her emotional state of mind is immediately after he has raped her again and again and again in her past. Her reservoir of experience and knowledge with this man is nothing but abuse—physical abuse, sexual abuse, forced abuse, anal abuse—you know what her emotions were. I can't imagine her emotions would have been any higher. That emotion, and that emotional state of mind as such, that was hot blood, rage, anger, resentment, terror, or fear as to cause one to act on impulse—well, I really don't think we're talking about an issue here.

Dr. Nelson told you this morning those doctors respectfully disagree on whether it's an irresistible impulse, but no one disagrees that what she did that night was an impulsive act—Nelson conceded to you today, Dr. Gwaltney conceded it to you yesterday, of course Dr. Feister said that it was an irresistible impulse and Dr. Miller Ryans said it was an impulsive act. When I was going down the criteria with Dr. Ryans of post traumatic stress disorder, I said "Doctor, is one of the features of post-traumatic stress disorder impulsive activity," and he says "You're absolutely right." So there's no issue here about the impulsivity of her actions.

I would submit to you based on the credible evidence in this case, based on the testimony of all the doctors, and when you look at this instruction you can eliminate, before you even go back there to deliberate this case, malice is out of the case. Malice has no place in this case.

Where does that leave us with when malice is gone? Well, we're down to unlawful wounding. Unlawful wounding. Well unlawful wounding, ladies and gentlemen, does require a specific intent and that is to say that if you find there was a cutting, you have to also find that at the time she acted that she had the capability, she was rational enough and her thinking was logical enough that she could have formed the specific intent to maim, disfigure, disable, or kill. I don't know that anyone is ever going to know a hundred percent what was going through her mind that night in the state she was in, in that diseased state of mind, in that altered state that she was acting in that night. But Dr. Gwaltney said to her, he said "Lorena, most of the cases that I handle, when a woman is in that situation, she picks up the knife, she goes back there to kill him." She said, "Oh, I didn't want to kill him. I didn't want to hurt him. I didn't want to be raped anymore. I didn't want to be raped anymore." If you believe that that's what that woman felt at that moment when she went into that room and did that act. The verdict is not guilty. If you don't believe she had the capability of formulating the specific intent as required under this instruction, your verdict, ladies and gentlemen, is not guilty.

Now there's a suggestion here that was alluded to and I gotta deal with it up front about the defense is coming at you two ways. We're gonna throw self defense on the table, if you don't like that, they will try a little irresistible impulse. Well let me make it very clear to you. Our feelings about this case is whether you look at the irresistible impulse instruction or the self defense instruction, it really makes no difference. You know why? Because the instructions tell you that you have to look at the situation that she was in that night as she saw it, not as the reasonable man out here on the street or one of you would have seen it, you have to look at this from her perspective.

You've heard the expression walk a mile in her shoes. Well I'm asking you, based on the evidence you've heard about this girl's background, I'm asking you of everything that you've heard in this case without any dispute, without any rebuttal, that she was a good girl, she was a good Catholic family, she was raised properly, she came to this country. Yes, she saw an opportunity here and she wanted to be here and she met the man of her dreams. She met a guy that could sit on any poster in the United States for the United States Marine Corp. I guess they don't come any handsomer than John Bobbitt. He's ramrod straight, and when he walks in the room, everybody notices him.

Well, she fell head over heels in love with him, but she'd always been taught by her family, she'd been taught by her mother that marriage is forever. She had been taught not only about the sanctity of marriage but the greatest thing she could give to this man that she loved was a child. She wanted to give him that child more than anything else and at that stage of the marriage, well they—there were some problems going on. They had not escalated to any great extent of some of the battering at the end of the relationship, but she wanted badly to please him and do everything and she blamed herself all the time when things went wrong. That was instilled in her.

We're talking about a good girl here. We're not talking about a girl that's a sleep-around. We're not talking about a girl that's cruising the bars of Manassas looking to pick up men. No one has said this in this case, and it's got to be said. That girl on that night was in her home where she had a right to be. Everybody will concede that. She wasn't cruising the bars. She wasn't looking for action. She was in her bed where she had a right to be.

I mean, that seems to me one of the most important things about this case. She wasn't stalking her husband. She wasn't planning to go down and confront him or catch him with another girl. She had made up her mind she was going to get a separation, she was going to get a divorce. The last thing she read that night was the rape literature. The last thing she read that night, she fell off into a dreamless state—a dreamlike state I believe they said in the state's report—you know what the last thing was on her mind. You know what was on those pamphlets right next to where she was sleeping. Rape, abuse.

You heard it from Bonnie Alexander. You heard from Beth Wilson. They're not going around the country appearing on television shows. They're not making themselves unavailable to Dr. Nelson because they've got commitments on the Stern Extravaganza or some other show. They came forward because they wanted you to know the truth. They came forward because they saw this girl and they know the hell she was going through. The evidence is compelling, the evidence is overwhelming. This girl was crumbling, she was falling apart, she was falling into pieces.

With respect to the insanity instruction, insanity in Virginia is defined essentially is if she was able to understand the nature, character, and consequences of the act and perceived that it was wrong and that she possessed a will sufficient to restrain any impulse to do the act that may arise from the diseased mind then the Defendant cannot rely on the doctrine of irresistible impulse.

Ladies and gentlemen, in plain and simple language, it means this. It means you have to find that she operated with a diseased mind. And the doctors told you the other day what's identified in the manual and these major mental disorders. Post traumatic stress disorder, major depression which three of the doctors found, or even major depression which Dr. Nelson found, all constitute major mental disorders which are in the legal jargon, diseases. If you believe she was suffering from that at the time of this offense, if you believe further that because of that mental disease that she could not resist the impulse to act and that she committed that violent act because she couldn't resist that impulse, then the verdict is not guilty by reason of insanity.

I've already told you essentially that the doctors are not in disagreement except for the ultimate issue—the ultimate issue as to irresistible impulse. Let's look at the evidence itself. Remarkably as I sat there being accused of offering you two defenses, I really have to shake my head because the Commonwealth has come at you with two theories in this case. Have you noticed that? The one theory of the case is we want you to believe the state doctors who believe Lorena Bobbitt, talked to John Bobbitt and all his family members. But they totally disregard everything that came from the Bobbitt family and from John suggesting that she was the aggressor, she was the person committing the assault and that John was just a good husband and a victim of circumstances.

On the other hand, they bring in 7 or 8 witnesses from

the Bobbitt family who tell you just the opposite and here they're accusing the defense of offering you a two prong attack. I will tell you, the burden again is on the Commonwealth and when their own evidence is in hopeless conflict with each other, they never meet the burden. I was even wondering and perhaps you were when they brought in the Bobbitt family, was that really to rebut some of the things that we had said in our case or was that to rebut the conclusions of the state doctors who said that it was rape and three years of abuse. The Commonwealth's calling them both and they're at odds with one another. What do these witnesses tell us. I'm just willing to briefly hit on some things that I recall from the conver—not the conversation, but the testimony of Dr. Gwaltney and Dr. Rye that I took in my notes. Forgive me if I make a mistake and if I don't have it correct but I think it's pertinent and relevant for your consideration. Dr. Gwaltney I believe testified that before the rape she had good reason to be afraid. And why was that? And this ties right into the self defense instruction about she has to believe reasonably that something has occurred and that she is in danger of something happening. Well, the evidence is unequivocal. He made the threat. I will find you wherever you go, separation or divorce makes no difference. Wherever I find you, whenever I find you, I'm going to have sex with you. I'm going to have it the way I want to have it. That was the threat. And that just doesn't come from Lorena from that stand. Remember Diane Hall? Diane Hall was the lady she took the boxes down to. And Diane Hall told you here the other day and she testified in the last trial that Lorena told me that week that he was going to track her down.

The truth, ladies and gentlemen, is like a smoldering ember in the fire. When you blow on it and blow on it, it gets brighter and brighter. And that's really the case in the defense. Every witness, witness after witness, told you about her emotional state and what she was going through.

My good friend Paul Ebert and Mary Grace O'Brien. I tell you, they're excellent prosecutors. They're the best that there is. But they've got a tough case. They've got a real tough case. They got a rock in a hard pile and they've found themselves in this case walking both sides of the street and no matter which way they turn they get hit. Let me tell you, ladies and gentlemen, what's really significant here, what is really important here—the experts agree there was an impulse, they all agree she had a diseased mind, they all agree she was threatened, they all agree she was frightened and the significant thing is they all agree that she went through a period of time there in that house where she was disoriented.

Now, there's no doctor, there's none of us, I think it's more than a gamble, I think it's pure speculation for any of us to say when that disorientation started. We know one thing. It was probably one of the most bizarre acts that has happened in this country in a long, long time. Everything about this case—it is so unique, what she did, going out of that house with a Gameboy, a penis in her hand, everything about this case is crazy and bizarre. This is a classic case of irresistible impulse. An absolute classic case. If there was ever a case that was made for irresistible impulse, this is the one.

And that's another thing. The fact of the matter is they have attacked [Lorena's] credibility repeatedly. [But] independently of all the witnesses that we presented to you, the police investigated, corroborated, and confirmed everything she was saying. That was why the state doctors ultimately concluded that she was telling the truth and that John Bobbitt had no credibility.

Let me tell you about the Bobbitt family, and I really want you to draw on your own personal experience here. They had something very traumatic happen to someone that they love, John Bobbitt. Mrs. Biro, the two young brothers love John Bobbitt. They're supportive of John Bobbitt, and I say to you that that is a natural inclination. I don't hold that against them. If someone in your family is attacked, injured, if someone points a finger at someone in your family, you close ranks, you solidify, and that's normal and that's human. I have no issue with that.

But respectfully, when you go to evaluate the testimony, understand—and I'm not talking about just their testimony, but the instruction tells you when you evaluate the testimony of all witnesses in this case you look at it—is there some bias? Not intentionally. No one's coming in here to lie to you but is it perceived in the way that they want to see it. I don't know how else to tell you. You've got to evaluate that when you're evaluating Todd. I'm sorry. That's the way it is. You've gotta judge this evidence with credible, credible witnesses.

Connie James. Connie James came forward as, I guess, the surprise witness for the Commonwealth. She came in here and she said maybe 1989, early 1990 she worked at a nail salon, she was very goods friends with Lorena, their husbands were in the military together and socialized together, good friends. Then went on to say that at one time they had this conversation—the way she spins this conversation is that she jokingly said to Lorena, gee, if I caught my husband running around I'd shoot him. Lorena is supposed to have said back in response to that, I'd cut his D-I-C-K off [spelled out]. The word is so repulsive, I don't want to do anything but spell it to you. It's American slang; it's repulsive. It's interesting to me about the manner in which this lady came forward to you in the last month before this trial started. She tells you that she first heard about this through the news and she called the radio station. Then, very interestingly, she is put in touch where she is contacted by, I think, it's a Mr. Ericson who she says reluctantly was the publicity attorney for John Bobbitt. You've got to see a little agenda developing right here, ladies and gentlemen. I mean, right off the bat this case has got nationwide coverage—talk shows, television, Stern Extravaganza, everything. I suggest to you there's an agenda here.

John Bobbitt. The first thing I would like to tell you about John Bobbit is, unfortunately for my good friends at counsel table representing the Commonwealth, everytime he came in the courtroom, he dropped a bomb on them that they weren't expecting. He presented himself here last week and you put a witness on the stand, you're representing him to be an honest credible person, and he tells you about the Victoria Secret underwear, he tells you that after a night of drinking—and he doesn't think he was all that bad after he ate at Denny's, he thought he was pretty clear—came home, put his friend to bed, made sure he was fully accommodated, and went in and laid down on the bed and said he kind of fell asleep and at some point he says "I remember I kept wanting to have sex but I was so tired, gosh, and I got on top of my wife but then I fell asleep." On cross examination I says well now, John, did you ever rape your—oh no. No. I didn't rape her. Well now if he gets on top of her and he starts the sexual act and then he falls asleep, how can he tell us what he did.

But the bomb was dropped to the state's detective. The state's detective, Detective Weintz, he and Investigator Morgan, when they first went to see John, they asked John about that night and what he did and John initially told them that there was no sex. When he was really pushed on that he said well—he says, you know, sometimes I have sex in my sleep. That's an interesting statement. That's an extraordinary statement. Sometimes I have my sex in my sleep but I don't really remember it. And he says oh, and the last time I had sex with my wife was—was last Sunday before my friend Robbie got here.

Well that's statement number one.

And then, ladies and gentlemen, they went back to see him and you know why they went back to see him? They did a little investigation on their own. They had the forensic test. You remember the nice lady that came from the forensic lab that testified about the smears and the swabs—so that he knew John was lying

They go back July 13 to see John. "Come on in, fellas. I'm just writing—writing my autobiography, let me get my notes out and I will gladly talk to you, so let me see here, you want to know whether—no, I don't believe we had any sexual intercourse, I really don't remember . . . What was she wearing? Oh, I don't remember that. She was under the covers. I don't remember what she had on."

Nobody's going to swallow that. Nobody's going to buy that. And they say you know, John, we've got the test results and immediately, never forget it, Detective Weintz stands with his finger in the air and he said [click] just like that he changed. And he said, "Yeah, I don't want to lie to you. Yeah, I got on top of her and well I penetrated her and I had an orgasm."

It's almost as if, ladies and gentlemen, and I mean this not tongue in cheek, but if John said it's raining outside, everybody in the room would run over to the window and look up at the sky just to make sure.

I called him as an adverse witness and when he took the stand I asked him—I gave him every opportunity—I said John, do you remember the Marine Corp incident? You were back in the car and door knocked your wife down. You remember she made a complaint about that. John, you remember driving off and he kind of vaguely remembered that and I said do you remember Kathleen? I guess he didn't want to remember Kathleen Williams. Kathleen Williams got him to fill out the questionnaire. Documents don't lie, ladies and gentlemen. Documents don't lie. Whose signature is on here? John Bobbitt.

John Bobbitt's testimony and his representations to you is like a house of cards. When you take the finger of truth and just brush it by that house of cards every so slightly, the structure collapses. It's vanished. It's gone.

My colleague, and boy she's done a bang up job in this case, Lisa Kemler hit it on the head when she said a reign of terror. A reign of terror. That's just what it was. The abortion, I would only bring this to your attention. The notion that she was upset for a day, upset for a day, was—it is so absurd, it is so ludicrous, that you ladies don't have to hear more about that subject matter. Dr. Feister came into this courtroom, she was on that stand for about five, five and one-half hours, I guess. Direct, cross, direct, cross. You're going to have to judge Dr. Feister's credibility. I don't think she was impeached by credible evidence. Respectfully, there was a disagreement—there was a disagreement of conclusions, but there was nothing about her testimony that was discredited.

Everyone has agreed with Dr. Feister of the major depression, two of the doctors have agreed to post traumatic stress disorder, and Dr. Nelson feels that that now is her situation. She's suffering from two major mental diseases. What she said and what is fully supported by all this evidence is that in the last week to ten days from all of the evidence, from all of the independent witnesses, from Inman's records, from what she was told, the health of Lorena's mind was decreasing downhill rapidly. The increase in fear was magnified by the threat that John had made that he was going to find her, he was going to carry out the act of rape whenever he wanted. It was her opinion that, going in to this event on the morning of the 23rd, having all of these thoughts on her mind, having exhibited all these symptoms, that when she underwent the horrendous stress of the rape that she broke. She snapped. She did not have the wherewithal at that moment.

To me this is so obvious it's got to be obvious to you. We're talking here in a clinical atmosphere of a courtroom and we're talking about goal-oriented acts and picking up a knife and walking into a room, I mean you would think we're talking about a healthy mind of a healthy individual who is not operating with any background material, who has not been the victim of repeated vicious attacks for three years. I suggest to you if you've got the healthiest mind in the world that you're in a state of hysteria and disorientation from everything I've read and heard when you're raped. When [she was] in this unhealthy state of mind, can there be any question she could not control her impulsive act.

I think the evidence is overwhelming, I think the evidence is compelling, I think the conclusion is inescapable ladies and gentlemen.

I want to tell you one final thing before I sit down. I want to thank you again for your patience. Sure do appreciate your consideration. Lorena has not been out west writing, she's not been on the talk circuit. This lady is ill. And every doctor has told you that. This lady has been stripped of all dignity, of all self confidence, she's been done in by the man she loved, the man that she tried to be a good wife to, the man she was faithful to, and as a result of all this battering, she needs a lot of help. She needs your help. And I would say to you that by your verdict, ladies and gentlemen, you can restore perhaps not all of that confidence. That's not going to heal things, that's going to take time. But by your verdict you can restore a little bit of self respect so she can walk out of this court room not heaving and crying as you saw her last week but with her head up. It has been a tremendous ordeal. I know in my heart you're going to do the right thing. And that's because justice, ladies and gentlemen, is for all. For the weak as well as the strong. Thank you.

INFORMATIVE—
COMPELLING—
SCINTILLATING—
NON-FICTION FROM PINNACLE TELLS THE TRUTH!

BORN TOO SOON (751, $4.50)
by Elizabeth Mehren
This is the poignant story of Elizabeth's daughter Emily's premature birth. As the parents of one of the 275,000 babies born prematurely each year in this country, she and her husband were plunged into the world of the Neonatal Intensive Care unit. With stunning candor, Elizabeth Mehren relates her gripping story of unshakable faith and hope—and of courage that comes in tiny little packages.

THE PROSTATE PROBLEM (745, $4.50)
by Chet Cunningham
An essential, easy-to-use guide to the treatment and prevention of the illness that's in the headlines. This book explains in clear, practical terms all the facts. Complete with a glossary of medical terms, and a comprehensive list of health organizations and support groups, this illustrated handbook will help men combat prostate disorder and lead longer, healthier lives.

THE ACADEMY AWARDS HANDBOOK (887, $4.50)
An interesting and easy-to-use guide for movie fans everywhere, the book features a year-to-year listing of all the Oscar nominations in every category, all the winners, an expert analysis of who wins and why, a complete index to get information quickly, and even a 99% foolproof method to pick this year's winners!

WHAT WAS HOT (894, $4.50)
by Julian Biddle
Journey through 40 years of the trends and fads, famous and infamous figures, and momentous milestones in American history. From hoola hoops to rap music, greasers to yuppies, Elvis to Madonna—it's all here, trivia for all ages. An entertaining and evocative overview of the milestones in America from the 1950's to the 1990's!

Available wherever paperbacks are sold, or order direct from the Publisher. Send cover price plus 50¢ per copy for mailing and handling to Penguin USA, P.O. Box 999, c/o Dept. 17109, Bergenfield, NJ 07621. Residents of New York and Tennessee must include sales tax. DO NOT SEND CASH.